Gutenberg Two

Gutenberg Two

Edited by

David Godfrey and Douglas Parkhill

Press Porcépic Ltd.   Toronto   Victoria

First Edition 1979
Second Edition, revised 1980

The opinions of any individual contributors expressed in this book do not necessarily represent the policies or opinions of the institution with which the contributor is affiliated, nor of the editors or other contributors.

This edition is published by Press Porcépic Limited, Toronto and Victoria, with the assistance of the Canada Council. Typeset on a Compugraphic Editwriter 7500 and partly written and edited on word processors.

A *Softwords* book.

Printed in Canada

2   3   4   5   83   81   80

Cover design by Roberto Dosil

Canadian Cataloguing in Publication Data

Main entry under title:
Gutenberg Two

ISBN 0-88878-190-3 (cloth)
ISBN 0-88878-191-1 (paper)

1. Canada-Social conditions-1965-*
Addresses, essays, lectures. 2. Mass media-
Social aspects — Canada — Addresses, essays,
lectures. 3. Data transmission systems —
Addresses, essays, lectures. I. Godfrey,
Dave, 1938·   II. Parkhill, Douglas.
HN107.G88   1980   971.064   C80-091206-3

TABLE OF CONTENTS

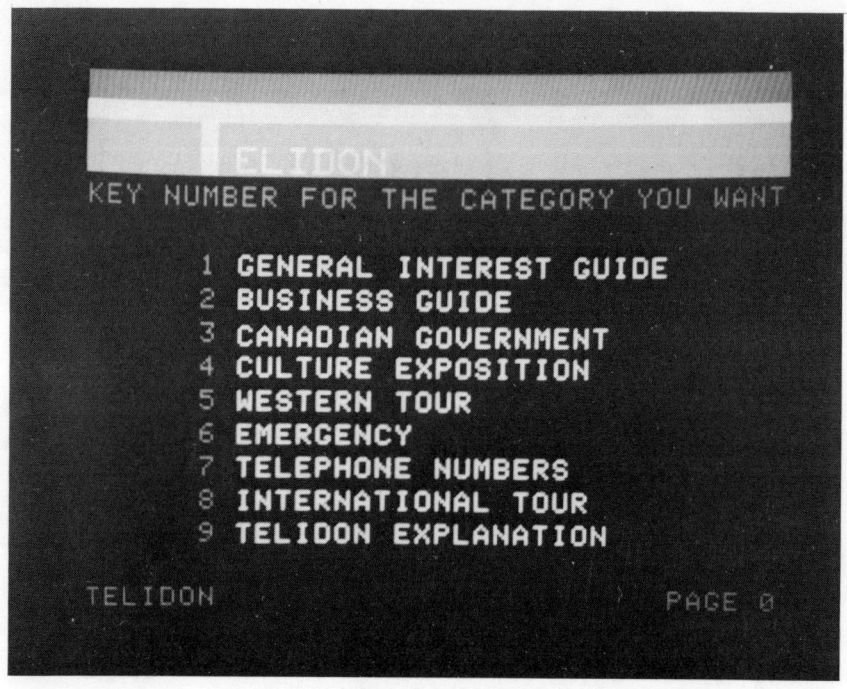

Plate 1. The potential of TELIDON is enormous. Using special graphics software developed by the Department of Communications, TELIDON presents the best colour graphics displays of all videotex systems. The following black and white photographs give some idea of its range.

STOCK MARKET

key number for the category you want

1 Stock Prices Weekly Range
2 Toronto Stock Exchange Index
■ Montreal Stock Index
■ New York Stock Exchange Index
■ Dow-Jones U.S. Average
■ Statistics Canada Report

The Financial Post   page 2415

FUN GUIDE: NORTH

KSAN INDIAN VILLAGE
WAC BENNETT DAM
MOUNT ROBSON
X-COUNTRY SKIING
TERRACE LAVA BEDS

FOR INFORMATION CONTACT TOURISM B.C.
more...   668-2300

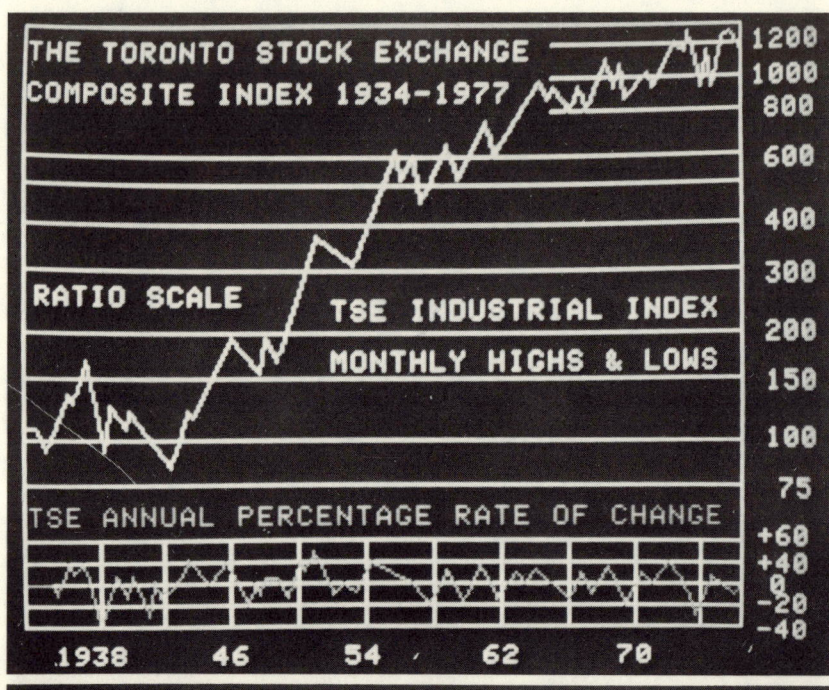

THE TORONTO STOCK EXCHANGE
COMPOSITE INDEX 1934-1977

RATIO SCALE

TSE INDUSTRIAL INDEX
MONTHLY HIGHS & LOWS

1200
1000
800
600
400
300
200
150
100
75

TSE ANNUAL PERCENTAGE RATE OF CHANGE

+60
+40
0
-20
-40

1938   46   54   62   70

FUN GUIDE CENTRAL B.C.

■ BARKERVILLE
■ RODEOS
■ DUDE RANCHES
■ CANOEING
■ FISHING
■ HUNTING

TOURISM B.C.

FOR INFORMATION CONTACT: 666-2300
more...

SIR MACKENZIE BOWELL
1894-1896

Bowell had a brief, bitter humiliating period in office. His career in Parliament was undistinguished although he was a tenacious, informed and effective debater.

But he could not command allegiance. Seven of his cabinet grew dissatisfied with his leadership and resigned. He failed to find replacements Terms were imposed upon him. He had t take the seven members back, and agree resign at the end of the session.

TELIDON

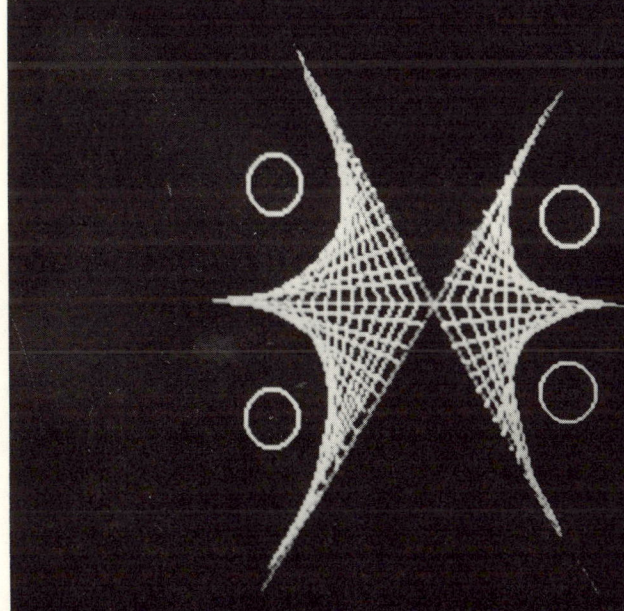

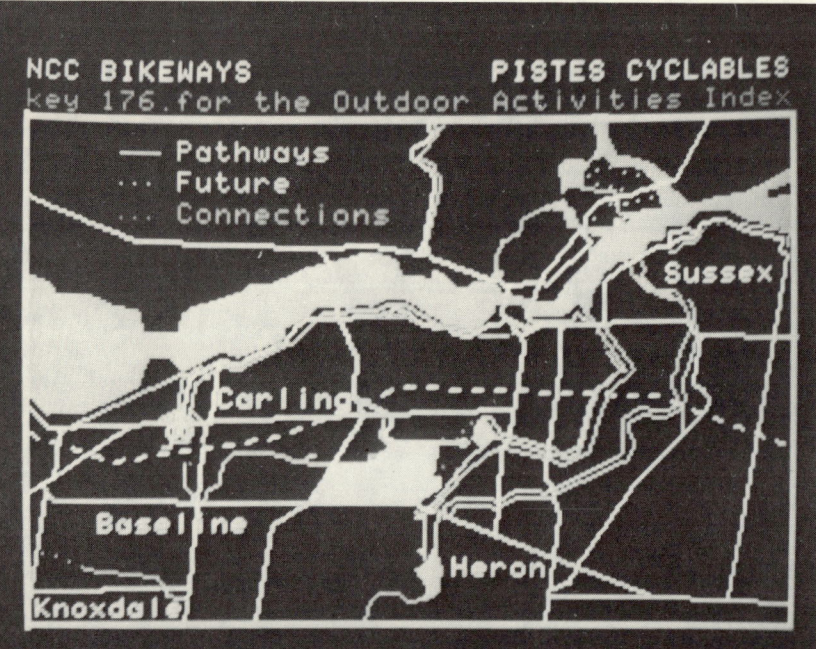

NCC BIKEWAYS   PISTES CYCLABLES
key 176.for the Outdoor Activities Index

— Pathways
... Future
... Connections

Sussex

Carling

Baseline

Heron

Knoxdale

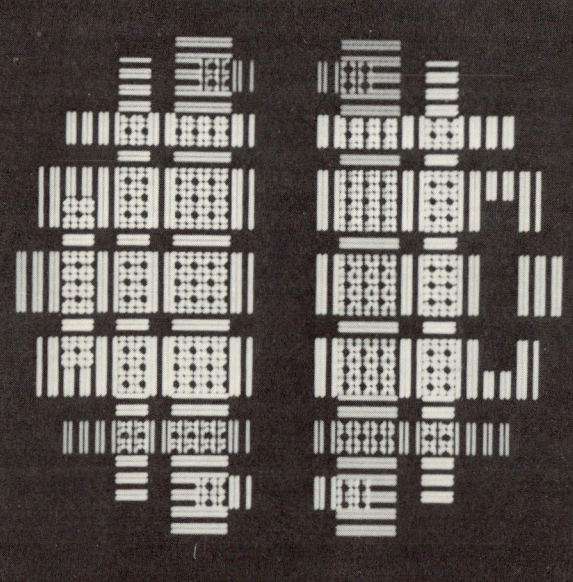

INTRODUCTION All Information In All Places at All Times
David Godfrey

The Taste of Space

McLuhan put his telescope to his ear;
What a lovely smell, he said, we have here.

A. J. M. Smith

There is something very satisfying in that couplet. In one stroke, Smith reduces McLuhan to a foolish and human figure. But is it really McLuhan we wish to see reduced, or is it that vast maze of wires, electronic sounds, networks, microwaves, databanks, punchcards, idiotboxes, satellites, and remote-control robots which some have termed communications, but which often seems more like aerial bombardment?

Now another major change is about to take place. Not just a few more degrees of heat under the bubbling pot, but a quite magical change, a change almost as exciting as the first telephone must have been in rural areas, but with an impact far more fundamental. The basics of our social life are going to be changed to a degree that they have not since the well-born German goldsmith, Gutenberg, began that mysterious ten-year process that led eventually to the creation of quickly reproducible, absolutely similar, metal type—letting any handy wine-press be turned into a bookmaking machine and putting more than a little panic into those with heavy investments in monastaries and scriptoriums.

All information in all places at all times. The impossible ideal. But the marriage of computers with existing communications-links will take us far closer to that goal than we have ever been. *Gutenberg Two* is a key to the technology of the new maze. We make some predictions about the social rearrangements the new maze will force, look at many aspects of the current maze from the vantage point of the new technology, observe some of the ways in which the current maze will be tipped over and ploughed under, and present a firm set of regulatory principles for ensuring that Canadians receive the maximum benefits from the new structures and powers that are suddenly going to appear all about us.

For that new maze will make the current one seem like a child's plaything. Fortunes will be lost; fortunes will be made. Many an old institution will go under; many a new one will spring up. Authors will drift back into anonymity; librarians will gain vast new powers and respect; teachers will understand at last what drove the Luddites and some of them will teach themselves how to destroy cable-lines. We will all learn to be TV producers just as we once all learned how to write. Pollsters will do serious battle with parliamentarians and the staunch, free-enterprise newspaper owners who fail to adapt or merge will suddenly learn, as their profits disappear, why artists, musicians and book publishers love and loathe the Canada Council. The great corporate battles and mergers of the decade will be among telephone companies, cable companies, publishers, data processors and advertising agencies. Communications lawyers will become rich as the regulations are constantly rewritten and revised. Like the 16th century, it will be an age of magic and an age of litigation, power struggles and sudden reversals of fortune.

The first chapter of this book presents a fairly long-term scenario of life within the new maze, culminating in the great crisis of 2005. What about the short term, say the next ten years?

Scattered about the house, by 1990, will be six or seven NABU's*, with the older ones in the basement, of course. On the surface, a NABU will look like a Colour TV hooked up to an electric typewriter with a few other strange boxes on the side. But each NABU will let you access a vast number of databanks, or send a message to your Aunt Sally in Moncton, or see if there are any messages from any members of your 1927 Maserati Fan Club around the world, or check the price range on 30-foot sloops and sell some of your Bellstar stock if you find a sloop you like and are ready to dicker—by NABU—with the owner, or access a step-by-step recipe for Beef Wellington (free, courtesy of the beef-growers co-op), or continue with your course on Aztec Art, or requisition the old 1987 Stanley Cup (Winnipeg vs Montreal, final game, second period, Meeker's highlights only, please), or compare your daughter's marks against some regional norm.

There will be similar NABU's in sports clubs and game clubs, as well as union offices and business establishments. These would, of course, be refined and expanded for their more specialized purposes.

It's just a name, although Nabu was the son of Marduk, the sun-god of Babylon at the time of Hammurabi; as the god of writing, he gave understanding and wisdom; his symbol was the stylus of the scribe. Those who demand acronyms might accept Natural Access to Bidirectional Utilities.

In essence, there is nothing that new in this respect of the technology, although we have assumed a number of minor marriages (for example, between the video-disc and the computer). The mechanisms that now allow a Ford dealer in Victoria to check with all the other Ford dealers on the continent for a 1975 transmission for a large truck, compare prices, and put in the order, will basically suffice. The impact factors will be the rapid fall in prices of components such as memory and central processors, the standardization of information protocols, and the increase of transmission channels.

The impact of falling prices is fairly obvious, although startling in an age of inflation. Many of the major components have come down 30% a year for over two decades. As Madden makes clear in Chapter Two, it's like finding a house that cost a million dollars available now for only a few dollars, and with much of the cost of up-keep gone also.

But standardization of protocols is equally important. What we are proposing is the possibility of the owner of that truck being able to bypass the Ford dealers if she choses, send a message to all possible owners of the missing transmission (within, say, 150 miles), and dicker by NABU with them. Then, once delivery is made, installation of the transmission could be done with the help of a manual/course selected from a number of possibilities and presented on the NABU in the workshop.

At the moment, the Ford dealer can't even easily communicate with the Chrysler dealer network. The early networks were private. The new ones must be public. The six or seven NABU's in a home should reflect the passage of time, additional capabilities, and the influence of style, fad and fashion; they should not be required because a large number of private networks have been allowed to grow and develop their own non-compatible protocols.

Standardization is important because the duplication it avoids will save the consumers billions of dollars. It is also important because each NABU will be capable of sending information rather than simply receiving it. For example, let us assume that Elie, Manitoba (one of the first towns to be wired-up with optical fibre), decides that it's going to create a regional history. Instead of an editor, or local historical committee deciding what must be chopped and what must be crammed-in in order to meet the printing budget, all the members of the community could contribute their own reminiscences. An editor might be appointed to set up all the cross-indexes (so that a scholar in Winnepeg or Toronto 20 years later could run a quick search for specific areas of interest), or to arbitrate disputes among contributors as to when the first town hall actually did burn down, or to suggest a consistent spelling, but the basic construction of the work would be by the contributors and access to the work would be available to all. And the arrangement of the work would be flexible, not limited to the rigidities of the book. Digitalization of sound recordings might mean that the viewer had a choice between reading a contributor's words and hearing them; digitalization of video tapes might also mean that the viewer could call up specific images interspersed with the text. What did Ulysse Richard, Elie's Councillor, look like back in 1979 when TELIDON put Elie on the map?

The multiplication of available transmission channels, as Alphonse Ouimet points out in Chapter Five, will be another act of sorcery that will have to be used with care lest the potential of the revolution disintegrates into what we might call the multi-track wasteland. Hundreds of TV channels will be nice, but will we use them more wisely just because there are more? Perhaps. Historically, Canada does have some advantages.

To a large extent Canada is already an electronic nation: 96 percent of all homes have television and telephones and we made 22 billion telephone calls in 1977 (1). Statistics Canada hasn't yet started keeping figures on sales of home computers, but there is no major city without at least one home computer store. The CIPS Computer Survey (2) shows over 8,251 major installations in place. As Ouimet points out in Chapter Five, the advent of optical fibre and satellite modes of transmission will mean not only a possible hundred-fold increase in the number of channels available, but also at last a switch in ideology from mass to complementarity. By complementarity he means that many audience sectors can be served simultaneously and that we need no longer submit to the NBC/CBS/ABC battle to find the lowest common denominator and feed it mindless garbage.

We also have an historical recognition that communications generate identification and mutual benefit. By acknowledging early the existence of this technology, and putting some risk capital into TELIDON, the federal government has actually gained a year or two of lead-time for the private sector, and industry seems to be ready to take advantage of that lead (3). By putting together the complete package, hardware, software, systems and regulatory concepts, we could have an export that should pay for at least a few of our Florida vacations.

And we have, in Innis and McLuhan, the two most important theoretical approaches to communications. In the Epilogue, I deal briefly with Innis's basic duality: time-oriented versus space-oriented communications, but there is another aspect of his theory which is important.

One of the important elements that distinguishes the comments of Harold Innis on communications from those of McLuhan is the emphasis Innis places on unit-cost and thresholds. McLuhan lacks Innis's economic intensity and tends to ignore not only these apparently small factors but also the way in which the nature of institutions depends upon such factors. Chapter Four uses these two factors to examine the different forms that institutions have taken in television, radio, book publishing, newspapers, etc. It is apparent, for example, that the hundreds of book publishers in Canada owe their existence to the fact that the threshold cost of setting up and getting the first list of books out is comparatively minimal. At the same time, we have had a major battle between CNCP and the telephone companies brought before the CRTC and the Cabinet, a battle which essentially rests on the fact that CNCP cannot afford the threshold costs (of many billions) to duplicate Bell's network and so must petition the regulatory bodies to gain access to that network.

In the new maze, the unit costs per message will be very low, in the pennies, even without advertising subsidy, while the threshold costs of establishing a national network will be staggering. Provided that satisfactory regulations are introduced, however, as Chapter Three makes clear, the threshold cost of becoming an information producer will also be very low—less than the current cost of producing a single book. Thus, a whole range of publishers or information providers will come into being once the networks are in place. Fotheringham will not need *Maclean's* to reach his audience, nor will Pierre Berton need Jack McClelland. But advertisers may need them both when the *Sun* and the *Province* fold and new avenues to consumers are required. By the time the *Sun* does fold, the smart reporters will have already picked their area of specialization and alone, or in small groups, or in co-operatives, or by going to work for Starbell on salary or contract or a royalty-basis, will have become information providers. If consumer groups, or woman's groups, or Ford-owner groups, or religious groups don't like what's happening, they will be able to establish their own information group and become publishers—with an initial investment of less than $10,000.

Thus, although *Gutenberg Two* concentrates on the technological innovations, which are fascinating, we have tried to be open to the creative possibilities. Nor, especially in Chapter One, have we ignored the psychological factors likely to inhibit these possibilities or divert them towards unwanted ends.

One strange thing noticeable at most displays of segments of the new technology described in this book is that children under fifteen participate eagerly and naturally while people over eighteen tend to hold back and be unwilling to take those first steps that will let them participate in the experiment.

If there is a key term that arises in discussions of the impact of these new technologies, it is "interaction" or one of its variations: two-way, non-passive, bi-directional, participational, etc. The exciting concept is that the technologies make possible—at last—individual production of information without major investment. So why do "adults" hold back?

I think there is a fifteen-year-old barrier and it arises from the young adult's slow realization that although there is a great deal of information available now, none of the *speakers* know "me", nor are there many *listeners* for what "I" have to say. All the charts seem to agree that people have less and less faith in the existing media and that, although they are absorbing more and more data from mass media such as television, they are more and more suspicious of the validity of that data (4).

The first century of the printing press saw vast diversity (5) and if there was fear, it came from the established social structure. The last two or three decades of innovation in electronic media seem only to have confirmed the individual's suspicions and fears of the media establishments.

Despite McLuhan's optimism, the approach of the global village seems to have aroused a tribal fear of what one might call the global witchdoctor, a Doctor Strangeband who will somehow manipulate the entire complex, mysterious, almost magical system for his own purposes.

Deep in the bowels of some mountain, the evil doctor will monitor all communications with a vast computer and then slowly shape the world towards his own ends. The fact that the computer has been developed by military, government and large corporations lends some justification to the dichotomy between I and Them which is part of many individual reactions to the information revolution. Things were bad enough before, adults seem to say, what will happen when more powers are available? Why should one believe that an information revolution will actually benefit the individual?

The book, which also was once considered an invention of the devil, has prospered recently despite many predictions of its demise. There were over 591,000 new titles produced around the world in 1976 (6). One of the reasons that trust in the book has remained high is that variety does exist, not only of product but of producer. More and more community and religious groups are producing their own books, knowing that their own members will trust that information because they know from whom it comes.

Television, by contrast, has not yet delivered on its promises of diversity. The major reason is unit-cost. Saskatchewan might feel that its own citizens ought to have some access to the production side of information and might take some strong steps in that direction, but what they run into is the forty-thousand-dollar-an-hour barrier. A minimal hour of television at a professional level costs at least $40,000 to produce. Assume an average level of even two hours per day and one arrives at an interesting figure: in a year the average viewer absorbs material that cost at least $30 million to produce. In fact, of course, the original production costs were far higher, but if one wishes to provide a possible substitution on the basis of original productions one must confront a figure like that: $30 million per annum.

Saskatchewan's original experiment was funded to the extent of only $1.5 million (7).

Not only can one predict from those figures the failure of the Saskatchewan experiment to replace more than a minute percentage of the existing non-regional information sources, one can also begin to understand the fifteen-year-old barrier.

Until that age, the individual does not differentiate in depth between the local environment and the screen-world. Take away your child's TV set for a few weeks and the real complaints will come not from missing a segment of "Mork and Mindy" or "Justice League", but from the social deprivation of not being able to banter about those actions and heroes and new rock stars on the school playground.

Formal recognition of that differentiation between our-world and screen-world may come with a rush somewhere between fifteen and eighteen, but by that time the individual is usually addicted to TV. The alienation that takes place is somewhat unusual: the viewer distrusts more and more of the information and yet depends on the medium. The fear of Dr. Strangeband's system then seems rooted in the individual's own statistical inability to break the pattern of dependency.

What we watch rarely portrays people we know, places we know, problems that are our problems, nor is it produced by people we know or have any direct influence upon. When we do get up at 6:30 a.m. to watch our friends perform on the local Cable station, the tackiness of it all seems only to confirm the difference between the screen-world and our-world. The studio is small; the camera shots are all straight on; there is no applause and the MC is obviously bored out of his skull. The dependency then remains fundamentally a dependency on information produced by strangers, about strangers, in a strange place and in a manner mysterious and very very expensive. And yet it is pleasant and enticing; we cannot walk out of the wasteland.

Of course, some do break free and more may, but if you feel you are free of this addiction, ask yourself some simple questions. How many hours of TV did you actually watch last week? Of those hours, how many had you decided well in advance to watch because of your interest in the specific subject? How many did you watch because of habit? And how many did you watch simply because the set was on?

Promises of diversity and innovation connected with new computer/communications systems will have to deal with the false promises made for TV as a new system thirty years ago and the reality of similarity, repetition and banality which TV acutally delivered.

It is the contention of all of us in *Gutenberg Two* that this information revolution will deliver on its promises, given that certain complexities are understood by the general population.

There are three such complexities discussed in this book. Two of these are fairly obvious. The revolution we describe as Gutenberg Two is based not on a single invention like moveable type (8), but upon an interaction of many technologies, some of which are current inventions and all of which have to be understood to grasp the *process* of Gutenberg Two.

The relationship between the technologies and society is the second complexity. This relationship tends to be like an iceberg in that the great mass of impact is invisible while the visible portion, such as a specific ruling of the CRTC, appears angular, destructive and unnatural. Why can't a northern community set up its own antenna and beam down whatever it wants?

In order to know what is *going* to happen, we have to first understand a complex set of technologies about which even the experts have difficulty in making firm predictions. Then, in order to have any real influence on the future, we have to haul and heave the iceberg into drydock and understand the structures produced by society's use of these technologies: the past and current relationships between society and media technologies. Then we can try some predictions. Those two are complexities which can be grasped.

But the third complexity, symbolized by the fifteen-year-old barrier, is psychological. Individual responses will probably play as large a role in this revolution as the other two factors, but these are far harder to define or quantify.

The structure of this book then, although it bears in mind the need to make the two major complexities clear to the average reader, is also influenced by our (limited) awareness of the psychological factors involved.

Chapter One, indeed, begins with this problem. What will it be like to live within Gutenberg Two? How will an individual adjust to the changes that technology is making inevitable? Or will society decide that the "inevitability" is something that should be brought under control and abruptly terminated, not simply regulated, but aborted?

Chapter Two provides a guide to the major terms and concepts underlying the technologies which will combine to produce Gutenberg Two as well as the specific case of "Julia's Dilemma."

In Chapter Three, Douglas Parkhill puts the iceberg in drydock and suggests a blueprint for reshaping it while we still have a chance. Assuming that the technologies will develop and that our major goal ought to be maximum participation in information-creation as well as maximum access to information, he suggests guidelines that society, through its governments, must implement and implement quickly, if that goal is not to be distorted by minority or even dictatorial control of the new systems.

Chapter Four returns to the present and examines the existing media in terms of their current impact upon us and their relative profitability and power, and in terms of their vulnerability to the new technologies. One of the obvious axioms is that those media corporations most vulnerable will be most likely to recognize that vulnerability and to attempt to implement regulatory changes or marketplace control by domination in order to ensure their survival and growth. Such activities may become quite desperate, but will not necessarily contribute to the greatest possible distribution of the greatest possible variety of information.

Chapter Five looks at a specific segment of the iceberg: television; and at the social implications of the technological innovations and options of that particular sector of the revolution. Any global strategy will have to absorb a number of such sectoral strategies.

Education is normally considered as quite distinct from the media. But a contrary case is made in Chapter Six. Leacock said that all one needed for a university was a good, large library and a reading room. The printing press made possible not only the grammar book, but the grammar school and the concept of correctness of grammar of a number of low-class, disdained, vulgar and probably savage tongues such as English, French and German. In a mechanical age, education became a growth-industry, gathering in large numbers of people engaged in what really can be considered as hand-labour. The mechanization of education is an inevitable part of Gutenberg Two; there will be no greater cries of protest than those that come in the next few decades from manual labourers of the educational field. Teachers will at last understand the plight of the handweaver.

Chapter Seven may seem somewhat out of place in a book otherwise dedicated to analysis and forecast. What has a guide to home-computers got to do with these larger questions? Quite a bit. If cheapness of creation is indeed going to become a crucial factor, then surely we ought to be able to see some evidence even now; the home computer symbolizes that cheapness of access. For $2,000, you can buy what would have cost hundreds of thousands in 1960. More importantly, however, the home computer represents a psychological factor. People who buy them may buy them for different purposes: to play games, to keep up with their neighbours, to learn BASIC, or because their children insisted; but whatever the purpose, the result is essentially a demystification of the technology.

Assuming that there are truly creative, innovative and liberating possibilities hidden in this technology, yet recognizing that some of the largest corporations extant are going to be seriously threatened by the implications if this revolution is allowed to run "out of control", nothing is going to be more important than the average citizen overcoming the mystifications of technology that lead in the extreme to a fear of Dr. Strangeband. That is not to say that the evil Doctor does not exist, for there are any number of scenarios for this technology that are probably more frightening than any that uninformed terror-mongers have been able to conceive, but there are also a number of scenarios that could lead to a new enlightenment. Only hands-on experience will let the average citizen see the difference, see the absolute necessity for a set of guidelines similar to those suggested by Douglas Parkhill. As the new technology comes into the production and distribution stage, information about it will be primarily in the hands of the existing media. Given that their own survival is involved, they will face a major test of their objectivity. So when your child says "I'd like an Apple or Sorcerer for Christmas this year," don't laugh them off; for in this revolution, ignorance will not be bliss.

The final chapter is a glossary. One proof of the existence of Gutenberg Two is the vocabulary which now exists at the specialist level, but has not yet entered common parlance. *Cliche, stereotype, freedom of the press, news,* and many other terms were once similarly the property only of printer specialists. ROMS, *chips,* TELIDON, *silicon,* VLSI, *Electronic Highways, databankers, content/carrier separation* may now be phrases known only to specialists of a new kind, but their entry into common parlance is only a matter of time.

There has been a great deal of co-operation among the contributors to this book and an attempt to build upon one another's definitions and concepts. If you do get tangled in the terminology at this point, however, the glossary will help you find your bearings once again. As in any subject which is indeed "news", these unfamiliar phrases must be utilized.

The final effect of the newness of the theories and data here presented is that a large number of questions remain unanswered. We cannot apologize for that. All this book attempts to do is to present a proper base for debate. Unlike many debates however, the content of this one will soon influence the debate itself. Polls of a complexity we can now only imagine, *about* the direction of the technologies, will soon be made available *by* the technology. In the Epilogue, we will briefly raise some of the questions which only an understanding of the content of a book such as this can bring into prominence.

Within this technology, all the weight is on the side of diversity, innovation, low threshold costs and minimal message costs. It will take great blindness on the part of society to allow any special interest groups to overcome those natural tendencies. But they will want to, and it has been so long since we have been able, as individuals and small communities, to have any say over the media structures and content that perhaps we are too long out of practice to begin. Let us hope not. Let us hope that this book and others like it begin a process of reversal which ensures that the creative use of these inevitable changes wins out over the forces of self-interest, uniformity and centralization.

REFERENCES TO THE INTRODUCTION

1. Voyer, R.D. and Edwards, B.L., "The Wired Country" (unpublished);Statistics Canada 56-203 shows that in 1977 Canadians made an average of 1,536 local calls per phone and 63 toll calls per phone.

2. *1978 Canadian Computer Census,* Canadian Information Processing Society, Toronto, p. 27.

3. Telephone companies, newspapers and cable companies in Quebec, Ontario, Manitoba, Alberta and British Columbia are already involved in projects of various kinds. The government expects to spend $9 million to assist industry in these projects. See *A Scenario for the Implementation of Interactive Computer-Communications Systems in the Home,* Science Council, Ottawa, July, 1978.

4. *The Film Industry in Canada: Report,* prepared by the Bureau of Management Consulting for the Department of the Secretary of State, Arts and Culture Branch, Ottawa, 1977, pp. 76-77.

5. The fact that 40,000 editions, more than 10 million copies, were printed in the fifteenth century alone indicates the rapid growth of the book trade. From Hirsch, Rudolf, *Printing, Selling and Reading: 1450-1500,* Otto Harrassowitz, Wiesbaden, 1967, p. 105.

6. From *United Nations Statistical Yearbook, 1976.*

7. Humphries, Donald, "Saskatchewan TV network revived", Toronto *Globe and Mail*, 29 June 1979. A new pay-TV corporation (composed of the Saskatchewan Government, three cable TV companies and Credit Union Central) will pay $1.1 million for all assets of the Co-operative Programming Network. The provincial government (which must continue CPN operations in a manner agreeable to the new consortium) will assume all CPN debt, reported to be close to $3.5 million.

8. A case could be made that Gutenberg's invention also represented improvements in a number of technologies, including paper-making, metallurgy, casting and metal-cutting and punching, rather than a single specific creation.

1 JULIA'S DILEMMA
John Madden

It was a beautiful spring morning in Vancouver. Julia opened the patio doors . . . puffy white clouds trooped jauntily across the deep blue sky, and the sun shone down on two small blossoming cherry trees, which interrupted an otherwise unbroken luxuriant green lawn. It was a small garden, but a private one—one which held many fond memories for Julia.

How could she leave it now? And how could the sun shine today, of all days, when she and countless others must make this terrible decision? It should be raining, pouring, pelting, the heavens should burst asunder and wash the blossoms from the cherry trees. But no; it was sunny, placid, calm, idyllic; the kind of day that turned Easterners, still knee deep in slush and mud, green with envy.

In Australia it would be autumn. She tried to imagine it, but could not. Some of her friends told her it was very pleasant—just like a depopulated California, they said—but it wouldn't be depopulated for long when all the world's BF'ers moved there. Anyway she much preferred the muted, hazy colours of the B.C. outdoors to the bold, bright colourings of the tropics and sub-tropics.

But that, she told herself, must not influence her decision. Older generations retained their attachment for their native land, but the youngsters—and Michael was only fifteen now—would adapt quickly to a new environment. It was of Michael's future that she must think, and that was why she felt she was about to vote with the modern, forward looking intelligentsia, a vote which would automatically entail their move to Australia. But something told her that her own instinct to stay put, to remain with the Humanity Firsters, could well turn out to be the right decision even for Michael.

But if it turned out to be the wrong decision, would Michael understand? Or would he just think that she had been selfish or shortsighted or both? Perhaps she was only trying to avoid responsibility by involving her son much more in the decision.

Michael was in the garage, working on his jalopy. She would go talk to him, but she knew what he would say, indeed he had said it already. Michael thought the Humanity Firsters were a bunch of nutty psychopaths who thought that everyone, even the friendly computers, were about to do them in. "Let them go hoe their own potatoes," he would say, "as for me, I will do as my AYEE suggests." If he could have his way, he would be in Australia already. Michael loved tinkering with things mechanical and electrical. He would sit for hours conversing with the computer to learn how this or that object worked. He never chose the instruction routines which featured a human mediator—an essential feature for so many learners—but preferred to dialogue directly with the computer. Of course unmediated learning was much cheaper, but Julia, who was a learning mediator herself, would willingly have paid the extra expense.

Lately, however, there had been some signs of change in Michael. He was becoming less of a loner, spending more time with friends—even girl-friends. Perhaps he too would come to regret leaving their small but comfortable home in Vancouver. If there should be a war in five or ten years, as many believed would happen, Vancouver just might escape the holocaust, but all of Australia was almost certain to be affected—or so they said.

Somehow she would have to get across to Michael all the pros and cons of each option. She would have to be quick, and use any material which was at hand—and she would have to be fair—although she was unsure what being fair meant when faced with such a complex and emotional decision. At least she could honestly say that she hadn't made up her own mind how to vote.

But how should she begin her discussion with Michael? Should she talk to him about the theory of evolution, of the origins of our sensitivities and emotions? Or should she discourse on relevant parts of the history of philosophy—something she was well qualified to do as a course mediator on the subject? She knew that a discussion of the history of computer development would hold his interest—unless he knew it all already. All of these subjects she felt, contained insights into the problem which faced them. Perhaps, on the other hand, she should start by recounting a story she had never told Michael in any detail before—the story of the father Michael never saw, and of her own life, particularly that part which began when she was Michael's age.

She thought back to when it had all begun, on a June day in 1987. Her parents had gone out and she was alone, watching "Banana Boat" on TV. It was supposed to be funny, and it had been her favourite show, but suddenly, from some chance remark of one of the characters, she had realized that every word and every action on the screen was carefully planned to get the viewer mentally prepared to receive the message, subtly introduced into the framework of the plot, that it was essential to ration fuel oil since imports of oil from the Middle East had recently ceased altogether.

She had supposed the message was a sensible one, but somehow it made the show itself seem trite and boring. She had reached for the little hand held controller that looked like a small pocket calculator and switched off the TV. Nothing to do! Perhaps she should have something to eat, she had thought. But she wasn't really hungry—just bored. She keyed in the box number of her personal electronic mail box for the fourth time that day, just in case someone had written. Nothing there, as usual. She had tried her general electronic mail box, the one reserved for her general and advertising messages, to see what advertising had accumulated for her. A message flashed on the TV screen while a Chopin Nocturne came movingly through the sound system.

BORED WITH LIFE, AREN'T YOU JULIA! EVERYTHING SEEMS PERFECTLY
PLANNED, YET SOMEHOW NOTHING SEEMS IMPORTANT. HAVE YOU
TRIED THE OTHER LIFE? LIVE DANGEROUSLY!
TAKE A CHANCE! DIAL 728-3760-528 TO LEARN MORE.

She had followed the instructions, and one thing had led to another. Now, here she was, almost twenty years later, facing a crucial decision once more. Only this time there would be no turning back.

She got up and walked towards the garage. Michael was busy changing the electric drive motor for the right front wheel of his fifteen year old jalopy. Parts for it were hard to come by these days. Last year he had managed to locate some of the old-style battery cells the car required by sending a personal query to all owners in North America of the same model car who were under 26 years of age. He thought those under 26 would be more sympathetic to his problem. Besides, it had cut down on the computer mailing costs by a factor of three. Someone in Alabama had replied and, after a bit of haggling over the price, the deal was closed. The batteries had arrived two days later at the parcel pick-up office. He had inspected them carefully before authorizing payment and being permitted to take the batteries away.

This time he hadn't been so lucky. The motor bearings were not available. Fortunately, the specifications for the bearings were still on computer

15

file, so the part could be manufactured without difficulty on a computer controlled milling machine. Still, it was expensive, and he had had to wait two weeks as he could not afford to pay the 20% surcharge which would have given him priority, same day service. He had hoped that his mother would pay the surcharge for him, but the several broad hints he had dropped had either passed unnoticed or else she had deliberately ignored them (he wasn't sure which). Since he was by nature an independent boy, he had accepted the two week wait philosophically.

Now he was busy installing the bearing. He had been fortunate in acquiring a complete set of maintenance video discs when he bought the car with his mother's help two years ago. He was now playing the video disc containing instructions for motor bearing replacement, mimicking exactly the actions of the mechanic on the screen, stopping the action with a foot pedal whenever he wanted to inspect a particular frame with extra care, or if he got behind the action on the screen.

"Everything going together well, Michael?" Julia said, poking her head into the garage.

"Yes thanks, Mother," he replied, "She should be ready to roll in 23 minutes according to the message on the TV screen, but it will probably take me a bit longer."

She carried on out into the garden. The brief conversation had been on the usual perfunctory level. Both were absorbed in their own thoughts, their own actions, their own lives.

She wheeled about in panic. What a fool she was! Had she not decided that today she would engage Michael in the most important decision of his life? Yet, she had just talked to him as if today was a day like any other. And he, who knew that today she was to make the all important decision, had given no hint of curiosity. She rushed back to the garage and threw open the door.

"Oh, Michael," she said, a little louder than was natural for her.

"Yes, Mother," came the reply, with just a hint of bored resignation.

"Michael, er . . . uh . . . uh . . . I . . . we . . . have an important decision to make today."

Silence.

Michael came out from under the car and stood up slowly wiping his greasy hands on the sides of his coveralls. "I know, Mother," he said.

Silence again, as they stood looking at each other.

"I . . . I . . . would like us to make the decision together," she said, and added hurriedly as she could see him start to reply, "but I'm not ready to talk about it yet . . . I . . . well . . . I want to get my thoughts in order first. Perhaps we could have an early dinner tonight and tackle the problem together after dinner."

On the instant of speaking she had realized what she would have to do. She would compile a record, laying out the whole subject, which she and Michael could review together. It was the kind of thing she put together for her especially bright students all the time, only this time the issue was crucial. How she wished she had thought of doing this last week or last month! Time was so short—only eight hours—but still she did know where appropriate material could be found.

Michael's reply broke in on her train of thought. "I would like that very much, Mother," he said evenly—but she was not fooled by his attempt to appear unemotional. Pleasure... relief... even love could be detected in his reply, evoking almost uncontrollable emotions in herself. "OK," she said, and turned away quickly and fled out the door.

Outside in the garden she slowly regained her composure. She must adopt a rational approach! Slowly she walked into the house and sat down before the large-screen animation panel. Deliberately, she pulled out a small note pad.

Item one would be Lasqueti Island and the history of the Hiramites—that was after all how Michael came to be born. She had initiated a search of old records and, after several attempts, was able to find what she was looking for in the record of the old parliamentary committee on privacy for the year 1989.

The old film brought back memories of the June day in 1987 when she had heeded the urging in her computer mail to "Live Dangerously", and had dialled the number 728-3760-528 on the old fashioned TV control box one had in those days. (Curious, wasn't it, how time gives new meanings to old words. She recalled seeing a few of the old dial telephones when she was in primary school. Now everyone either pushed buttons or spoke the numbers directly into the telephone, but people still referred to it as "dialling" a number.)

Well, she had dialled the number, and onto her TV screen had come a genial looking middle-aged man dressed in hiking boots, blue shorts, and a red shirt. He had the slightly vacant look of someone reading from a script placed behind the camera. These days they wouldn't be so crude as to broadcast the same message to every viewer who answered the same call. The computer would piece together a film strip tailored to the particular psychological profile of the subject.

"If you are between the ages of fifteen and twenty," the genial man in the blue shorts had said, "I have a challenge for you." He had gone on to explain that the current unrest, boredom and unhappiness were due to society being too large, too complex and too bureaucratic. "Human understanding is simply not possible in such large groupings as we now have," he intoned.

"Over millions of years man existed in tribes which probably varied in size between five and five hundred people. All members of the tribe knew each other personally. Each knew how much trust he could place in his fellow man in times of war and in times of peace. All our inherited behaviour patterns are attuned to life in such a simple society, for it is known that it takes hundreds of thousands of years for significant inherited changes to become fixed in a large population. Our inherited behaviour patterns are essentially those of our forbears who formed the first cities some 150 generations ago at the dawn of recorded history.

"Our ability to learn customs which enable us to satisfy most of our inborn behaviour pattern in a 'civilized' world is a marvel of animal adaptability. But life in large communities can never be wholly satisfying, as mankind wasn't really designed for such a life.

"Shed your boredom! Shed your frustrations! Join me and my companions in a true community of equals on Lasqueti Island in the sunny Gulf of Georgia! Live the life of honest toil and true friendship, the life your forbears led before you. Think it over carefully and then leave me a note in my electronic mail box. I will contact you directly. But remember, there is only room for 120 people, and (pause) 103 (the number obviously inserted by a computer generated voice) people have already enrolled."

With a long sincere look, and a reminder that his name was Hiram Walker, the figure had faded from the screen, and the message ended, just as the final chord of the Chopin Nocturne in the background was played.

Julia had decided to enroll almost immediately. The objections of her parents had only made her the more determined. Having yielded to the extent of promising that she would return home if she was unhappy, she extracted the necessary $10,000 "founder's fee" from her father and set off.

At first she had enjoyed herself immensely, even though she was puzzled to find that they were a community of only 27, not 120 as had been promised. When questioned on this point, Hiram Walker, who turned out to be at least as genial as he had appeared to be on TV, had mumbled something about children under the thrall of their parents being unable to get away.

She had soon found a steady boy friend, Eric Loopstone, and since the policy of the community was to encourage couples to have children, they happily complied. Julia was pregnant within six months of her arrival.

Ah, those innocent, happy days. They seemed carefree and idyllic in retrospect, particularly as she and Eric had been consumed by mutual love. What passionate nights they had had! The emotion, long since forgotten, brought a hot blush to her face and a momentary increase in her heartbeat.

But all had not been idyllic. The mosquitoes had been bad whenever the wind had dropped, and the bed bugs had been horrible. Absolutely nothing would seem to remove them except the chemical repellents which were initially banned on the commune. After a full year of acid debate, insect repellents, in limited quantities, had finally been allowed.

Winter was somewhat dreary and wet on the island, and several times she had thought how convenient it would be to have her television information and entertainment system in front of her—but the community considered the system to be the embodiment of all that was wrong with society; so there were no systems.

She had not been accustomed to reading from books, and found them generally dull, and the reading hard on her eyes. While television surely was an evil influence, she had told herself, it seemed all its uses weren't evil. On the Lasqueti Island farm they were living without even the weather reports which could have been so useful. They also lacked electronic mail facilities, so Julia had to write letters home, and delivery sometimes took weeks, since the post office was really only set up to handle parcels.

But most of all, she missed the educational programs. Since she had been working on the farm, she had become interested in knowing more about farming, and she had developed a lively, but largely unfulfilled interest in the history of farming too. She had recalled somewhat ruefully that the program catalogue at home contained literally hundreds of programs on these two items alone.

Julia's first pregnancy had reached its term in October. It had been a difficult delivery, and the local doctor had been hurriedly called. The baby died on the way to the hospital. The doctor told her afterwards that had she been wearing the little electronic monitoring device that other prospective mothers usually wore in their last three months of pregnancy, the baby would have been saved.

She had returned to the community farm and to Eric with a heavy heart.

Some months later, serious dissension had broken out in the group. It appeared that a parliamentary enquiry concerning advertising and the individual's right to privacy had unearthed the fact that Hiram Walker, amongst others, had had illegal access to medical, educational and financial files. He had used the information from these files to decide to whom he should transmit his film advertising the community.

The medical and educational files had been used to select potentially bored and restive young people, the financial files to determine whether their parents might be able to make the needed financial contribution.

There had been an intense loyalty to and liking of Hiram Walker in the community. Indeed, members of the community referred to themselves as Hiramites. He was by turns resourceful, cheerful and philosophical: a father and a friend. He had held the community together through some difficult times and no one doubted the sincerity of his purpose.

Walker had admitted his error, but excused himself on the grounds of

19

necessity, and the fact that others made use of the same files for nefarious ends (as the parliamentary enquiry had shown). Why shouldn't he use the files to a really useful end, he had asked. His defence convinced most of his followers, though a few left at that time. Somehow though, the community was different afterwards. There had been an almost fierce suppression of further discussion of the issue—a suppression instigated not by Walker himself, who seemed almost to long for an occasion to air his past sins—but by his more ardent followers, of whom Eric was one of the most impassioned.

Meanwhile, the old debates had continued in new forms. Ploughing in the community had been conducted using magnificent Clydesdale horses imported from a rich farmer in Alberta, and a rather crude but nonetheless effective hand plough which Eric had cut, welded and bolted together using drawings from an old farmer's almanac. The problem was that the horses could only plough an acre a day, and in between times they consumed a lot of hay. It was Julia's Eric who had once more resolved the ensuing debate by suddenly appearing with an old Massey tractor, recovered from an abandoned farm outbuilding and quietly reconditioned even while the argument raged.

Those who had opposed the use of tractors had quietly accepted the inevitable.

It was ironic that in Eric's quiet victory lay the seeds for his own end.

Julia had become pregnant again in the late winter, but this had only increased her anxiety. She had felt she would do anything to have the baby survive, but despite (or perhaps because of?) his leading role in the mechanization of the colony, Eric would not entertain the thought of her using an electronic monitor. Slowly, she and Eric were drifting apart, and Julia came to see herself as the victim of a psychological entrapment, a victim ensnared moreover by illegal means as the parliamentry enquiry had clearly demonstrated.

She had returned home that September. Michael had been born six weeks later.

The following spring she had received a short note from a friend on Lasqueti, enclosing a tattered picture of herself which Eric had apparently carried with him to his death. The old Massey tractor had overturned onto him while he was using it to pull stumps on a steep hillside. Oddly, she had been hardly affected by his death at the time; her grief and regret came later. The Hiramite colony and Eric with it had seemed so remote, so distant. Almost as though they were on another planet.

Two worlds! Would the Humanity Firsters and the Brains Firsters succeed in creating two worlds equally remote? She thought they would. And just as the Hiramites had had intense arguments within their own group as to the extent they should make use of new technology, so too there would be factions within the two basic divisions urging compromises. Indeed the thought struck her that the compromise groups were perhaps the only hope for the long term survival of humanity. That, more than anything else in the history of the Hiramites, should be the message she tried to convey to Michael in this first section of the record. She must keep it short, but not too short since he had, after all, a personal involvement in this part of the presentation.

As the old parliamentary enquiry film rolled on, she found, much to her surprise, that it even contained shots of herself and Eric working together in the hay fields. She forced back the emotion that flooded her. Time was short.

Unfortunately the Hiramites themselves had kept no visual records of their activities, so that parliamentary enquiry film, much of it garnered by the press at the time, was all the original material she had to work with, though she could, and did, insert shots of herself recounting experiences, and of old keepsakes from the colony.

After three hours of hard work, she assembled a reasonable half hour history of the Hiramites, and of Eric's and her own involvement in the movement. She felt sure that Michael would grasp the message of the importance of technology to human well-being—he was conditioned to believe in that anyway—but would he understand the nobility, the essential humanity (with all its warts) of the Hiramites? Might he not just be confirmed in his bias towards a move to Australia?

How could she convey her own conviction that although the Brains Firsters, or BF'ers, understood well the importance of electronics technology and of artificial intelligence, they seemed to be totally confused in their understanding of what she had been taught were fundamental limits on the elasticity of human nature.

Perhaps she should start by describing the ways in which today's electronic circuitry mimicked the human brain, the way it simulated forgetfulness, and the way it injected emotion? But after wasting almost an hour reviewing on her monitor news clip after news clip which described these marvels of the past fifteen years, she realized she didn't really understand it, and hence could not possibly edit together a convincing record for Michael.

It was to history she must return: her own first love. Although history might not repeat itself, it must surely provide some important pointers to the future.

Suddenly she remembered the so-called Harvard lecture series. Although Harvard no longer existed as a university campus since people could no longer afford the luxury of coming to one place for the sole purpose of learning and researching, the venerable name lingered on, having been acquired at some expense by a large publishing house. The "Fellows" of Harvard were now scattered literally around the world. The original fellows had dissipated the endowment, first in publishing books with no hope of sale and finally, as an understanding of the future caught up with them, in rather stilted computer-aided learning routines. Unfortunately, they had not realized that in the meantime the population at large had ceased to be text literate but was instead image literate. That is, their understanding of the world around them was once more conditioned by images and sounds as had been the case with their distant ancestors. People just didn't read much anymore.

The publisher had replaced many of the Harvard fellows just a little faster than he decently should have with a strange collection of ex ad-men and film directors.

These new arrivals were able to transform the material of the remaining scholars into a sensational series of educational sequences on a great variety of topics. Of course, initially there had been a great deal of resistance to the association of ad-men with a venerable institution, but this resistance slowly faded once it was realized that when their creative talents were harnessed to important educational goals the results could be, to say the least, highly beneficial.

Julia quickly asked for the series on the history of modern thought by a certain Professor Venables. She scanned quickly through the introductory sections on Charles Darwin and the acid debate surrounding the acceptance of the Theory of Evolution and then lingered over the discussion of what Venables called the Great Sociobiology Debate. She recalled it now from the time she had studied the series in earnest a decade ago. Venables spent a long time describing it—indeed it was apparent he had been directly involved in the debate which lasted through the 1980's.

She could never understand why the debate had raged so long and fiercely. Once a person accepted the theory of evolution, it seemed only natural to her that one would assume that aspects of human behaviour were passed on through the genes just as much as the shape of the nose or the colour of eyes was passed on.

But no, it seemed that the facts conflicted with what were, at the time, commonly held religious and philosophical beliefs, so that it took a generation for the idea to be accepted despite the massive evidence accumulated by people like Konrad Lorenz and Edward Wilson (1). Every adult now knew that the ability to learn and adapt behaviour accordingly was nothing but a highly refined evolutionary tool which promoted survival. They knew that behaviour was an intricate mixture of inherited behaviour patterns fortified and filled out as to detail by a process of learning.

Surely every school child knew this by now too! Michael should not need reminding. Yet it was a crucial point in her presentation. Julia accordingly diverted to search for a good illustrative example to hammer the point home. She finally fixed on two five minute sequences and inserted them deftly into the growing record.

The first sequence showed some film of experiments with inexperienced turkey hens responding to their first brood of chicks. The role of inheritance in the hen's behaviour was demonstrated by showing that they treated anything that moved in their nest as an enemy unless it uttered the specific call of a turkey chick. Small stuffed animals fitted with a loudspeaker through which the correct call notes were piped were shown being carefully mothered. On the other hand, there were gruesome scenes of a deaf hen turkey murdering her chicks as soon as they hatched (2).

A clear, if somewhat chilling, demonstration of an inherited behaviour pattern, she thought.

Examples of inherited behaviour in mankind were unmistakable but more subtle, and hence difficult to show in a short period of time. She finally chose a film clip from a Harvard lecture series in which the professor reviewed and demonstrated the extraordinarily close similarity of human expression via body movements amongst humans everywhere, including isolated tribes (studied in the 1960's) and relatively cultured civilizations. She supplemented this with a brief lecture by Noam Chomsky himself of his findings about the basic similarity of human languages everywhere, and his demonstration that certain thought patterns must be inherited. His theories had received additional confirmation in the intervening twenty year period, but she liked the direct and convincing way in which the old man expressed himself.

Julia hoped that these two clips would remind Michael that even if the wrong choice rationally led to man's certain extinction, man could not, would not always make a rational choice. His survival in the past 100,000 years had depended on certain pre-programmed responses, and most of these pre-programmed responses were as surely incorporated in his genes as was the colour of his eyes and the shape of his chin. She programmed a pause into the record. She would stop here and discuss this point with Michael if necessary.

She assumed that Michael had already learned about the discovery of the structure of the DNA molecule by Crick and Watson in 1953. But she could never recall the number of different inherited characteristics the human genetic code permitted. She had no head for numbers, but Michael did, and he might want to know. The information system was soon able to remind her that some ten trillion (10^{13}) different characteristics could be inherited, more than enough to encode the vast inheritance of physical and behavioural characteristics with which man was born.

But if she was prepared to discuss the idea of inheritance of behaviour with Michael, she positively shrank from the idea of any discussion of computer technology. Even the history of its development put her mind into a state of confusion. But time was now very short. Only about two hours remained, and it was essential, she thought, that both of them review together the events which led directly to the dilemma which faced them.

Julia asked for sources of technical history, and was reminded by her AYEE that she and Michael had sat in on a presentation to the Computer Historical Society (B. C. Branch) by the father of one of Michael's friends. The presentation had been rather amateurish, but it was sincere and probably accurate too, as far as it went.

When she called it up on her screen she realized she had forgotten just how amateurish it was. Just like a TV program from the 1970's. About half the time the historian was simply looking into the camera and talking, with no relevant graphics or films to help make his point. No background music either, for that matter. How on earth could the speaker ensure himself of a receptive audience?

She watched the clip begin:

"What might be termed the computer takeover was so gradual that it had passed almost unnoticed by the general public until the last few years. It is now known that the takeover started early. Even by the 1960's, chess programs with grand master qualifications had been developed. There were interesting reports, too, in the late sixties and early seventies of people preferring to answer medical questions posed by a computer, over the same questions posed by a doctor or a nurse. The computer, it seemed, was unfailingly polite.

"There were also cases of impoverished children from ghettos who burst into tears over the kindness and consideration shown them by a computer instruction program which did little more than make such comments as 'That was well done, Johnny, now let's try the next problem.' It was easy to program such comments even in those days. Some children said they had never had such a kind human teacher.

"Another ominous, but relatively undetected indicator of the future, was a program written by a professor at MIT in 1966. It was capable of real conversation (using a typewriter and a TV screen). The conversation was not very enlightening, but, rather significantly, it was copied from a technique developed by a psychologist several decades earlier as a method of quieting troubled employees. The technique was to turn each statement by the speaker into a question based on the previous statement. If for some reason the interviewer (or the computer) was unable to turn the statement into a question, he simply inserted an innocuous comment such as 'Very interesting. Please continue.' or 'Can you elaborate on that.' In this way, the employee was encouraged to get what troubled him off his chest.

"Once computer experts combined forces with the sociobiologists, they made much more deliberate attempts to program emotion and creative thought into the computer. The latter capacity was spurred by the development of cheap associative memories which came into common use in the early 1980's and by the need for more sophisticated robot machines to do society's work.

"All these added capabilities were, of course, made possible by a half century of phenomenal price reductions which saw the price of the basic unit of memory decline from a cost of about $30 in the early 1950's to about three hundredths of a cent in 1980 and, amazingly, continuing on down to thirty millionths of a cent in 1990. The fact that inflation has caused this cost to double since 1995 should not let us lose track of the enormous significance of the change in cost of this most basic unit of intelligence.

"The only vaguely comparable phenomena in recorded history are the drastic reductions in cost and the increase in availability of energy which largely took place over a one hundred and fifty year period starting in the late 18th century, and the combined developments of the printing press and, about four hundred years later, a period of drastic reductions in the price of paper. It is safe to say, however, that the significance of these two development pales by comparison with that of electronic memory.

"Inexpensive speech synthesizers were already available in the 1970's, but they were relatively crude devices with limited vocabularies and rather unnatural sounding speech. By the mid 1980's, the synthesizers produced speech which was unrecognizable as artificial and by the late 1980's they were commonly available with "emotion control", which permitted changes in syntax and tone of voice appropriate to various levels of different emotions. Even mixed emotions were permitted. Indeed some mixture of emotions was normally necessary to achieve the desired tone of voice."

Even as she sat there, watching and listening, Julia wondered if the words she was hearing had been artificially synthesized or whether she was in fact listening to a faithful recording of the speaker. She knew that either was possible and that tests had proven that the detection of which was which was impossible for the human ear.

The speaker intruded on her thoughts. At least things had not reached that stage where the computer knew what she was thinking!

"Perhaps most important to the evolution of the computer was the development of programs which recognized speech reliably and which were capable of translating speech into another language. Progress had been relatively slow on both these fronts for years until the idea of personalized speech recognition and translation devices was generally accepted.

"Although any quality speech recognition program could detect clearly enunciated speech by the early 1980's, it was found that programs could be written which gradually adapted themselves, by a continual process of error correction, to virtual 100% accuracy in recognizing the speech of a single individual. Much of the development work for such programs had come about from an earlier need for a device which unmistakably identified a human voice with a person, thus permitting voice "signatures" to be used for electronic funds transfers. The later development of "personal" speech recognizers led to translators which were familiar enough with an individual's thinking to grasp the idea he wanted to get across, and thus avoid the sort of confusion early translation programs had with such phrases as: 'The spirit is willing but the flesh is weak,' which, after translation into Russian and back into English came back as, 'The wine is agreeable but the meat has spoiled.'

"By that time (the mid 1990's), some people came to regard these programs almost as alter egos. They even abbreviated alter ego to A. E., and referred to the hand held portable terminal they used to access their personal routines as their A. E.'s. At first this was thought to be a joke. Soon, however, the spelling was changed to Ayees, and people all but forgot the origin of the word as their reliance on the ever more sophisticated and personalized routines increased.

"Much care was taken by individuals to adjust the voice response units of their AYEES to have a tone pleasing to their ears. There were even cases of people getting married who couldn't speak a word to each other without using their AYEES, since they spoke different languages. In such cases great attention was paid to tailoring speech synthesizers to sound just like the loved one, when speech from that source was translated.

"By the year 2000, the AYEES had been developed to the point where, by the purchase of a special attachment, widows were able to carry on conversations with their dead husband's alter ego computer, although not with their actual husbands, who were indeed biologically dead."

Julia stopped the sequence there. The man was not so bad after all, especially considering that he was an amateur, but she must think of another way of reviewing more recent events. Michael's attention could not be held to the same sequence much longer.

Was it really only three years ago that the serious trouble had started? It seemed as though the constant tension had gone on forever. But it was in the year 2003 that the dependence of many people on their AYEES became very noticeable. Hucksters were selling personal advice modules to run on AYEES which turned out to have been partially financed by commercial operators who were causing the advice given to be biased in their favour.

There had been some strange mistakes too. In one famous case, a young man had been supplied with part of a female personal advice module by mistake. Although he said afterwards he had thought at the time it was strange advice, he had followed his AYEES' instructions to go out and find a handsome male sexual partner. After this case came to light, stricter labelling laws were brought into effect.

Instances such as these had triggered widespread public discussion of mankind's growing dependence on computers. Then it had gradually come to light that the dependence was greater than anyone had realized. Programs which adapted to and learned from new circumstances had been known since the 1960's. By the late 1980's, they were in general use for a wide variety of tasks. By the year 2000 they had grown to a level of sophistication which no man could any longer comprehend. Personal advice tendered by the computer was by no means infallible, but the statisticians had proved beyond doubt that on average it was better than advice tendered by a human.

The Humanity First (HF) movement sprang into being almost overnight. The Humanity Firsters claimed that human instincts and human behaviour patterns were designed for the preservation of the human race, and that computers posed a definite threat to the future of the human race. The more radical HF'ers proposed the destruction of all computers. Some started by throwing away their own AYEES (and were soon confounded by the opposition). Others suggested that if certain program changes were made to the personal advice modules of the opposition party, then all might be won over to the same opinion. As soon as word of this idea (or plot—depending on your personal viewpoint) got out, bitter accusations and counter accusations were hurled back and forth and a sort of guerilla warfare began.

The opposition party were at first less well organized and less vocal. Most of the intellectual elite opposed the HF movement as a typical rear guard attempt to impede progress, and they warned of the poverty, strife and misery which would result if the HF'ers had their way. They pointed, also, to the steady accumulation of order and intelligence over evolutionary history. Mankind had emerged as the supreme intelligence on Earth over millions of years. In the last few hundred years, his store of knowledge had increased at a phenomenal rate. Now, from his own brain, he had created a new, superior intelligence. We should be grateful, they said, for the sense of security which reliance on a superior intelligence had brought us. We were truly entering the golden era of mankind.

Once the movement was strong and important, historians had scurried to trace (incorrectly Julia suspected) the popular roots of this philosophy to an editorial which had appeared in 1978 in what was at the time a wide-circulation, news magazine (called *Time*). This editorial had recently been widely quoted by both sides. It was easy to find several film clips of it. Julia selected one produced by the Humanity Firsters. The Chopin musical accompaniment vaguely reminded her of her introduction to the Hiramites. However this time it was the *Marche Funebre* which played in the background. The text rolled slowly across the screen, and was simultaneously read by a man with a deep bass voice:

> We are still in control, but the capabilities of computers are increasing at a fantastic rate, while raw human intelligence is changing slowly, if at all. Computer power is growing exponentially; it has increased tenfold every eight years since 1946. Four generations of computer evolution—vacuum tubes, transistors, simple integrated circuits and today's miracle chips—followed one another in rapid succession, and the fifth generation, built out of such esoteric devices as bubble memories and Josephson junctions, will be on the market in the 1980s. In the 1990s, when the sixth generation appears, the compactness and reasoning power of an intelligence built out of silicon will begin to match that of the human brain.

> By that time [the 1990's], ultra-intelligent machines will be working in partnership with our best minds on all the serious problems of the day, in an unbeatable combination of brute reasoning power and human intuition. What happens after that? Dartmouth President John Kemeny, a pioneer in computer usage, sees the ultimate relation between man and computer as a symbolic union of two living species, each completely dependent on the other for survival. The computer—a new form of life dedicated to pure thought—will be taken care of by its human partners, who will minister to its bodily needs with electricity and spare parts. Man will also provide for computer reproduction, as he does today. In return, the computer will minister to our social and economic needs. Child of man's brain rather than his loins, it will become his salvation in a world of crushing complexity.

> The partnership will not last very long. Computer intelligence is growing by leaps and bounds, with no natural limit in sight. But human evolution is a nearly finished chapter in the history of life. The human brain has not changed, at least in gross size, in the past 100,000 years, and while the organization of the brain may have improved in that period, the amount of information and wiring that can be crammed into a cranium of fixed size is limited.

> That does not mean the evolution of intelligence has ended on the earth. Judging by the record of the past, we can expect that a new species will arise out of man, surpassing his achievements as he has surpassed those of his predecessor, *Homo erectus*. Only a carbon-chemistry chauvinist would assume that the new species must be man's flesh-and-blood descendants, with brains housed in fragile shells of bone. The new kind of intelligent life is more likely to be made out of silicon (3).

How accurate the writer had been in his predictions—yet how complacent about the stress this self-inflicted challenge would place on humanity. Clearly, there was much more to the Humanity Firster's position than "carbon chemistry chauvinism." A basic change in man's instinctual behaviour patterns would seem to be required.

She herself would outline the more recent history for Michael she decided, using as an aid only this rather lurid version of the *Time* editorial.

She would tell Michael that it was the Humanity Firsters who eventually found a name for their oppositon. They called them the Brains First movement, or BF'ers for short. The fact that BF was also a popular shorthand for 'bloody fool' had not been lost on either the coiners of the expression or the general public. By then it was too late for the BF'ers to change their name. Though they did subsequently adopt the name "People for Progress," it never caught on.

The polarization of society on the issue had been swift and terrible. Mutual suspicion gave way to open hostility. Both sides developed militant right wings. The mass of people in the middle were bombarded with hate literature from both sides, and prominent members of both movements were subject to bombings and kidnappings. Social pressures to join one group or the other became intolerable. Neutral personal advice modules for AYEES simply were not available. Computer advice was slanted one way or the other according to the source from which the module had come. Now no one was sure whether or not his advice module might have been sabotaged. Indeed, many Humanity Firsters didn't believe that a personal advice module could be programmed to advise against its own continuance, so that the HF'ers were frequently in a state of near hysteria and chronic indecisiveness as they relearned old habits of decision making without "real" knowledge.

By 2005, it had become apparent to both sides that they were headed for an armed, computer-controlled conflict. Almost 80% of the world's population were thought to be HF'ers, but they comprised, by and large, the poorer, less powerful people. Predictably most (though by no means all) computer experts were BF'ers, as were many government leaders and university professors. Their strength was far greater than their numbers would suggest.

After lengthy debate in the assembly of the United Peoples, and extensive polling of the populations of the world, it was finally agreed that the only solution, temporary though it might turn out to be, was segregation.

Julia, as with all other adults on Earth, had received top-priority notice in her personal mail box 59 days ago.

There was to be no more killing. Each person was to have sixty days in which to declare his or her allegiance to the HF or BF movement. All BF'ers would be moved to Australia which would become exclusive BF territory. The rest would continue where they were.

Julia snapped out of her reverie with a jolt. Only an hour to go to complete the record. Michael would be getting hungry soon. She consulted her AYEE for dinner suggestions, specifying something that Michael particularly liked, but which was easy to prepare and available from food already stored in the house. She had forgotten about the Cornish game hens stored in the irradiated microbe-free storage bin for some months, but on being reminded of them, quickly decided to program them into the dinner.

She got up and walked through to the kitchen. Julia had only to insert the game hens and the vegetables she wanted in the appropriate microwave oven compartments and specify the dinner time for 6 pm, for the food preparation to be essentially complete. She quickly set the table and, as an afterthought, selected a bottle of light red wine and pulled the "plastifram" cork to give the wine some time to breathe. At $50 even for this comparatively ordinary bottle of wine, this was a luxury in which Julia seldom indulged. She headed quickly back to the screen room and sat down. Then, on an impulse, leaving the editing/recorder on, she walked purposefully up to her bedroom and closed the door.

She drew the curtains carefully shut and pulled her old video-disc machine out of her walk-in closet. Then, from her chest of drawers, from beneath a pile of sweaters and T-shirts, she withdrew a video-disc wrapped only in a department store wrapper. Placing it on the machine, she sat on the end of the bed and watched intently as the screen came to life.

It was a recording of Sol Feldman, one of the founders of the Humanity Firster's movement, and one of the first assassinated some three years previously. The disc itself was about ten years old, and dated from the time that Sol had first risen to prominence as a philosophical mediator, popular at first primarily in California (his home State) and British Columbia. With the passing of the years, his views had become somewhat more strident, and he had dissociated himself from his former more moderate views. As a result, the disc was hard to find now. Both BF'ers and HF'ers denounced the views he formerly held with almost equal passion, the more so as a significant fraction of the uncommitted population had become adherents of his earlier philosophy.

In his earlier days, Feldman had been a Maslowian, that is an adherent of the views put forward by Abraham Maslow, the American psychologist, and by Ruth Benedict, the American anthropologist, but he had refined and updated their views in the light of more recent scientific findings about human and animal behaviour. No one was quite sure why he had subsequently abandoned his former mentors. He himself had said shortly before his death that he believed it was too late to establish a state of implicit trust in a society grown corrupt from easy living and dependence on technology. It was necessary first, therefore, to rid the world of computers, which did so much to make life easy, before even attempting to establish a better society. Detractors felt that his new, much more combative approach to world organization was due to the fact that his wife (who had been matched to him by computer) abandoned him and their three children to join a free-love cult headed by the designer of one of the more successful of the early AYEE units.

But Feldman's earlier philosophy still exerted a strong pull on Julia, though she was nervous about letting others know of her interest. It seemed clear that the future polarized socieities of the BF'ers and the HF'ers, threatened as they would be from the outside, would not tolerate the retention of such subversive material, although there was as yet no law against possessing or viewing it.

Feldman's voice spoke clearly and strongly.

"My friends, you ask me how we can achieve a harmonious society?

"I tell you it cannot be done through charity and self-denial. Nor yet can it be done through elimination of hard labour; nor the establishment of equality for all mankind; nor through the accretion of great wealth for all mankind; nor through the love of God or Allah or Buddha.

"While all of these activities or goals can help, one must remember that they have been tried before without conspicuous success. The wells of self-denial and charity eventually run dry. Idleness is the handmaiden of boredom and discontent. Equality is a meaningless term unless it is specified in what respects people shall be equal. Only equality of opportunity has any logical basis and even this important principle is devilishly difficult to apply. As to wealth, there is no evidence to show that once societies are wealthy enough to provide their members with food and shelter, additional wealth leads to greater overall happiness, though it would appear that individuals derive happiness from having greater wealth than others in their own society. Nor does the history of religious wars lead us to associate religious zeal with social harmony."

Downstairs a door banged shut. There were footsteps on the stairs. Julia halted the machine just as Michael opened the door. She turned from Feldman's frozen face to meet Michael's quizzical look.

"You left the video machine running downstairs, Mother . . . and anyway, what are you watching up here?"

Julia's mind raced in panic. If she showed him this old disc now without his having seen the material she had so carefully prepared downstairs, would he just laugh at her for being interested in an old fool? If so, all her plans would be shattered. Yet, Michael was impatiently awaiting a reply. In the circumstances, she had no time to fabricate a lie, so she decided to make the best of it, and tell the truth.

"It is an old video-disc of Sol Feldman," she said.

"Isn't he the guy who was assassinated three years ago?"

"Yes, he is, but . . . " she was going to explain that the record predated Feldman's more militant phase as an HF'er, but Michael broke in.

"Oh good. Is this from his Maslowian period?"

Julia could hardly believe her ears.

"Hey, Kathleen says that he was quite a guy then. Her parents often talk to her about him. Did you know him too, Mom?"

There seemed to be a new respect and warmth in his tone as he sat down to watch the disc with her.

Julia's mind set off in new directions. How well did Michael know Kathie Mansbridge? Were Kathie's parents, then, followers of Feldman? Even if they were, which way would they be opting? Would they stay here or go to Australia with the BF'ers?

Treating her silence as assent, and possibly sensing her confusion, Michael put one arm around her. With his free hand he restarted the machine and Feldman's face became animated once more as his famous address continued.

"To understand how to achieve a harmonious society one must first understand what are the limits of human plasticity and what are the needs and drives which are fundamental and which cannot be repressed or altered without gross distortions resulting . . . "

Julia watched Michael as he sat, his attention absorbed by the screen, while Feldman described the once famous Maslowian hierarchy of human needs, starting with the basic physiological needs of oxygen, food, shelter, etc. and moving upwards through the safety and security needs, the belongingness and love needs, and the esteem needs, to the need to be able to achieve one's potential to the full, the self-actualization need. Feldman finished his discussion of the needs-hierarchy with a direct quote from Maslow himself:

> The logic of facts, however unclearly seen, has been unmistakable; inexorably, the therapist has been forced to differentiate more basic from less basic wishes (or needs, or impulses). It is as simple as this: the frustration of some needs produces pathology, the frustration of other needs does not. The gratification of these needs produces health, of others not. These needs are inconceivably stubborn and recalcitrant. They resist all blandishments, substitutions, bribes, and alternatives; nothing will do for them but their proper and intrinsic gratifications. Consciously or unconsciously they are craved and sought forever. They behave always like stubborn, irreducible, final unanalyzable facts that must be taken as given or as starting points not to be questioned. It should be an overwhelmingly impressive point that almost every school of psychiatry, psychoanalysis, clinical psychology, social work, or child therapy has had to postulate some doctrine of instinctlike needs no matter how much they disagreed on every other point (4).

Then Feldman attacked those who interpreted the needs-hierarchy to mean that increased wealth in a society would necessarily allow its members to shift their emphasis from the more basic needs towards the self-actualization need, with a steady increase in happiness and harmony resulting.

Not necessarily so, said Feldman, quoting Fred Hirsch, "the esteem-needs depend primarily on social status, and status is not easily shared. If antiques were plentiful, people would no longer acquire them as a status symbol, and would look elsewhere for scarce commodities"(5).

Then he skillfully switched the topic of discussion to sociobiology.

"For millions of years man has evolved in such a way that his inherited behaviour favours the survival of his race. Will he now calmly pass over his superiority on the evolutionary scale to an inanimate product of his own hands and mind?"

"You bet he won't! Not without a major struggle." Julia watched Michael closely for signs of scorn or disbelief, but he sat motionless, glued to the screen. What was the boy thinking? How she wished she knew him better!

Feldman's voice penetrated her consciousness once more.

"Fifteen years ago, people said computers could not learn, or show emotion or demonstrate an appreciation for beauty. Now we know better, and with this knowledge has come the slow realization that not only can all of those qualities which we view as being "essentially human" be programmed, but indeed they *are* to a rather large extent programmed in us. In fact, as we now know, man's actions at a given time are determined by a combination of inherited traits, accummulated learning which lends specificity and individuality to those traits, and the physical and chemical state of the body and brain!

"But don't listen to our philosopher friends who say 'Aha! A nasty determinist theory! If you spread such beliefs, no one will accomplish anything. They will just lie around doing nothing, saying that their fate is determined for them, so they need only wait to see what happens!'"

Julia chuckled to herself at the thought of a world full of people lying about waiting for something to happen.

Initially, philosophers and religious leaders had been unable to understand that the brand of determinism of which Feldman spoke did not imply a resigned acceptance of one's lot. Far from it.

She had enjoyed making this very point herself as a learning mediator, and realized fully how difficult the basic concepts were to grasp. Absorbed in the subject as she had been, it seemed blatantly obvious to her that the very behaviour patterns which are part of the inherited baggage of mankind prevented him from lying about waiting for the world to react on him.

However, Feldman had done much to relieve the fears of the clerics by pointing out that there would always be a certain irreducible element of chance in the working of the brain. Even in the year 2005, it was not possible to define all the relevant variables such as blood viscosity and pressure, temperature, external visual and aural stimuli, etc., with sufficient precision to predict the outcome of the decisions which could go either way, although the outcome of many human decisions was, of course, easy to predict.

33

The main body of philosophical and subsequently of theological thought, although rejecting Feldman's later extremism, absorbed his contention that since man was happiest when his inherited behavioural patterns were able to find appropriate release, it behooved man to understand as accurately as possible just what the nature of those behaviour patterns and of the appropriate release mechanisms were. Yet somehow things had gone terribly awry.

The people and the politicians, in pursuing their own interests, had wandered further and further away from activities which benefited the society at large. Julia wanted to blame them and to react angrily at their greed and short-sightedness for placing Michael, herself and billions of others in the predicament they were in today.

But Julia realized that no one and yet everyone was really to blame. It was complexity that had done them in. Every increase in the standard of living, every increase in the number of human beings supported by the global system was won at the price of an increasingly complex network of interrelationships until it could almost be said that a change in anything caused an unpredictable change in almost everything else. In such circumstances, everyone could do what they wanted and claim it was in the public interest that they do so. Thus, AYEE development had proceeded without regulation, not because the dangers were not foreseen, but rather because no one could reach agreement on what the specific dangers and remedies were. In the meantime, enormous fortunes were made in AYEE manufacture by a few large corporations, and the profits had been used to acquire control of much of the rest of the world's economy.

Now Feldman was off into the Benedict-Maslow concept of social synergy. His speech, she knew, would only last another ten minutes.

"I never knew Ruth Benedict. I wish I had. She was a poet and an anthropologist. Before she died in 1948, she achieved considerable renown for her anthropological writings, yet it was an unpublished manuscript, recovered by Abraham Maslow, which won her lasting fame.

"In her professional life she studied a number of very different cultures and societies, and became known for her thesis that each human culture was a separate whole and that individual aspects of a culture, such as religious practice and marriage rites, had to be viewed in the context of the whole culture. Comparisons of specific rites and customs with those of other cultures were, she maintained, non-productive.

"Yet she too was bothered by the question I posed at the beginning: How can we achieve a harmonious society?

"Some of the societies she had studied were obviously more harmonious than others, and after deep thought and study, she felt she had found the key to social harmony. It lay not in the individual customs, rites or religions of the more successful societies, but rather in the social structure itself. She noted that the societies she admired as being relatively harmonious and happy were those where social customs and laws were so shaped that the dichotomy between selfish and unselfish actions was reduced to a minimum. Inhabitants of such societies had only infrequently to decide whether they should do something for the common good *or* something for their own good. Usually, by one activity both ends could be achieved. Benedict applied the medical term *synergy* to this social concept, and wrote of societies high in social synergy as being those so structured that more often than not individual and community welfare resulted from a single activity. In low-synergy societies, individual and community interests were frequently opposed.

"The need for esteem is, as we know, an important need of all normal humans. A telling example of the role that bestowal of esteem can play relative to social synergy was given by Maslow from his personal experience as follows:

> I remember my confusion when I came into the Blackfoot society and tried to find out who was the richest man, and found that the rich man had nothing. When I asked the white secretary of the reserve who was the richest man, he mentioned a man none of the Indians had mentioned, that is, the man who had on the books the most stock, the most cattle and horses. When I came back to my Indian informants and asked them about Jimmy McHugh, about all his horses, they shrugged with contempt. "He keeps it," they said, and as a consequence, they hadn't even thought to regard him as wealthy. White Headed Chief was "wealthy" even though he owned nothing. In what way then did virtue pay? The men who were formally generous in this way were the most admired, the most respected and the most loved men in the tribe. These were the men who benefited the tribe, the men they could be proud of, the men who warmed their hearts.
>
> To say it another way, if White Headed Chief, this generous man, had discovered a gold mine or stumbled across some pile of wealth, everyone in the tribe would have been happy because of his generosity. If he had been an ungenerous man, as happens so frequently in our society, then the tendency would have been as it is for our friends who have suddenly acquired great wealth; it is apt to set them over against us. Our institutions encourage the development of jealousy, envy, resentment, distance, and finally a real likelihood of enmity, in a situation like this (6).

Julia put her arm around Michael and squeezed him gently. The answering squeeze told her that he was aware of her and in sympathy, but his concentration remained focused on Feldman's image and words. She marvelled at this. How could this fifteen year old mechanical genius of a son of hers focus on philosophy? And did he understand what was being said, or was he merely mesmerized by the skillful delivery? She must find out before she showed it to him again (in its proper sequence this time), after dinner.

"My friends," Feldman had almost finished his speech now, "we have learned much since Maslow's time, but we have forgotten a lot too.

"In Maslow's day they knew that social synergy was much easier to achieve in small groups, but we have ignored this fact and formed even more centralized, more complex industrial and political groupings. And for what? In a search for economic efficiency? To flatter the self-esteem of our leaders who became bigger chiefs in the process? There is strong evidence to suggest that wealthier societies are not, on the whole, any happier than their poorer neighbours. Wealth is not a basic human need, although food, shelter and self-esteem are. And if the opportunities did not exist, our leaders would not thirst after ever more power and influence.

"While we are able, we must use our new found wealth of artificial intelligence to help decentralize our society, to give individuals and groups a sense of independence and self-sufficiency, while at the same time keeping them conscious of the effects of their actions on others. For nothing can be more certain than the strife which will result if the human need for self-esteem and self-reliance is ignored on a large scale.

"Computers and communications can be constructively used to promote the efficient co-ordination of the otherwise independent activities of small groups working on various aspects of a related enterprise, whether it be the manufacture of auto parts or the provision of banking services. Our perception of what can be entrusted to local initiative and what must be co-ordinated centrally will have to become much more finely tuned. With a good communications network there will be time to consult, where previously consultation was impossible. With a good computer, it will be possible to provide products and services in a variety which is better attuned to individual needs and preferences.

"Computer and telecommunications technologies are *not* neutral and unbiased. They do present mankind with opportunities for satisfying his instinctive drives which would not otherwise be presented. Of these drives, the drive for status is notable in that it is the only drive which is almost inevitably a win/lose situation. One man's gain in status is likely to result in someone else losing status, and vice versa. The other drives, those for security, material well-being, affection, self-fulfilment, etc., need not be win/lose, but can be satisfied, in a well-organized society, so that co-operative rather than competitive efforts are most rewarding.

"Do not, my friends, assume that the system will automatically ensure that this most vital of new technologies is put to good use. You must take the time to grasp it, to understand it, and to help decide how it will be wisely used to benefit us all."

Sounds of thunderous applause came over the loudspeakers, and the scene before them showed a massive crowd assembled outdoors somewhere in the barren hills of California . . . .

But the world had not listened to those words of Feldman's, and now, ten short years later, society was being split asunder, polarized on the crucial issue of the continued supremacy of mankind. Feldman himself was one of hundreds of victims.

Australia or Canada? Machines or men? She realized that these weren't the issues any longer. Only Michael's survival really mattered to her now. Where should they go to ensure that?

Julia's AYEE sounded the call to inform her that dinner was ready. She and Michael rose without a word and went downstairs to eat.

REFERENCES TO CHAPTER 1

1. Further information on sociobiology can be found in Wilson, Edward O., *Sociobiology: A New Synthesis,* The Belknap Press of Harvard University, Cambridge, Mass., 1975.

2. These experiments were first conducted by Schleidt and Schleidt. They are reported in Konrad Lorenz, *Evolution and Modification of Behaviour*, University of Chicago Press, Chicago, 1955, p. 36.

3. Jastrow, Robert, "Toward an Intelligence Beyond Man's", *Time,* 20 February 1978, p. 47.

4. Maslow, Abraham H., *Motivation and Personality* (2nd edition), Harper and Row, New York, 1970, pp. 78-79.

5. Hirsch, Fred, *Social Limits to Growth,* A Twentieth Century Fund Study, Harvard University Press, Cambridge, Mass., 1976.

6. Maslow, Abraham H., "Synergy in the Society and in the Individual", *Journal of Individual Psychology,* Vol. 20, 1964, pp. 153-164. Reprinted in Maslow, *The Farther Reaches of Human Nature,* Penguin Books, Harmondsworth, England, 1975, pp. 191-202.

2 SIMPLE NOTES ON A COMPLEX FUTURE
John Madden

Julia's world is not a pure figment of my imagination. It is based on a known and foreseeable series of scientific technical advances, primarily in the field of computer technology.

It would be misleading to describe these developments in terms of a sudden breakthrough, although in a historical perspective from two or three hundred years hence, the last half of the twentieth century (during which the major developments occur) may well appear as such. They are, rather, the result of a long series of continuous improvements, with here and there a major breakthrough such as the invention of the transistor.

In this chapter, I have attempted to provide a scientific background and perspective on computer and communications development so that the technical reality of Julia's world, which spans the last two decades of this century and the first decade of the next, can be more readily assessed.

COMPUTERS AND MICROCHIPS

Shortly after the Second World War, when computers were in their infancy, it was estimated that twelve computers would be adequate to satisfy total U.S. demand. This estimate was later raised to fifty (1).

In retrospect, these figures are ludicrous, and should serve as a useful lesson in humility for those who try their hand at technical forecasting. There were an estimated 88,000 computing installations in the U.S. by the end of 1971, about 3,600 in Canada, and about 160,000 installations worldwide. By now, such number counts are almost meaningless. Since 1971, when the first computer on a single chip measuring less than 1/50 of a square inch was produced, microcomputers have been manufactured by the hundreds of thousands and are finding their way into a bewildering array of equipment, from TV games to automobiles. How could the forecasters of thirty years ago have been so wrong?

It was ridiculously easy when you think of it. Early computers cost millions of dollars, consumed many kilowatts of power, required large rooms with special cooling equipment to house them, and were notoriously unreliable. Hardly the sort of beast one would invite into one's home.

The price of executing an instruction on a computer has declined by a factor of about 1,000,000 since the early 1950's. It is as though you saw a beautiful mansion for sale in 1950 at a price of a million dollars and came back today to find it for sale for about a dollar. Not only that, but you would discover that unlike the mansion of thirty years ago which required many servants to maintain it, and which was continuously experiencing failures in the heating, plumbing and electrical systems, the mansion today would cost only pennies to maintain while its essential systems were so reliable that you would not expect to experience a failure during your lifetime or that of your children.

Of course, if you could buy a house for $1.00 you would treat it very differently from a house costing $1,000,000. Likewise, the computer which now sits easily on a thumbnail may perform almost identical functions to the roomful of tubes which characterized its ancestors, but there the resemblance ceases.

The returns are not yet in on what the computer will do for and to us. We know that NASA could not have launched a rocket to the moon without computers: we are told that computers are becoming an indispensable tool in cancer research and we strongly suspect that many multinational conglomerates would come unstuck without the computer, but all of these were made possible by computers costing in the $100,000 to $10,000,000 range. We haven't yet seen the end of the price reductions, nor realized the impact on our lives of being able to buy a computer on a chip for less than $10.00.

Computer development did not really get into high gear until transistors started to become commercially available in the 1950's. Then it became possible to amplify and switch a signal or to produce chains of electrical pulses without having to power thousands of little heaters, one to each vacuum tube. The consequences in terms of size, power consumption and reliability (though not, initially, in the speed) of electronic computers was enormous. Prices came tumbling down and circuit reliability, after a slow start, soared upwards.

Early transistors were manufactured primarily from a relatively rare element called germanium, but silicon, the most abundant element on earth, soon became the dominant element used in transistor manufacture. (One can buy a four inch diameter wafer of 99.999999% pure silicon—enough to make many thousand transistors—for less than $10).

In the early days, transistor manufacturing was almost a black art. The technology is tricky and reproducibility of transistor characteristics, an essential requirement of mass production, was difficult to obtain.

To begin with, materials of very high purity are required. It is necessary to introduce very small quantities of specific impurities to well-defined small regions of the basic material and to attach electrodes in appropriate places. These impurities, or "dopants" (the elements boron and phosphorus are two commonly used dopants), alter the electrical characteristics of the silicon and make it behave in such a way that it can be used to switch or amplify electrical currents or signals. The characteristics of the transistor (such as its switching speed, the amount of input signal needed to cause it to switch, or if it is designed as an amplifier, the degree to which the transistor output will faithfully match its input) are vitally dependent on the purity of the basic material, the concentration of the dopants, and the thickness and shape of the different regions of the transistor, each of which must have a reliable electrical contact to permit attachment to other circuit elements.

It is small wonder then that transistor manufacturing, particularly in the early days, was somewhat of a hit or miss affair. In fact, the standard manufacturing process was (and by and large still is), to make a large number of transistors and test each one. Those whose characteristics match the design specifications within approved tolerances are accepted. Those which come close might well be dumped in a second bin to be sold at a lower price as low grade transistors. The rest are thrown out.

A very important number, then, in determining the manufacturing cost of a transistor is what is called the "yield", or the percentage of good transistors produced. In the early days, yields of 5 to 10% were not uncommon. The manufacturing cost of the transistor therefore was 20 to 10 times what it would have been with a 100% yield. Not surprisingly, great effort was exerted in improving yields—primarily through the use of cleaner manufacturing environments, more carefully controlled doping processes, and the development of transistor designs which were less susceptible to manufacturing irregularities.

Yields improved steadily, and the price of transistors plummetted, while their quality and reliability improved. But then an interesting thing happened. Starting in the middle 1950's, people began to ask themselves why it would not be possible to put other essential electrical components— resistors and capacitors in particular—on the same piece of material as the transistor, in this way saving the trouble and expense of connecting the bits and pieces together after manufacture.

By that time the technology of the photographer was being introduced into transistor manufacturing, except that whereas the photographer would take a relatively small negative and project an enlarged image on photosensitive paper, the transistor manufacturer did the reverse. He drew out on a piece of paper the boundaries of an area which (for example) might represent the collector of a transistor. This pattern was then reproduced many times on a large piece of paper, which was subsequently photoreduced

41

onto a very small piece of film. This film "negative" was then used to project the images required to delineate the essential components of hundreds or even thousands of transistors onto a "substrate" of basic material (silicon for example) coated with a suitable photo-sensitive layer. The next step was to etch away the unwanted areas of the photo-sensitive layer and process the exposed areas to produce the desired effects. The same basic technique was repeated until the number of layers required to fabricate a complete device had been built up. The substrate was then cut up into "chips" to form hundreds or thousands of individual transistors.

This manufacturing technique, which is called photolithography, turned out to be admirably suited to development of the idea of producing other circuit elements on the same substrate as the transistor. The Integrated Circuit (or IC) was born. Of all the electronic widgets and gadgets (including radio and television sets), none offered so promising a market for the IC as the computer. For a single computer uses thousands, even hundreds of thousands of transistors, while a radio or TV set uses only a handful.

There is another good reason why computers spurred the development of integrated circuit. Computers tend to use a few basic circuits over and over again, and almost all of the transistors used in a computer are used as switches; that is, they are either "on" or "off." Such transistors are easier to make than those which are used in most amplifiers, where the output signal must at all times be a constant proportion of the input signal or else the amplifier "distorts" the signal. In other words, not only was the market potential for IC's used in computers very high, but also the manufacturing yields were likely to be good since these IC's were relatively easy to produce.

Thus, the marriage between the computer, and what came to be called the solid state electronics industry, was consumated. Computers were the fuel that fired the industry. The other applications were spin-offs.

The Economics of IC Manufacturing

With the introduction of integrated circuits, the problem of manufacturing yields, which had been beaten back to manageable proportions in transistor manufacture, raised its ugly head again. The more complex patterns being etched on the substrate used up a larger area, increasing the probability that somewhere in that area was a speck of dust or a material imperfection sufficient to render the device useless.

For this reason, and because the cost of processing a silicon wafer is roughly constant (in the $100 range) regardless of the number of individual circuits on the wafer, or of the diameter of the wafer, there has been a strong push both to increase the density of circuits on the chip and to increase the wafer size.

For example, one integrated circuit, produced in 1964, contained 14 transistors (plus 10 resistors and two capacitors) on a chip measuring 0.07 "x 0.07", yielding a density of under 3000 transistors per square inch. The INTEL 8748 microcomputer (1977), contains some 20,000 transistors on a substrate measuring 0.22 x 0.260 inches—for a circuit density of 350,000 transistors per square inch.

For similar reasons of manufacturing economy, the diameter of the silicon wafer substrate used has increased steadily from 1 inch in 1964 to 3 and 4 inches in 1978, with a diameter of 6 inches or more predicted for 1985. The technical problem here is to maintain uniformity and purity in crystals of such large diameter.

The limits on circuit density are set by the fineness of the lines which can be reliably reproduced by the photo engraving process used to define the deposition patterns on the chip. Present technology routinely produces circuit elements a few millionths of a metre across. The limit on how fine a line can be reproduced is determined by the wavelength of the light used to project the image. By moving from the ultraviolet light used today to shorter wavelength x-rays or to electron beam projection, line widths can be reduced by a factor of ten (permitting equivalent circuits to be compressed into one hundredth the area).

Thus, the enormous progress in computer development over the last twenty years, paced as it has been by developments in solid state electronics, is due not so much to a series of technological breakthroughs, as to hard-slogging attention to detail and the gradual elaboration of better manufacturing techniques. There is considerable wisdom as well as humour in the definition of a "breakthrough" as "three fall throughs in a row."

It was, therefore, simply a matter of time before the techniques needed to produce high yields were developed to the point where somebody said, "Why not put a whole computer processor on a single substrate (or chip)?" History doesn't record how many times someone asked the question and was laughed out of his boss's office before a Californian firm called INTEL produced the first "computer on a chip" in 1971, three years after the company's foundation by a small group of scientists and engineers. By 1977 the company had 8,000 employees and was doing $282M a year in business!

The number of circuit components per chip has approximately doubled every year since 1959, and this startling progression shows every sign of continuing at least until 1985. The combined effort of circuit density increase and other technological improvements can be seen in Figure 2-1 where the price decline in computer memory is plotted from 1973 onwards.

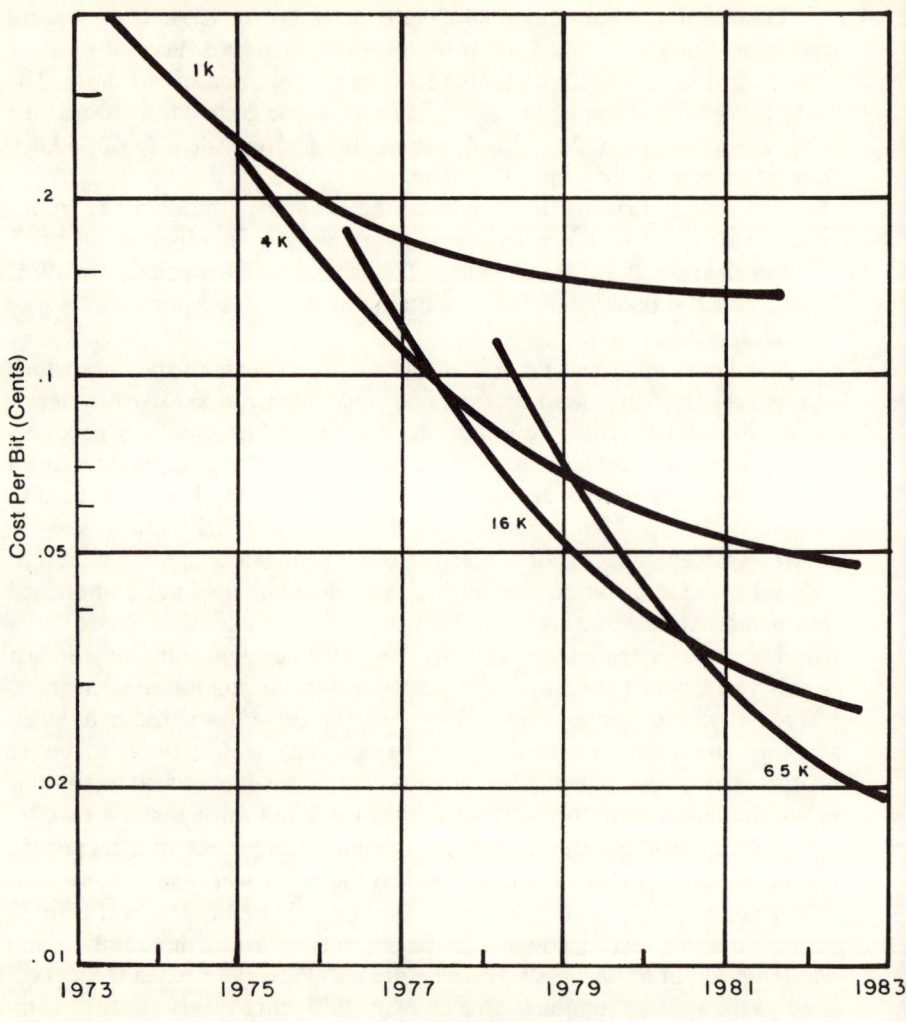

Figure 2-1

This figure, which is reproduced from an article in *Scientific American* (2), clearly demonstrates the way each large scale integrated circuit decreases in price as development costs are written off and new competitive products reach the market. Much more dramatic, though, are the overall price declines resulting directly from the increasing number of memory elements economically contained on a single chip. Industry insiders are virtually unanimous that price decreases will continue at least until 1985. Many see price declines continuing well beyond that time.

The following hypothetical example provides some insight into the economic forces which drive the micro electronics industry. It costs roughly $100 to process a single silicon wafer, regardless of its size or the number of circuit elements it contains (3). It is likely that a single wafer would contain several hundred microcomputers of which, on average, there would be 40 of acceptable quality. The manufacturing cost, in this instance, is therefore about $2.50 per chip. Yet such chips may sell in the $100 to $300 range. Why?

Profits from successful products can indeed be high (the risks are high too), but apart from the usual additional overhead expenses and middleman mark ups there is another very important reason for the price spread. The cost of tooling up to produce the first chip is very high indeed, particularly so when the circuit being produced is as complex as a microcomputer. Circuit development may take several years and the costs are normally closely guarded corporate secrets, but a ball park figure of $1M for a reasonably sophisticated microcomputer complete with minimal support software would not be too far out.

If the full manufacturing and marketing cost for such a chip is five dollars, the required sales price to recover the original investment as a function of the number sold is clearly strongly dependent on the estimated market. For example, if the estimated market was only 5000 chips, a selling price of $205 would be needed just to break even. If the estimated market was 10,000, the corresponding price would be $105. A market of 100,000 chips, would suggest a price of $10 (4).

Looked at another way, if the manufacturer estimates the market for such a chip at 10,000, and prices his product accordingly, and if he then sells only 5,000, he will realize a $500,000 loss. If, on the other hand, he sells 50,000 chips, then he makes a $500,000 profit.

From this sort of an analysis it is easy to see how the manufacturer of a pocket calculator chip could afford to reduce his price by a factor of 10 or 20 (as has happened) once his initial investment has been paid off. But of course he won't reduce his price unless competitive pressures force him to.

Given these kinds of economic conditions, that is, very high market entry costs and low unit manufacturing costs, it is difficult to imagine that there will not soon be a considerable thinning out of the number of competitors in the industry. With rapidly falling production costs, it is necessary for companies to increase sales volumes correspondingly just to maintain gross company revenues at a constant value. The sort of growth that a company like INTEL has experienced can only be achieved by even greater sales growth.

This problem has been addressed by Gordon Moore, the president of INTEL. His estimates of the 1976 market and of the potential 1985 market are shown in Table 2-1. Based on current growth rates, the industry will be capable of *producing ten to one hundred times more circuit functions than the market he foresees for them.* While some other industry spokesmen believe he is overly pessimistic, the outside observer might reasonably conclude either that there will be a tremendous scramble to introduce new applications for low cost computer power or there will be hard times ahead in the industry, or, more likely, both.

I. Circuit-function usage—1976

	Functions per Unit	No. of Units	Total Functions
Computer mainframe (logic)	50 000	2 000	0.001×10^{11}
Minicomputers	10 000	20 000	0.002×10^{11}
Semiconductor memory			$2.0 \quad \times 10^{11}$
Pocket calculators	3 000	3×10^7	$1.0 \quad \times 10^{11}$
Electronic Watches	1 000	3×10^7	$0.1 \quad \times 10^{11}$
Total			$3.0 \quad \times 10^{11}$

II. Estimated circuit-function usage—1985

	Functions per Unit	No. of Units	Total Functions
Data-processing systems (logic)	10^5	10^5	0.0001×10^{13}
Semiconductor memory			$0.6 \quad \times 10^{13}$
Calculators; including scientific computers	3×10^4	3×10^7	$0.1 \quad \times 10^{13}$
Watches	2×10^3	2×10^7	0.04×10^{13}
Video games	10^5	10^7	$0.1 \quad \times 10^{13}$
Automobiles	2×10^5	10^7	$0.2 \quad \times 10^{13}$
Total			$1.0 \quad \times 10^{13}$

Table 2-1*

Source: IEEE *Spectrum*.October 1977, p.43.

*A circuit function is defined as a circuit element of the complexity of a single unit of computer memory (i.e. a bit), or of a gate (another basic computer building block).

It can be noted from Table 2-1 that the automobile is a major projected consumer of circuit functions. This is now close enough to fruition to be a virtual certainty. A German manufacturer is already using a microprocessor to provide an automobile seat control with a memory, and Cadillac offers a computerized instrumentation system. More productive uses for the computer, such as in the control of carburation, fuel injection, exhaust gas recirculation and spark timing were introduced in 1978. Relative to a slightly more distant future, it is worth noting that the Japanese are already testing a model of a complete traffic guidance system which will guide the driver as to the optimum routing to reach his destination (taking account of existing traffic conditions) and optimize the timing of the traffic lights to help speed all motorists to their destinations.

Although its major impact will probably not be felt until after 1985, it seems likely that the telephone and data communications system of the future (there are over 380 million telephones in use in the world) will be a significant user of microprocessors.

Another market for computer power is one which might be broadly defined as the pattern recognition market. The process by which human beings are able to recognize both speech and visual patterns is complicated and difficult to emulate using electronic brains. But it can be done, though at the cost of a lot of computing power. However, once the hardware required to do the job declines in cost from $10,000,000 to $10, a wide variety of applications become feasible. The AYEE which was in common use in Julia's world is an example of the sorts of devices which could be available in the not too distant future.

Machines which will read the pages of a book and speak the words read—an invaluable aid to a blind person—have already been developed. Security devices capable of detecting any movement in the field of vision of a TV camera and raising an appropriate alarm are also available, though they are expensive. They will become much cheaper.

Voice recognition systems capable of recognizing a limited vocabulary have been available and in use for some time. As these systems become cheaper it will become increasingly common to find oneself in conversation with a computer when phoning to enquire about the weather, an airline schedule or the price of eggs.

Automata, or robots, will be able to take on more complex chores. The president of General Motors recently estimated that within ten years computers will control 90% of all new machines in General Motors' manufacturing and assembly plants (5). A robot lawn mower, trained to mow your lawn unattended and (this is the major problem) safe enough to be entrusted to do so, might be generally available in about the same time frame.

There are thus many new applications of computers which could serve to keep the micro-electronics industry growing at the pace it needs to continue as a healthy industry, while, at the same time, greatly changing the complexion of the society in which we live.

Over the last two decades we have moved from transistors to integrated circuits, from integrated circuits (IC's) to "medium scale integrated circuits" (MSI's), and from MSI's to "large scale integrated circuits" (LSI's). But the circuits continue to get smaller, and the number of circuit components routinely included on a single chip seems to grow inexorably larger. Industry insiders talks now of "very large scale integrated circuits" or VLSI's to indicate a further increase in circuit density. The list of superlatives must soon run out. Perhaps industry and humanity at large will be content to call a halt at "super large scale integrated circuits," or "jumbo circuits?"

Whatever the name, the gradual march to ever cheaper computing power will continue to rely on the further miniaturization of electronic circuits. When current techniques for reducing costs have run their course, perhaps by the mid-1980's, a new type of circuit which operates at temperatures close to absolute zero and requires even less power and space than today's silicon based microcircuits, will probably be starting a new round of dramatic price decreases. These devices make use of a phenomenon known as the "Josephson effect." Josephson devices are under active development by IBM and others (6).

The price of computers will continue to decline because manufacturers must keep cutting prices in order to survive in the intense, competitive micro-electronics market, and because the market for cheap computers itself continues to expand enormously as more and more new uses become economically viable with each price decline.

Will mankind be any better off when computers are almost as common as grains of sand? Many say yes, and picture a Utopia where hard work is all done by machines and man spends his time indulging his creative talents and energy in an atmosphere of peace and harmony. However, the history of Utopias is not encouraging. To most Utopian writers of the nineteenth century, our productive capacity today seemed more than adequate to permit mankind to enter a golden age—yet still that Utopia escapes us. The reasons why this should be so are now familiar to most of us, and were touched on in the previous chapter.

MAN VS MACHINE INTELLIGENCE

When computers first struck the popular imagination in the early 1950's, there was a good deal of discussion of the possibility that machine intelligence would displace mankind. However, it was soon discovered that computers were really very dumb objects. Although they could do arithmetic very quickly indeed, they only did exactly what a programmer told them to do; no more and no less. Furthermore, computer instructions had to be painstakingly detailed, a frustrating characteristic for humans who are used to giving instructions to other humans in which most of the detail is both unnecessary and unspoken.

Thereafter, the world of super intelligent machines was abandoned largely to the science fiction enthusiasts although researchers continued to work quietly and productively in the background. The issue rose again to public conscience through the vehicle of science fiction, most notably in the movie version of Arthur Clarke's *2001*, where the HAL takes on a will of its own.

In the Feb. 20, 1978 issue of *Time*, the issue was raised again in a factual context. Jastrow's editorial from that issue was quoted in full in "Julia's Dilemma."

We must not be surprised at finding Jastrow's message a little disquieting. After all, our instincts, we are told, are for the promotion of our survival and that of our species. The survival of a bundle of silicon chips, however superior its brain, cannot be expected to be of much interest to us. And although we may program a robot to regard human life as sacred, the spectre of Arthur Clarke's HAL computer is not reassuring.

Joseph Weizenbaum wrote wisely when he wrote "The limit . . . of the extent to which computers can help us cope with the world of human affairs is determined by our ability to assess our situation honestly, *and our ability to know ourselves*" (italics added) (7). Despite the fact that we do not yet understand the workings of the human brain in detail, we have learnt a lot about the way our social behaviour is determined over the last few decades. The science of sociobiology, defined as "the systematic study of the biological basis of all social behaviour" (8) has been interpreted by some as a philosophy which sees man as an obedient slave.

As the story of Julia makes clear, I believe that the findings of the sociobiologist deserve much more attention than many philosophers and religious authorities seem prepared to give them. It is to be expected that some early claims in a new field will be exaggerated or just plain wrong. It appears to the writer, however, that the general thrust of the sociobiological argument provides the only available consistent and rational explanation of human behaviour which does not require the direct intervention of one or more benevolent or malevolent deities. It even does much to explain our search for and belief in deities.

The findings of the sociobiologists are quite consistent with the steady progress which has been made by computer scientists in the field generally known as *Artificial Intelligence*. The words of one of these scientists, Patrick Henry Winston, are worth pondering:

Myth: Computers Can Never...

It hardly matters how the sentence is finished because the standard proof is as weak as it is inevitable. Stripped of obfuscation, it goes like this: "Computers cannot because no one has thought of a way to make them..." The elusive qualities most frequently proposed by the critics of computer intelligence include learning, introspection, and aesthetic feeling, all of which suggest a certain unfamiliarity with the literature.

[Some] programs... already manifest these abilities to some degree. Their competence certainly leaves much to be explored, but doors are swinging open nevertheless.

Of course to believe in human superiority is a tradition. Once our earth was the center of the universe, now it is an undistinguished planet. Once our creation was direct and divine, now some people believe it is the good luck of the primates. Once our intelligence was unchallenged, yet someday computers may laugh at us and wonder if biological information processors could be really smart. Beware of those who think it can never happen. Their ancestors hassled Galileo and ridiculed Darwin (9).

The more we learn about the workings of the human brain, the more computer scientists will be driven to emulate the processes in a computer. As the preceding quote suggests, there do not appear to be any insuperable technical barriers.

In order to have an intelligent conversation with a computer, it should, as Raphael observed in 1976, be able to:

(1) accept facts and questions, and make appropriate responses, all in the form of natural English;

(2) store, remember, and make efficient use of a large amount of data—at least thousands of elementary facts;

(3) answer questions that require it to figure out the logical consequences of the facts stored explicitly in its memory; and

(4) operate conversationally—e.g., via a time-sharing computer terminal—without frustrating delays.

Although no system yet developed has all four of these capabilities, a significant degree of success in each of the four areas has been separately achieved by various systems. In the next few years we should begin to see these capabilities combined and improved, producing the first true, complete question-answering system (10).

Raphael might have added a fifth condition, namely the ability to recognize human speech and to synthesize human speech in reply. The use of keyboards and T.V. screens or printers is, after all, a rather clumsy and artificial way of entering into a conversation.

Of the two, speech synthesis is by far the easiest. Though it is far from trivial to do it cheaply and well, Texas Instruments did succeed in putting a child's educational toy called "Speak and Spell" on the market in the United States in 1978 which was capable of synthesizing speech with a clear, if slightly mechanical voice. The total cost of the device was about $50.00.

Speech recognition, however, is a much harder task. Because of the variability of human speech, particularly as to tone, speed of talking and accent, it is difficult to build a reliable speech recognition program, particularly one with a large vocabulary. Speech recognition systems which, after hearing the speaker pronounce the numbers 0 to 9 several times, will then correctly identify the number spoken, have been in commercial use for several years. In the future it seems probable that regular conversations with computers will be mediated by a speech recognition program which has stored in its memory the appropriate parameters for recognizing speech of particular individuals. This will be the beginning of computer programs which become personally identified with individual humans, in the sense that one will be able to say "This program understands what I say, but it doesn't understand what you say." The existence of an extensive digital communications network will mean that even someone far from home can access his personalized computer routines by giving some appropriate identification. Quite possibly even the identification will be performed automatically by examining the voice pattern.

The actual understanding of the meaning of the speech once the words themselves have been understood poses a problem of yet another order of difficulty. Computers are programmed in special languages which are by and large devoid of hidden meanings and ambiguities. Human languages have no such simple properties.

Much effort was expended in the 1950's aimed at developing automatic translators from one language to another. The result was abject failure. The example given in Julia's Dilemma of the computer translation of "The spirit is willing, but the flesh is weak" is only one of a series of famous incidents from the early attempts. Raphael (10) gives another example which points to the sophistication of some of the early translation routines. This example came from Harvard in the 1960's. The sentence given was "Time flies like an arrow." The computer program produced the following four possible meanings:

1. Time moves in the same manner that an arrow moves.
2. Measure the speed of flies in the same way that you measure the speed of an arrow.
3. Measure the speed of the flies that resemble an arrow.
4. A particular variety of flies called "time flies" are fond of an arrow.

When one reflects on the factors contributing to human comprehension of the words of others (a process which is by no means infallible), one realizes that knowledge of context, and of the interests, knowledge and mood of the speaker are all important contributors to the deciphering of meaning in any circumstances.

Once again one can see the need for personalized "Alter Egos" which contain vast stores of information on the traits of the individual they serve, to make the reliable interpretation of human language possible. Rather large quantities of computer processor chips and computer memory could be consumed in this task, not to mention the enormous labour involved in creating workable computer programs. As suggested in "Julia's Dilemma," such capabilities are probably two or three decades from realization, but in the meantime there will be some interesting developments along the way.

NEW DEVELOPMENTS

From the point of view of the home user, some of the more interesting devices which are now becoming available, and which lie on the developmental pathway towards the realizations of electronic alter egos, are home computers, videotex, teletext and video-discs.

Home Computers

The early home computers are not of great interest to the average householder. They are somewhat daunting pieces of hardware, requiring the knowledge of special languages and techniques. They are fun for those with a technical bent to play with, and have found practical uses in small businesses and as text processors in the home, but in their early forms they are not expected to achieve large penetrations into the household—certainly nothing approaching the penetration of TV sets and telephones, both of which can be found in over 95% of Canadian households.

However, home computer technology will almost certainly be merged with videotex technology over the next five or six years, and at that point household penetration is likely to increase sharply. Video discs too are likely to play a key role in what will emerge as an electronic home information and recreation centre.

Let us examine these developments so as to better understand the services which might be expected in the near future.

Videotex, Teletext and TELIDON

These three technical terms are worth understanding. The systems they represent could be the mainspring of some significant changes in our lives over the next decade. They are at the cutting edge of the changes that silicon chip technology is bringing to us, and as such are likely to be the focus for the hopes and fears with which the new electronics both tantalizes and taunts us.

The words videotex, teletext and TELIDON all describe information systems which are designed for mass market home and business use and which make use of an ordinary TV receiver as the primary (but not the only) output terminal.

The systems are all adaptations of old, well-tried computer techniques to a mass market, a market which, for the first time is accessible due to the precipitous drops in the cost of the essential electronic components—memory and microcomputers. The words videotex and teletext essentially describe two different ways of delivering the signal to places of business or to households, while TELIDON is the specific name given to a system developed in Canada, which is capable of operating in either a videotex or a teletext mode. A basic teletext and videotex adapter is expected to add $100-$200 to the price of a colour TV set by 1983 or so.

The word *teletext* is normally used to refer to a method of delivery which makes use of the spare signal carrying capacity in existing television broadcasting channels to make somewhere between 100 and 300 "pages" or "TV screens of information" available to persons tuned to that channel and equipped with the appropriate teletext receiver.* The user typically accesses a page by keying in the number of the page he desires and waiting until the page is transmitted from the TV station, at which time the electronics in the receiver will "grab" the page and display it. The two principal disadvantages of such teletext systems are the relatively small amount of information which can be made accessible (even 300 pages is not very much), and the relatively long time a user must wait after requesting a page before he can view it; average wait times of twenty or thirty seconds and maximum wait times of a minute or so are not unusual.

Indeed, the average wait time and the number of pages accessible are directly related. Depending on the details of technical implementation of the service, the TV transmitter will broadcast from one to six pages a second (the British teletext service which started in 1975 broadcasts at about 2 pages a second). Thus, for a system with 100 frames which broadcasts at 2 frames per second, it can be expected that any given frame will be broadcast every 50 seconds. On average then, a user can expect to wait 25 seconds (and a maximum of 50 seconds) to view the frame he has requested. The more frames there are in the system, the longer will be the average wait time. It is possible to send out more popular pages, such as index pages, more fre-

---

The spare signal carrying capacity is found in what is called the "vertical blanking interval" or VBI, which is a pause in the TV signal transmission between the completion of one TV frame and the start of the next in order to allow the electron beam of the TV tube to move from the bottom left hand corner of the screen back up to the top right hand corner ready for the new frame to begin. Approximately 22 lines out of the 525 horizontal sweeps made by the electron beam occur during the vertical blanking interval. Several of these lines are, or could, be made available for teletext signal transmission.

53

quently, thereby reducing the average wait time for access to them, but such tactics do, of course, result in an increased wait time for pages not so favoured.

Nonetheless, despite their limited information carrying capacity, teletext systems have some significant advantages. Consider the following:

1. *Cheapness* It requires only a relatively minor investment on the part of a TV station to install and operate a teletext service. An additional investment in the $100,000 range will equip a TV station to insert teletext on its broadcast signal. This is a small cost compared to an average station investment of several million dollars in broadcast equipment. To this cost must be added, however, the cost of updating and maintaining the pages of information which are broadcast. The largest running fully operational teletext service, the BBC's CEEFAX, employs some 16 journalists working in two shifts. They insert an average of 200 pages of updates a day.

2. *Subtitling* By reserving the appropriate number of pages (one page for each language), the system can be efficiently used to provide subtitles to the regular TV programming when teletext is operated in a "transparent" mode, that is, a mode which allows the regular TV to show through the text as a background. This service has obvious educational uses as well as being a boon for the deaf. Incidentally, the same technique used for sub-titling can be used to insert a "News Flash" or any other urgent message onto the regular TV program.

3. *Adjunct to TV Programming* As well as the more obvious uses of Teletext (to provide news, weather, sports, road reports, train and plane delays, TV programming information etc.), teletext has significant potential as an adjunct to the regular TV programming. For example, advertisers might use teletext to provide additional information on the products advertised such as the name and address of local agencies where the product is sold or additional technical information. Educators might want to use teletext to provide question and answer type tests (a "reveal" button on the user keypad permits certain parts of the teletext screen display to remain hidden until the reveal button is pressed), or to provide graphical or textual elaboration of an educational TV program.

It should be noted that the teletext system described is not the only form in which the service can be offered. If, as is the case in France, an entire TV broadcast channel is available for teletext service, it is possible to transmit 5000 or more frames with average wait times reduced to five seconds or so. Clearly, in such circumstances, a vastly expanded range of information can be provided, though even this enlarged figure is a long way from the millions of pages expected to be accessible using videotex type systems.

In Canada, although a full channel for teletext over-the-air broadcast could, with some difficulty, be made available in some areas, it seems more likely that full channel teletext would be "broadcast" using spare capacity on cable TV systems rather than over the air, though the latter option could be adopted in remote and rural areas where cable TV systems are uneconomical.

The term *videotex* is normally used to refer to systems which make use of the telephone system to deliver information, although, in Canada in particular, with its high cable TV penetration, two-way cable TV or even hybrid cable TV/telephone systems are possible.

The most important single characteristic of videotex systems is that they employ two-way communications, unlike teletext systems, where the user must wait patiently (or not, as the case may be) for the information he has requested to be delivered.

The consequences of the two-way communications capability of videotex are enormous. Not only does it mean that the technical barriers to the amount of information which can be accessed are essentially removed, potentially permitting access to millions of pages; but also, and perhaps more significantly, user feedback becomes possible, permitting use of the system for such purposes as remote banking, shopping, theatre and travel reservations and opinion polling. Nor has it escaped the notice of postal authorities that electronic mail is also possible with such systems.

From a commercial point of view, the two-way capability of videotex means that it is possible to identify the use that each terminal makes of the network, so that the user can be billed directly for the information or communications services provided. This is next to impossible with conventional teletext, although it could conceivably operate on a monthly subscription basis by encrypting the signals transmitted and renting out a signal "descrambler." Such techniques are already used by Pay TV networks.

But videotex systems can be made charge-selective relatively easily, even to the point of associating a particular charge with every information page. Such a pricing strategy permits the information provider to establish his own price for the information provided. This capability has led many to speculate on the arrival of a new era in which every person can afford to be his own publisher in that he can have cheap and easy access to the videotex system for getting his information into circulation while there is also a ready mechanism in place for him to collect revenues from users of the information he provides. (Users would likely pay for the information they access via their telephone or cable TV bill or via a credit card account.) In fact, an important characteristic of videotex systems is that it costs as much to format and insert information which is seen by one viewer as it does if one million people see it. Furthermore, unlike TV and radio, where similar economies of scale virtually dictate their use as "mass media" catering to small, special interest groups only with difficulty, videotex does not suffer from a shortage of delivery capacity, thus enabling small group interests to be catered to with relative ease.

The two major disadvantages of using the telephone system for videotex are its relatively limited signal carrying capacity, and the fact that use of the telephone line for videotex potentially, at least, prevents its use for normal telephone service. The limited carrying capacity of the phone line means that, although textual information and (thanks to development associated with the TELIDON system) some graphical information can be transmitted with reasonable speed, photographic or complex graphical information is transmitted too slowly to be transmitted in any quantity while the user waits. This constraint is unimportant for many applications, but it does restrict the value of the system for such applications as merchandising catalogues where extensive use of photographs is made. However, two-way cable or hybrid cable/telephone systems are not nearly as restricted as is the telephone in this regard. It should also be noted that digital telephone systems are now being introduced and that, although it is expected to be at least two decades before installation of digital phones is widespread, their installation will result in an effective fifty-fold increase in signal carry capacity (from 1200 bits/sec to 56,000 bits/sec). Optical fibres will also start to obtain significant penetration in a similar time frame, with an even more drastic resulting increase in signal carrying capacity.

The limitation imposed by tying up the phone line through use of videotex is not likely to be severe in the longer term, since a number of alternative technical solutions are available. These range from installation of a second phone line (expensive but straightforward) and the use of two-way cable, to the use of "data over voice" techniques to permit shared simultaneous use of the same telephone line for both videotex and voice.

TELIDON is the specific name given to an information system developed in Canada which is capable of operating in either a one-way teletext mode or a two-way videotex mode. It is not the first such system developed. There were a number of precursors to it, most notably in Great Britain. However, the TELIDON system was the first one to incorporate advanced computer graphics techniques into either a videotex or a teletext system. It is widely believed that it will provide the general model on which future videotex and teletext systems will develop, a situation which puts Canada, at least temporarily, in a position of technical leadership.

Some examples of TELIDON frames which give an idea of both the appearance and the variety of information which can be made available can be seen in plate 1, although the original will be in colour, of course.

TELIDON terminals, in common with some other videotex and teletext terminals, incorporate a microprocessor identical to the one used by many vendors of home computers. Indeed, because TELIDON requires a lot of computer memory to drive the display, it can be thought of as a rather powerful home computer which only lacks a computer program loading device, such as a magnetic tape cassette deck, and a full keyboard (instead of a twenty button keypad), to become a home computer in the traditional sense. Since these features can be easily and relatively cheaply added, it can be seen that home computer and videotex/teletext technologies are quickly merging. Chapter 7 gives some of the details.

Video-discs

Videotape cassette recorders have now become a familiar, if somewhat expensive, consumer product. They permit both the recording and the playback of TV pictures. Pre-recorded videotapes of popular (and often times pornographic) programs are available, generally in the $50 to $60 per tape range.

Video-discs use a gramophone-like disc instead of magnetic tape for playing back video pictures. They have long been promised, but only appeared on the North American market in 1978 for the first time. Within a few years they should be about half the price of the videotape recorders (VTR's), since they have only a sixth as many separate parts as the VTR's. Furthermore, video-disc signal quality should be considerably better. Individual discs should be substantially cheaper than videotapes since the discs are stamped out in much the same fashion as gramophone records; however, the video-disc owner will not be able to record his own programs, at least not with the first generation video-disc systems.

The use of video-discs (particularly those with a still frame capacity) for applications such as the one in "Julia's Dilemma" where Michael is able to obtain clear, step by step guidance on how to repair his car, seems a natural and most useful application of such systems. Indeed, in a society where we can expect to be thrust more and more into "do-it-yourself" home and equipment maintenance and repair, the video-disc could well become an essential tool, since the words and even the still pictures in conventional do-it yourself manuals often leave the inexperienced craftsman at a loss as to his next move.

Perhaps most exciting of all is the immense, information-storage capacity of video-discs. Encyclopedia publishers are already considering video-disc versions of their publications, and the possibility of storing whole libraries of music on a single video-disc has not passed unremarked. Used as a peripheral to a home computer, a single video-disc could contain a wealth of educational and entertainment programs which could be loaded into the computer for use as desired.

The incredible information-carrying capacity of a video-disc can be imagined when it is realized it is possible to store over 100 full length books on a single video-disc, costing 25 cents to manufacture in quantity.

A video-disc recorder would seem to be an essential element of the electronic home information and entertainment centre of the future.

The Intelligent Telephone

The era of the "plain old telephone service," or POTS as it is known in the trade, is fast disappearing, as the "computer on a chip" invades the telephone network and the telephone receiver itself. Many of the features in the following lists are already available to those connected to the newer, computer-controlled telephone exchanges.

1) *Treatment of Busy Lines*

A variety of ways of treating busy lines other than the transmission of the simple, but annoying, busy signal are possible. The prospective call receiver can be given an indication that someone else wished to call him, and may be permitted to transfer temporarily to the new caller, or to put him on the line simultaneously with the other caller while the call conflict is resolved. Alternatively, the blocked call can be put through automatically as soon as the line becomes free.

2) *Automatic Call Forwarding*

A person may go and visit his friend and have telephone calls automatically transferred to his friend's telephone.

3) *Abbreviated Dialling*

Commonly used, lengthy numbers can be replaced by easy to remember two digit numbers.

4) *Third Party Add-ons*

A subscriber at a third number can be added to an established two-way link for three-way conferencing.

5) *Control of Telephone Solicitation*

It will be possible to require those who solicit by telephone to use specially assigned telephone numbers. Those not wishing to receive telephone solicitations could then arrange to have calls from these numbers automatically blocked out.

6) *Number Tracing*

It would be a simple matter to record the phone numbers of either all incoming or all outgoing calls either for subscriber information, tracing of nuisance calls, or for police use. The potential implications for personal privacy are clear.

7) *Changing of Phone Numbers*

An important expense for telephone companies are the continuous changes of phone numbers as people move from place to place. With electronic and digital exchanges, new assignments of phone numbers no longer require the physical reconnection of wires at the switching office, but simply alteration of the computer memory in the table which associates wire pairs with a particular telephone number. This can be accomplished quickly and easily by typing in the relevant changes at a computer terminal.

Adding intelligence to the telephone receiver will start it too down a road where it starts to resemble a home computer. The French telephone authority announced in 1978 that it was planning to develop a cheap videotex terminal to incorporate into a telephone set. The primary purpose of this development is to be able to dispense with the traditional telephone book and use videotex as a telephone directory. However, such a device could clearly be used as well for more traditional videotex information activities and, if equipped with a full keyboard, would be a great boon to the deaf.

The Electronic Home Information and Entertainment Centre

All of the above mentioned devices and services point towards the development of what might be called electronic home information and entertainment centres, or NABU's as David Godfrey has referred to them in the Introduction. It seems likely that these centres will be assembled from separate components in much the same way that today's stereo systems are often an assemblage of separate speakers, amplifiers, tuners, record players and tape units.

The heart of the home information and entertainment centre is likely to be the TV set for some time to come, but videotex, teletext and home computer capabilities will be added, as well as video-discs and hard copy printers (of widely varying cost and capabilities).

Just as some people pay $150 or so for their stereo set, while others pay $2000 or $3000, so there will be a similar or greater price range for home centres. High quality videotex terminals and printers and such luxuries as projection television and high quality TV monitors with superior resolution and less flicker will combine to make high-priced systems desirable for those who can afford the cost.

COMMUNICATIONS SATELLITES AND OPTICAL FIBRES—TWO MAJOR NEW COMMUNICATIONS TECHNOLOGIES

This book emphasizes the implications of advances in electronics for the future. But electronics advances, while doubtless the most important, are not the only advances significantly affecting our ability to have rapid access to information and to each other.

Advances in space technology and in signal transmission using optical fibres, both of which have been enormously affected by advances in electronics technology, are also profoundly affecting the way we live now and the way we will live in the future.

Communications Satellites

The startling achievement of communications satellites is to make tele-communications almost independent of distance, for if a signal must travel 35,800 kilometres up to a satellite and then back down again, it makes little difference whether the destination for the signal transmitted is a mile away or on the other side of the ocean. Two important qualitative changes result from this:

1) the cost of long distance communications virtually ceases as an impediment either to exercising organizational control over a distance or to consulting and working cooperatively over a distance. Either way, life becomes even more complicated, as coordinating committees and bureaucracies multiply;

2) the technical impediments to widespread "swapping" of television programs are largely removed. In Canada we are accustomed to having access to four or more American TV stations either picked up off-air at border points by those close to the U.S. border or piped into cable systems. The use of multi-channel satellites to broadcast either directly to the home or, more probably, to cable TV head ends, raises the possibility of distributing all these signals and many others such as Pay TV, parliamentary proceedings, educational TV and British, French and other foreign TV (appropriately delayed to account for differences in time zones).

Communications satellites are now a well established part of the tele-communications infrastructure. They are used for communications over long distances, particularly where normal terrestial signal transmission is difficult.

By 1977, a scant twelve years after the first commercial communications satellite was launched, the Intelsat organization, a consortium of some 107 member countries, operated eight communications satellites with a combined capacity of some 36,000 voice circuits. A number of domestic satellite systems, including Canada's Anik series of satellites, added further to the world's total commercial satellite capacity.

Almost all communications satellites (including all INTELSAT and TELESAT CANADA vehicles) are geostationary, that is, their orbital period around the earth is precisely 24 hours, so they appear from earth to occupy a stationary or very nearly stationary position in the sky. The great advantage of a geostationary orbit is that earth station antennas do not have to track the satellite, but can instead be mounted in a fixed position.

A disadvantage of the stationary orbit is that it is only reached at an altitude of 35,800 km. Since signals travelling to and from the satellite travel at the speed of light (300,000 km/sec), it takes about one quarter of a second for a message to travel from the earth up to the transponder in the satellite and back. A telephone user must therefore wait for about one half a second for a reply if the telephone call travels via satellite in both directions. This delay causes a minor annoyance in a normal telephone conversation. Two hops by satellite can cause a significant annoyance, and are therefore avoided by the telecommunications carriers. It is possible to use the satellite for only one direction of a telephone conversation, and to use a submarine cable or microwave for the other direction, thus reducing to negligible proportions annoyance caused by transmission delay. About two thirds of trans-oceanic telephone traffic was carried by satellite by 1977.

The cost of satellite communications has been drastically reduced since Early Bird was launched. By 1979, the investment cost per circuit year had been reduced by a factor of 40 over a period of 14 years. Some of this cost reduction can be attributed to a progressive drive to reduce the weight of spacecraft components, some of that weight reduction being directly attributable to the reduction in weight and power consumption of electronic circuits already alluded to earlier in this chapter. Perhaps the most important factor has been the development of more powerful rockets, which enabled a greater weight to be economically hoisted aloft, thereby permitting a greater number of circuits to be accommodated in one satellite. More efficient signal transmission techniques have also permitted an increased signal carrying capacity.

It costs a lot of money just to lift a satellite into orbit. Launch costs normally account for ½ to ¾ of total satellite costs (exclusive of ground terminals). In 1976, it cost $12,500,000 to launch a 350 kg satellite into geostationary orbit and $40,000,000 to launch 1450 kg into the same orbit. In such circumstances, the importance of weight reduction is readily understandable. The space shuttle, which is the first re-usable launch vehicle, is expected to have a dramatic influence on satellite costs. Not only will the shuttle permit post-launch check-out and in-space repair, but launch costs will probably be further reduced by a factor of five or ten.

Canada's Role

Considering its size, Canada has played an active role in satellite communications. Her involvement grew directly from research aimed at improving terrestial high frequency (HF) radio communications in the north. It happens that reliable HF radio contact is dependent on conditions in the ionosphere,* but the ionosphere is characteristically unstable, and

*The ionosphere is the region of the earth's atmosphere extending from about 90 to 450 kilometres above the surface of the earth. This region contains several layers of ionized gas.

particularly so over the north and south magnetic poles. The disturbances over northern Canada can become so acute that not infrequently HF radio communication is blacked out altogether.

Hence Canada's particular concern to study the nature of ionospheric disturbances, which led research scientists to devise the Allouette I (launched in 1962), the first satellite which was not of either U.S. or Russian origin. This satellite was designed to make measurements on the ionosphere from the top side looking down—scientists already knew quite well what the ionosphere looked like from the earth, or bottom side. The satellite was so successful that it was followed by Allouette II and subsequently by the ISIS I and II satellites which conducted similar experiments.

The experience gained by these activities, compounded by the difficulty of providing a reliable communications system in the north, were important factors in Canada's decision to launch the world's first domestic geostationary communications satellite system. TELESAT CANADA was incorporated by statute in 1969 to carry out the task.

The first satellite, Anik I (Anik is an Inuit word meaning "brother") was launched on November 9, 1972. It was followed by two other similar vehicles to provide a total capacity (including stand-by circuits) of 36 TV channels or 43,200 voice circuits by 1977. The necessity of maintaining stand-by circuits in case of technical problems, and the fact that over "thin routes," that is, routes of low circuit capacity such as those to the far north, full voice circuit capacity cannot be utilized, means that the operational capacity of the TELESAT system is actually considerably less than the total capacity.

Nevertheless, the Anik satellites have made an important contribution to the Canadian way of life, particularly in the North where, almost overnight, colour television services as well as reliable long distance telephone connections to the south appeared in numerous far northern communities for the first time. In the south, Anik has served primarily as a vehicle for delivering network TV signals across the country, a function to which it is particularly well suited.

There has been much talk of direct TV broadcasting to the home, the idea being that each household or apartment building would be equipped with a small, cheap earth terminal, and receive its TV signals directly from a satellite. It is estimated that if an earth terminal market for hundreds of thousands (or some say millions) of earth terminals could be generated, then the unit cost of earth terminals would be brought down to a few hundred dollars. It is quite feasible to build a satellite capable of broadcasting twenty-five or more TV channels with adequate power to carry out such a scheme.

A recent and most significant development in Canada has been the elaboration of a direct broadcast satellite system which does not require the high powered (100 to 300 watt), and hence expensive, satellite previously thought to be necessary. Indeed, the new generation of Anik (Anik C) satellites scheduled for launch in 1981, which were not designed for use in a direct broadcast mode, may be usable for direct broadcast as a result of this development.

The effect of the declining costs of satellite communications can be illustrated by the following example, which makes use of INTELSAT statistics. The major cost reductions were achieved between 1965 and 1968 when costs declined from $32,500 per circuit year to $2,000 per circuit year. INTELSAT V will reduce the investment to $800 per circuit year, a factor of only 2.5 in eleven years. It seems likely that future cost reductions will take place at this leisurely pace. Even allowing for an approximate doubling of the INTELSAT V investment figure of $810 per circuit year to include the investment in ground terminals, and assuming a rather modest circuit utilization of 10%, the investment costs of the satellite system would be covered by a charge for a telephone call of only 3ᶜ per minute! Allowing for a markup to account for operating expenses and profit, one might in the near future expect to pay about 30ᶜ per minute for a conversation between Montreal and Cairo, or between Vancouver and Melbourne. This represents a ten-fold rate reduction over 1978 rates. If quick and cheap communications are a criterion of village style communications, then, in that sense at least, the world is indeed becoming a "global village."

But it is the combination of satellites with cable TV delivery systems which promises the greatest change in our lives. Assuming each TV channel broadcast over Canada requires four TV transponder channels, one for each major time zone, the investment cost of direct satellite broadcasting to cable TV head ends would only be about 30ᶜ per year per Canadian household. To this must be added operating costs, and the amortization of an earth terminal (costing several thousand dollars) amongst the local subscribers. Using a conservative estimate of $1.00 per channel per household per year, it can be seen that the cost of distributing ten network channels across Canada would be approximately equal to the total technical expenditures of the CBC in 1976 ($68,000,000), or $10 per household per year.

For this cost, coverage could be provided to nearly all in Canada (it is likely that many Americans would be able to access the signals too, of course). There are currently some 60,000 households in Canada with no TV reception, and a further 230,000 households which receive only one TV channel. For them, such a change would indeed be significant.

Optical Fibres

Optical fibre, is simply, very clear, very pure glass down which light can be transmitted for a long distance and still be detected at the far end. The glass is pulled out into long thin fibres, and is specially manufactured so that light rays travelling in the fibre cannot easily escape out the sides, but rather tend to get refocussed towards the centre line of the fibre. This is done by arranging for the index of refraction (which is a measure of the speed of light in a substance relative to the speed of light in a vacuum) to be lower at the outer edges of the fibre than it is at the centre.

Normal glass is not nearly clear enough for communications use. One can easily see why by trying to look through a piece of plate glass edgewise. All that can be seen is a green colouring. The sort of glass used for optical fibre communications can be likened to having a plate glass window a kilometre or more thick through which it is still possible to see the other side with little noticeable decrease in brightness.

If a source of light is attached to one end of a glass fibre, and a photodetector (a device for converting incoming light into electricity) is placed at the other end, the pulses of light sent out can be detected and transformed into electrical pulses at the receiver. That, in essence, is all an optical fibre transmission system does (11).

Such a system has some nice properties, which, in a nutshell, add up to low cost in many important applications.

Glass is just silicon dioxide, and silicon is the most plentiful element in the earth's crust. Furthermore, the glass fibres used are very thin—about the diameter of a human hair. A thimbleful of silicon will produce a kilometre of glass fibre.

Although glass fibre cables were initially very expensive, as most new products are, neither the materials nor the manufacturing process lead to expectation of a high price in quantity production. Indeed, it is expected that by the early 1980's the cost per kilometre of optical fibre cable will be comparable to that of the twisted copper pair, used in the telephone loop.

However, there is a startling difference in the signal carrying capacity of an optical fibre as compared to that of a copper pair, as can be seen from Table 2-2. Depending on the quality of fibre used and the spacing of repeaters, a single optical fibre can quite easily carry up to 4032 voice channels, a two hundred fold increase over the capacity of a copper pair used as a 24 channel trunk! Hundreds of hair-thin fibres can be economically combined into a single cable capable of carrying hundreds of thousands of simultaneous telephone conversations.

While it is the potential low cost combined with a high signal carrying capacity which make optical fibres so interesting from a telecommunications point of view, they have other interesting properties which render them valuable in special applications. Some of these properties are:

Table 2-2 Cost Comparison of Distribution Cables*

	Installed Cost/km	No. of Voice Channels	Repeater Amplifier Spacing	Installed Cost Per Voice Channel /km
Copper Pair	$50	1 (local loop) 24 (trunk)	10 km 1.8 km	$50 $2
Coaxial Cable (3/4" Cable TV Trunk)	$1600 - $3000	35 TV Channels 21,000 Voice Channels	0.5 km	$0.08 - 14
Optical Fibre	$3000 (1978) $50 (1980's)	1800 - 50,000	5 - 20 km	$0.60 - 1.67 (1978) $0.001 - 0.03 (1980's)

*As with electrical conductors, optical fibre systems will be specialized to various uses. There will be high capacity trunks with relatively expensive multiplexing electronics, and lower capacity systems using cheaper, low quality fibre and cheaper electronics. Hence, the figures used above should be considered as representative only.

1. Glass fibres are immune from inductive pick-up from electrical lines and apparatus, nor will they radiate electrical energy themselves. Problems of cross talk and of noise from power lines and lightning are thus virtually eliminated.

2. They have a very small volume relative to their signal carrying capacity, making them ideal for use in crowded urban areas where there is a

shortage of duct space for leading cables underground.

3. Their light weight makes them easy to handle. This property is particularly valuable for aircraft "wiring", where every pound of added weight counts. In one military aircraft it is estimated that cable weight can be reduced to 23 kg from 205 kg.

4. In many applications it is possible to send messages over ten kilometres without regeneration of amplication. This is an important advantage for telephone applications because most trunk lines between exchanges in cities are shorter than ten kilometres. Hence the need for repeaters is almost eliminated on short trunks between urban exchanges.

When optical fibres first came to public notice in the early 1970's (they were first developed in Corning Laboratories in the U.S. in the late 1960's), the difficulties of bringing the technology out of the laboratory and into general use appeared to be almost insurmountable. Not the least of these difficulties was the problem of splicing together two pieces of glass each the diameter of a hair, under real-life conditions, for example, in a dark, crowded manhole where the temperature is 20° below freezing, or atop a telephone pole in a driving rain storm. Amazingly, these and other problems are being solved with an ease which was not foreseen in the early 1970's.

Experimental optical fibre systems have been in place in Canada and elsewhere for several years already, and operational systems are starting to be planned and installed. The first operational systems apart from those used for special applications such as computer "wiring" or communications systems in power substations, will be glass fibre trunk circuits, carrying many signals simultaneously between switching exchanges in cities or over long distances between cities.

Replacement of telephone and cable TV wiring into the home is probably further away, although such an application could become economical in the mid-1980's in new subdivisions or in rural areas where cable TV systems using original cable are not economically viable. An optical fibre field trial is planned for Elie, Manitoba in 1980 to test out the concept of a unified telephone and cable TV delivery system in rural areas. It is jointly sponsored by the Canadian Telecommunications Carriers Association and the federal Department of Communications.

REFERENCES TO CHAPTER 2

1. Diebold, John, *Man and the Computer: Technology as an Agent of Social Change,* Frederic A. Praeger, New York, 1969, p. 48.

2. Noyce, Robert M., "Microelectronics", Scientific American, Vol. 237, No. 3, September 1977, pp. 62-69. This article and others on the subject

have oeen collected in one volume, *Microelectronics,* A Scientific American Book, W.H. Freeman & Co., San Francisco, 1977.

3. The figure $100 comes from an article "The Fabrication of Microelectronic Circuits" by William G. Oldham in the September 1977 *Scientific American.* It is representative of today's costs which have increased substantially over the estimated 1964 wafer processing costs of $10 (from C.L. Hogan, IEEE *Spectrum,* June 1964, p. 67). Higher circuit densities and much higher equivalent yields have necessitated much more carefully controlled processing equipment to reduce allowable tolerances on virtually all aspects of wafer processing. This trend will probably continue, and wafer processing costs can be expected to escalate further in the future, but not nearly fast enough to materially influence the overall precipitate reduction in cost of equivalent circuit functions.

4. The Motorola 6800 microprocessor, one of the more popular of the microprocessors on a chip, was introduced in 1974, at which time it cost $300 (U.S.), in single quantities. By 1979, the single quantity cost had gone down to $13.50 (U.S.), an average price reduction of 46% per year. When purchased in quantities of 500, the same device could be purchased for $8 to $10 (U.S.) in 1979. From *Computing Canada,* 1 May 1979.

5. IEEE *Spectrum,* January 1978, p. 45.

6. Anacker, W., "Computing at 4 degrees Kelvin", IEEE *Spectrum*, Vol. 16, No. 5, May 1979, pp. 26-37.

7. Weizenbaum, Joseph, "Once More—a computer revolution", *The Bulletin of the Atomic Scientists,* September 1978, pp. 12-19.

8. Wilson, Edward O., *Sociobiology: A New Synthesis,* The Belknap Press of Harvard University, Cambridge, Mass., 1975, p.4.

9. Winston, Patrick Henry, *Artificial Intelligence,* Addison-Wesley Publishing Co., Reading, Mass., 1977, p.252.

10. Raphael, Bertram, *The Thinking Computer: Mind Inside Matter,* W.H. Freeman & Co., San Francisco, 1976, p. 194 and p. 186.

11. Further information on optical fibre transmission systems can be found in the following articles:

Kapron, Felix P. and Koichi, Abe, "Physics of Optical Fibres of Communications", *Physics in Canada,* Part I, Vol. 35, No. 2, March 1979, p. 53; and Part II, Vol. 35, No. 4, July 1979, p. 75.

Boyle, W.S., "Light-Wave Communications", *Scientific American,* Vol. 237, No. 2, August 1977, p. 40.

Cook, J.S., "Communications by Optical Fibre", *Scientific American,* Vol. 229, No. 5, November 1973, p. 28.

Jacobs, Ira and Miller, Stewart E., "Optical Transmission of Voice and Data", IEEE *Spectrum,* Vol. 14, No. 2, February 1977, p. 32.

3 THE NECESSARY STRUCTURE
Douglas Parkhill

In the preceding chapters of this book we have been given a glimpse of the anatomy of the Information Revolution and the direction in which it seems to be evolving. Catalyzed by a host of new technologies like micro-computers, fibre-optics, digital communications, low-cost memory systems and very large scale integration, it is forcing together the hitherto separate technologies of computers and telecommunications and causing the emergence of what are loosely termed computer/communications systems. These in turn promise such a richness of information handling capabilities as to totally transform our conception of the possible. In fact, one could state with some truth that the principal limitation upon what we can accomplish with our technologies lies in our ability to decide what it is that we want to do. Some of the dimensions of that decision are explored in this chapter.

Before getting down to this exploration, however, a few words might be in order concerning the nature of the sorts of systems that emerge when computer and communications technologies are forced together. In this connection it is important to note that the idea of combination in the term computer/communications system implies much more than simply connecting a computer to a communications line. In fact, "merging" is a better term than connecting, since the ultimate promise lies in the evolution of integrated networks of information processing and communications hardward and software in which the boundaries between what is communications and what is processing blur and the two become, for all practical purposes, indistinguishable.

The characteristics, or more significantly, the capabilities of such merged systems are quite different from those of either of the parent technologies. In fact, the whole is much greater than the sum of the parts and constitutes in effect a new order of system or meta system.

In such a meta system, one finds a complex and constantly shifting mixture of different forms of information handling, some of which we today associate with telecommunications, others with data-processing, and many more which defy simple categorization and only become possible in a merged system. Many of the services remain to be invented, but any minimum list would certainly include conventional person-to-person and store and forward forms of communication including information, storage and retrieval and tele-mail; voice, video and computerized conferencing; information distribution, control and management; man-to-machine and machine-to-machine communications; information display and of course computation (1).

Computer/communications systems are often described as resource-sharing mechanisms analogous in a superficial sense to conventional resource-sharing utilities, electric power or gas networks for example. The analogy is a good one, but the order of magnitude difference in the complexity of the resources shared make the policy and institutional problems quite different.

In this case the resource is not a simple, easily definable commodity like electricity, but a nebulous something sometimes called "information power." This commodity is quite unlike any other, closely allied to the concept of intelligence, quite literally of infinite dimensions, and thus perhaps related more to mind than to any measurable physical entity. In fact, computer/communications systems could be regarded as mechanisms for both multiplying the human intellect without limit and extending it in space and time. As such, their influence is likely to pervade every human activity as a kind of Electronic Highway Network, channeling and distributing the very stuff that makes us human.

This has important implications for all of us since information is, in a very fundamental sense, the essence of human life and its communications and application in billions of different forms determines the nature of society. Consequently, quantum jumps in our ability to handle it are likely to be marked by fundamental changes in our affairs. These changes are now increasingly being compared to those wrought by the industrial revolution so that just as that revolution multiplied man's physical strength, the Information Revolution promises to expand his intellectual capabilities "with profound social and economic implications for every country in the world"(2).

These could include, given the right policies, major increases in the quality of life, the productivity of industry (especially the service sector), decentralization, and new opportunities for individual development. Education, the mechanisms for transfer of funds, trade practices, culture, public administration and transportation could all be made more efficient, more pleasant and more responsive to individual human needs. It is this incredible richness of function and service that makes the subject of the Information Revolution such a challenging and difficult field for the policy maker.

Many of the basic elements with which policy makers must deal are already receiving wide publicity. A small sampling for example, might include:

1. The "Cashless Society" and the "Financial Utility" with all that it implies for a more efficient and rational economic system.

2. True participatory democracy in which the town meeting concept is extended via the ubiquitous computer networks to embrace whole nations, and eventually perhaps, the world.

3. Individualized computer assisted instruction, providing each student with the equivalent of a private tutor embodying the best judgment and total experience of the world's greatest educators.

4. Medical Information Networks, for diagnosis, administration, case history information, and the evaluation and prescription of drugs.

5. Specialized information utilities designed to meet the needs of all the myriad occupational groups that make up our complex modern society.

6. Automatic publishing, computerized shopping and a whole spectrum of home entertainment and information services.

Some of the most exciting prospects are opened up by the developments in communications satellites that were mentioned by John Madden. In fact such satellites could ultimately have as great an impact upon the future of information networks as digital technology has had in bringing them to their present state. With communications satellites, distance is no longer a significant factor in the cost of providing communications services. Further, since they eliminate the need for expensive ground relay networks, satellites are the least expensive means for providing mass communications in the less developed countries of the world. Thus, for areas like Northern Canada, Africa, India and Brazil, it is possible to provide communications services of the most advanced type at a fraction of the cost of conventional systems. These include not only high quality television, radio and telephone communications, but also a wide range of data transmission services.

With the elimination of distance as a significant communications cost factor, some tantalizing new prospects are opened up for the exploitation of the Electronic Information Highway concept. Worldwide information networks have now become technically feasible and with such networks, the vital commodity which we have termed "information power" could be made available in any desired concentration everywhere on earth. A United Nations Information Utility, as the vehicle within which a multitude of international networks could develop and grow, would act as an electronic nervous system for the entire globe. In addition to enormously magnifying the operational effectiveness of the United Nations and its specialized agencies, such a system could bridge the knowledge barriers between the developed and under-developed areas of the world and ultimately bring the complete store of human knowledge within the reach of every human being.

Even with suitable safeguards however, we will still be faced with the supreme challenge of ensuring the aggressive and imaginative exploitation of our new computer and communications resources for the benefit of all mankind. This is no mean challenge, for it offers nothing less than the opportunity to leapfrog decades of normal development and move on a world-wide basis into the post-industrial society. In this new society, the universal availability of "information power" could magnify by orders of magnitude the economic and intellectual capabilities of all of us and lift the entire world in a quantum jump to an unprecedented level of achievement.

The wrong policy decisions could easily destroy this glittering promise and make the Electronic Highway Networks no more than computer/communications equivalents of today's commercial TV networks or, more ominously, dangerous instruments of repression. In fact, it requires little imagination to see how a totalitarian government could pervert the achievements of the information revolution into the omnipresent and irresistible instruments of control for a self-perpetuating fascism. The necessary structure, then, is the one which would make the potentially revolutionary benefits of computer power available to everyone and at the same time provide effective safeguards against the misuse of that power.

The possible applications of such a utility encompass every task for which conventional computers and mass communications systems are normally employed in addition to a host of others which only become feasible through the global coverage and multi-user features. Obviously, therefore, it would be presumptuous indeed to attempt a comprehensive listing at this time. Nevertheless, there are a number of obvious services which one could reasonably expect to see implemented at an early stage in the evolution of any U.N. system. These include global information networks, a United Nations Management System, an improved world weather network, educational services, a world health network and perhaps even a numerical control information utility.

THE MANY DIMENSIONS OF THE ELECTRONIC HIGHWAY

Unfortunately, the problem of selecting the "right policies" is complicated by the wide range of different systems with which we must deal; no single policy, institution, or regulatory structure is likely to be optimum for all. One dimension of this diversity has already been mentioned in connection with the many different types of "information handling" with which the Electronic Highway can be involved.

Another important dimension concerns the mix of customers served by computer-based systems. One can, for example, have purely private or in-house systems which serve only the members of a single organization; closed-user-group systems which serve a limited number of different organizations having a shared professional or business interest (such as airlines or credit unions); or, finally, public systems which serve an unlimited number of unrelated customers outside the owning organization.

In a society where videotex could soon bring computer/communications service to everyone, a particularly important dimension concerns the nature of the mechanisms employed for delivery of those services. The importance here, from the public policy aspect, arises not only from the number of possible delivery systems that exist (TV station, Cable, satellite, telephone, optical fibre, etc.), but also from the constraints which some of these mechanisms place upon the nature and quantity of the services that can be provided. Canadians ought to expect the best and most economical system, not one that is most profitable for any existing institution or corporation.

TWO BROAD CATEGORIES OF VIDEOTEX SYSTEM: EACH WITH UNIQUE CHARACTERISTICS

In this connection it is useful to consider two broad categories of system: viz., "broadcast systems" in which the information flow is in one direction only—from the information source to the customer—and "interactive," or "two-way," systems.

In broadcast systems, the information is transmitted in the form of an endlessly repeating sequence of individually coded frames or pages. By setting a code corresponding to the desired subject matter, a subscriber can seize or "grab" the appropriate page as it passes by his receiver, store it, and subsequently display or print it on his terminal. Such systems are selective in the sense that the subscriber sees only the information that he has requested, but are non-interactive since there is no communication back from the subscriber to the information source.

Since successive requests for information can require waiting while the entire database passes by, the amount of information in that database is severely limited by the permissible user waiting period. Normally this should not be longer than a comfortable human reaction time (about ten seconds max.), but times as long as 30 seconds seem to be accepted in operational broadcast systems like the British CEEFAX and ORACLE services.

The fraction of the broadcast channel available for information transmission also directly affects the database size. In the case of CEEFAX and ORACLE for example, the information service is shared with the normal TV transmission so that transmission of data is limited to certain unused scanning lines during the vertical blanking interval. The total database from which the subscriber makes his choice, consequently, is very small, 150 to 300 pages. On the other hand, if a full channel is available, as is the case with certain Cable delivery systems, as many as 10,000 pages might be offered without running into excessive waiting times.

In contrast to the broadcast systems, two-way systems permit users to interact directly with the databanks and make their selections from a theoretically unlimited number of pages. Moreover, instead of being limited to information retrieval, given the appropriate terminal equipment, users can also originate information and either send it for storage and subsequent retrieval or carry on a conversation with other subscribers. In addition, they can also access information processing and computing services and carry out a myriad of combined processing/communications functions such as banking, shopping, bill paying, playing games, going to school and making a reservation. In fact, interactive systems can be concerned with almost any service or function which can be related to the processing, storage, collection or distribution of information. Thus, they truly merit the accolade "information utilities."

DELIVERY SYSTEMS AND THEIR CHARACTERISTICS

Of course, not all videotex delivery systems can provide all of these services. This has some important implications for the "necessary structure" and it is worthwhile briefly digressing to examine the essential characteristics of the most commonly suggested media. Figure 3-1 summarizes the situation, but a few words of explanation may be in order.

Broadcast:

In the broadcast category, the three possible media are conventional TV stations, one-way cable systems and direct broadcast satellites; all of these may employ either the spare TV line or the full channel method of

Figure 3-1 Videotex Delivery System Characteristics

Parameter / Delivery System	SPARE TV LINE	FULL CHANNEL TV	TELEPHONE	2 WAY CABLE	HYBRID	SWITCHED FIBRE
Number of pages	150	10,000	NL	NL	NL	NL
Interactive	N	N	Y	Y	Y	Y
Services Information Selection	L	Y	NL	NL	NL	NL
1 way mail	L	Y	Y	Y	Y	Y
2 way mail	N	N	Y	Y	Y	Y
Software Delivery	Y	Y	Y	Y	Y	Y
Messages over TV	Y	NA	NA	NA	NA	NA
Information storage retrieval & processing	N	N	Y	Y	Y	Y
Analog TV Image communication	N	N	N	Y	Y	Y
Picture Phone	N	N	N	N	N	Y
Material — Graphics	Y	Y	Y	Y	Y	Y
Text	Y	Y	Y	Y	Y	Y
Telidon still image	Y	Y	Y	Y	Y	Y
Software	Y	Y	Y	Y	Y	Y
Limited analog TV frames	N	Y	N	Y	Y	Y
Voice	N	N	Y	Y	Y	Y
Unlimited analog TV frames	N	N	N	N	N	Y

NL—no limits L—limited NA—not applicable N—no Y—yes

transmission. Functions, as already mentioned, would be confined to the information retrieval category. But, in addition to conventional textual and graphical teletext, this could include facsimile, electronic newspapers and tele-software delivery. If a full channel were dedicated, per-channel pay-TV would be possible as well as a limited, single-frame, half-tone picture retrieval service using simple analog, frame-grabbing techniques rather than the TELIDON "picture instruction" technology.

Two-Way:

In the case of interactive services, the natural medium is the switched telephone system; it exemplifies the many-to-many, two-way communication network topology that is essential if there is to be widespread access to a wide variety of services provided by many different suppliers. This idea is illustrated in Figure 3-2. Any sort of graphical, textual or TELIDON-coded photographic material can be handled by this approach and the possible services exclude only television, whose moving pictures require band widths much wider than those available over telephone lines.

Two-way cable is another delivery alternative offering the same multiple supplier and range of service capabilities as the telephone system. In addition, the availability of wide-band channels can also make possible a number of TV services including scheduled pay-per-program pay-TV. The network topology of a cable-based system, however, would differ markedly from a switched telephone system. Thus, instead of providing unique physical connections between subscribers, a Cable system would employ a form of packet-switching in which the information frames would each be coded with the appropriate destination addresses and transmitted in sequence down the wide-band cable channels.

In the somewhat longer term, switched optical fibre networks offer the most exciting possibilities. Within a few years, such systems promise to provide subscribers with a local loop capacity of many TV channels for the price of a conventional copper loop capable of carrying only a single voice channel.

It has been suggested that the eventual result of the development of optical fibre networks should be the full integration of television broadcasting and information distribution systems into a wide-band, common-carrier network. Under this concept, television channels as well as information channels would cease to be a scarce and therefore rationed commodity, and would become instead readily available to anyone as a normal telecommunications offering. This development, by facilitating access to the distribution system by entrepreneurs and artists of all types, would in theory make it possible for anyone to be a TV producer. This in turn could lead to

INTERACTIVE TV SYSTEM

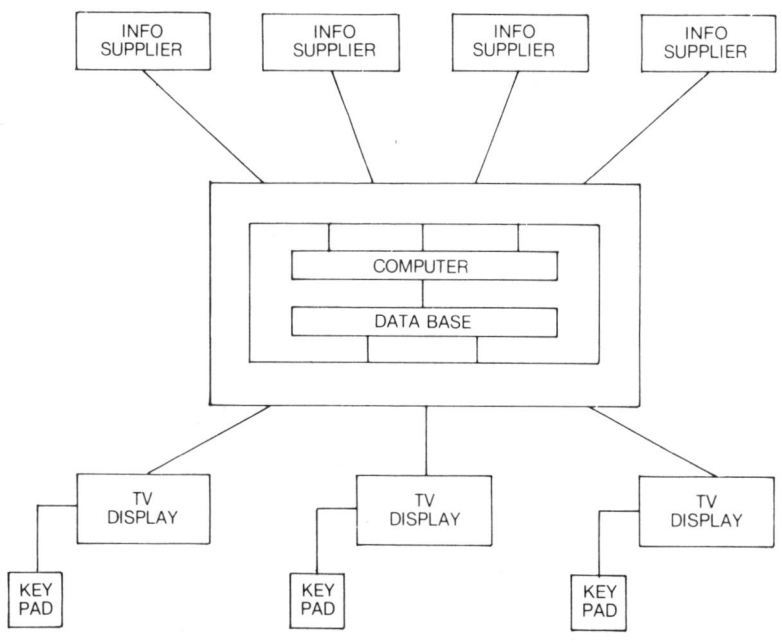

Figure 3-2

a proliferation of on-demand, pay-per-program, pay-TV services as well as making the picture-phone a viable economic proposition. Indeed, these possibilities are now being tested in an urban environment in the Japanese Hi-Ovis experiment and, for the first time in a rural location, will soon be undergoing tests in the Canadian Elie Field Trial (3).

Hybrid:

So called "hybrid networks" which combine the switched telephone system with full-channel broadcast systems also offer some attractive features. In such a network, the request for a particular frame of information is made using the telephone and relayed to the appropriate Information Provider by the telephone company. The responses are then bundled together and transmitted to the broadcast operator (Cable, satellite or TV station) who then transmits them as individually addressed packets in sequence over a wide-band channel to the subscriber. The general concept for a Telco/Cable embodiment is illustrated in Figure 3-3.

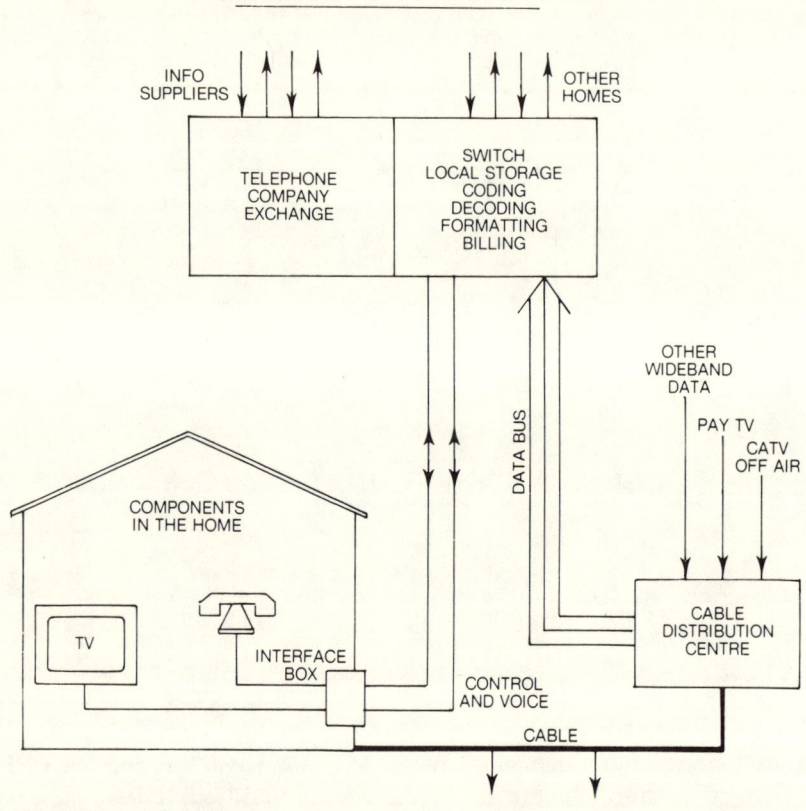

HYBRID CABLE/TELEPHONE DISTRIBUTION SYSTEM

Figure 3-3

Since the data-rate involved for an information request is generally much lower than for the response, the hybrid approach could turn out to be economically attractive to a telephone company. For example, it could reduce the local exchange load and more importantly, if a date-under-voice transmission technique was employed, make it possible to simultaneously use a customer's local loop for both voice and date service. For a Cable TV operator, the potential savings are even greater since he would be spared the possibly very high cost of modifying his one-way cable system for two-way operation. From the public policy aspect, the hybrid approach is also attractive since it gives both the Telcos and Cable companies legitimate, complementary roles to play in a mutually profitable enterprise. This could help avoid acrimonious franchise disputes, wasteful duplication of expensive facilities and the difficulties of regulation in a competitive duopoly situation. On the negative side however it should be noted that as all digital systems evolve, the exchange load problem for the telephone company will vanish anyway in the normal course of events. Also, the cost of providing the necessary multiplexing, signal separation and coding equipment could be quite high.

SERVICE SUPPLIERS

The delivery of services is of course only one of the many functions that must be carried out if the Electronic Highway is to become a reality. One other function has already been mentioned. This is the supplying of services; here the institutional options and problems involved are at least as great as for the delivery function. Indeed, as was predicted in the following quotation from a 1966 book, they could be even greater:

> When it comes to the service organizations, the problem is made more complex by the numbers and diversity of the organizations involved. Some will be very small, others extremely large. Some will confine their services to local geographic areas, others will be nationwide or even international in scope. Many will be fiercely competitive and others will be pure or quasi-monopolies. The range of services will be equally varied and will involve many businesses like insurance, banking and credit services that are currently regulated by numerous existing agencies—federal, state, and municipal. Complicating matters even further will be the growth of consolidated systems in which a single service organization performs many different functions. The tendency is already apparent in the banking business where many banks now offer integrated data-processing, billing and banking services to certain professional customers(4).

When considering these service supply functions, it is important to keep in mind that the services with which we are concerned are "information services," representing in the limit all of the infinite varieties of human thought. As detailed in Chapter Four, it is likely that they will become important alternatives to the orthodox media: newspapers, magazines, television, etc., and even the postal service, as basic mechanisms for both mass and personal communication.

Consequently, it would seem to be a fundamental principle of public policy in a free society to strive to maximize participation and diversity and strongly oppose anything which could foster concentration of control. For it seems obvious that such control of the electronic media, whether by the state or by private interests, would represent a serious threat to the freedom of expression that is the lifeblood of a democratic community.

Professor E. Parker of Stanford University emphasized the threat in the following words in a provocative paper delivered in February 1975 at the

OECD Conference on Computer/Telecommunications Policy:

> The difference between George Orwell's 1984 and a hypothetical
> participatory democracy with widespread sharing of political power lies
> in the question of who controls the sending and receiving of information
> in the society (5).

The answer to Parker's question in a free society, surely, is that no
control is either needed or desired other than that which ensures the free exchange of information in a truly open market place of ideas. It is therefore
of vital importance that we establish now, while systems like TELIDON are
still in their infancy, those fundamental principles concerning freedom to
publish and freedom from censorship that lie behind the time-hallowed
slogan, "Freedom of the Press." Indeed, we may want to go beyond this
and attack also the problem of commercial concentration. This would mean
developing appropriate bench marks to indicate when undue concentration
has been reached so that remedial action could be taken.

Maintaining an unregulated, truly competitive, service-supplier
industry and ensuring fundamental rights like "freedom to publish,"
however, will be impossible unless the service suppliers have guaranteed
access to their customers. This means that it is critically important that the
Electronic Highways, whereby such access is obtained, be open to everyone.
This implies two fundamental principles of open access:

(1)Equality of access to the services distributed by the Electronic
Highways insofar as this is technically and economically feasible.

(2)Non-discriminatory access to the highways at tariffed rates by
anyone for the provision and distribution of services.

CONTENT/CONTAINER SEPARATION

Since the services are distributed by regulated entities (Telcos, Cable
companies, etc., whose conditions of licence require that they meet all reasonable demands for service in their franchized areas), the equality of access
condition can be readily satisfied. In fact, in the case of the telecommunications carriers, both principles are implicit in their legal status as "public
utilities" or, as the Encyclopaedia Britannica puts it with reference to "the
law of public service undertakings":

this law places upon a public utility the extraordinary duty to render reasonably adequate service to all who apply. It is required to serve them up to the limit of its capacity, with capacity being defined as the limit of profitableness. It may not let customers' wants go unsatisfied. Nor, may it attach unreasonable conditions to contracts for service so as in effect to negate its duty "to serve all comers." Furthermore, it must serve without discrimination all customers similarly circumstanced. Finally, a public utility must observe more than ordinary care in the rendition of service in view of the dependence of the public upon such services and the hazards associated therewith (6).

In both Canada and the United States, the non-discrimination principle has received particular attention with respect to the issue of "Carrier participation in public data-processing." This issue first came to prominence in the late sixties and early seventies when there were attempts by Telcos to extend their data-communications activities and provide remote data-processing as well as communications services. These attempts were strongly opposed by data-processing companies who argued that for a Carrier to compete with its own customers constituted an intolerable breach of its obligations as a public utility and could lead to serious abuses. These, it was claimed, included a potentially dangerous concentration of power, cross-subsidization of the unregulated competitive services from the regulated monopoly sector, unfair competition, and, above all, opportunities for discriminatory treatment.

The issue was for all practical purposes settled in the case of the Canadian Federally Regulated Carriers in 1975 by the adoption of the arm's length subsidiary solution (7). This approach divorces the regulated telecommunications operations of the Carrier from its public data-processing business by requiring that the latter be carried out in an organization that is administratively and financially separated from the communication company. It is then up to the regulatory body to ensure that neither discriminatory treatment nor cross-subsidization exists.

The current Canadian approach to Computer/Communications Policy was expressed in April 1973 in a Federal Government Green Paper (2).

In the paper, the government opted for regulated provision of data-communications facilities by the existing carriers and competition in the service sector. Thus, with respect to the former, it was stated:

Statement 10
Within the scope of known technology no reason is seen to encourage the development of separate competitive transmission facilities and the established position of the existing carriers in providing transmission facilities should be continued.

The paper also stated the government's dedication to the concept of public rather than private networks.

Statement 4
It is a government objective to foster the continued development of efficient and reliable nation-wide systems of publicly-accessible data-communications facilities for use equally in the provision of, or access to computer or data communications services by, any sector or society.

The service sector, it was made clear, should be competitive and un-regulated except for certain minimal constraints that might be necessary to protect the public.

Statement 13
The government proposes to rely on competition policy to promote efficiency in the computer services and software industries, and to ensure that the resulting benefits are transmitted to the users of these services and to the Canadian public at large. Consequently the government believes that the computer services industry should remain unregulated except where constraints upon entry and participation may be necessary in the public interest and with the possible exception of some specific areas such as privacy, file protection, and perhaps liability and standards.

In effect, what we have here is recognition that in terms of regulation the marriage of computers and communications leads logically to a new fundamental dichotomy: a total separation of Container and Content, of the Electronic Highways and of the services that they distribute. Implicit in this separation are three conditions that are basic to any open-access policy:

1) a total ban on any Carrier involvement with Content;

2) an obligation on the part of the Carrier to meet any reasonable demands for service;

3) a legal requirement on the part of the Carrier to distribute the services of all suppliers on a non-discriminatory basis at authorized tariffs.

In exchange, measures would be highly desirable to clearly and un-ambiguously free the Carriers from any legal responsibility when the material carried might be deemed seditious, libellous, pornographic or slanderous under some statute.

THE DIFFICULT CASE OF CABLE COMPANIES AND BROADCASTERS

The foregoing conditions are really basic principles of common carriage and are generally accepted by the telecommunication carriers in Canada and the United States. Consequently, there should be no difficulty in applying them to any situation where the delivery system is the switched telephone network. However, in the case of broadcasters and cable companies there are potential problems, some of which are regulatory, others technical.

The regulatory problem arises from a dual function: the broadcasting industry and to a lesser extent, the cable TV industry have both traditionally been involved in both content and carriage. Indeed a case can be made that broadcasters are primarily content (or information) providers, and the fact that they also broadcast (or carry) the programming is more or less incidental to their primary preoccupation with content. This case becomes stronger with every increase in the penetration of cable TV systems, which now carry TV signals to urban households more often than they are received off-air (8).

Thus, instead of the carriage/services separation and freedom of access principles, we have a deliberate integration of services and distribution; the operators are fully responsible for content and there is strong control by the regulatory body of the types and numbers of services that can be carried.

In the case of broadcasters, this approach historically has been justified on the grounds that over-the-air carriage utilizes a scarce and valuable public resource, the radio frequency spectrum. As public property, this resource must be used in the public interest; the few who are granted a temporary licence to exploit it are consequently required to abide by certain rules designed by the state as part of its duty to protect that public interest.

The case for similarly regulating the use of cable TV undertakings is far more tenuous and, in the case of Canada, rests on a Supreme Court decision which defines those cable TV systems which distribute off-air signals as "Broadcasting Receiving Undertakings". This makes them subject to the Broadcasting Act and therefore to the regulations of the CRTC *even for their closed circuit services.* On the other hand, systems which do not include off-air signals in their offerings are not regarded as Broadcasting Receiving Undertakings and consequently are exempt from regulation under the Act.

When it comes to interactive TELIDON services, distributed by 2-way cable or hybrid systems, there is no rational reason for continuing to impose broadcast-based regulations. Indeed, for all of the reasons given earlier, a continuation of such regulation would constitute a dangerous infringement of basic human rights. Consequently, it is likely that the current CRTC policy which treats cable companies as broadcasters is nothing more than a temporary aberration that soon will be consigned to the garbage dump of history. When this happens, at least for interactive TELIDON services, cable TV companies will become common carriers subject to the same regulatory rules as the telephone carriers.

Unfortunately, however, when it comes to one-way cable, and terrestrial and satellite broadcasters, the solution is not as simple since we are constrained by some fundamental technical limitations that no amount of regulatory tinkering can remove.

As we have seen, when the vertical blanking interval technique is employed for information carriage on a conventional TV broadcast, there is a practical upper limit (of about 300 pages) to the amount of information that can be handled. With such a limitation, there is no way in which the access demands of all information providers could possibly be met; "open access" becomes an impossible dream.

In the absence of open access, however, how is it decided who shall have the privilege of access? John Madden has presented an excellent description of this problem and lists three alternatives:

1. Separate licensing by the CRTC of the vertical blanking intervals for each TV channel.

2. In cable systems, allowing the cable TV operator to insert his own information pages on any TV channel.

3. Giving the broadcast licensee control over the content of any information inserted into the vertical blanking interval of his channel. This would include the right to insert his own information (8).

Madden comes down on the side of option 3 and this writer agrees with his conclusion on the grounds of ease of regulation, maximizing public choice (after all most communities have many TV stations), and fairness to the broadcast licensee who retains total control of his authorized channel assignment.

A much more complex and difficult situation exists with respect to full channel, one-way, cable TV systems. As with the blanking line systems, the information capacity per channel is both finite and far below what would be needed to serve all Information Providers. Consequently, open access is impossible and again we are faced with the question of how and by whom access is to be controlled. On the other hand, unlike the blanking line case, the capacity is quite substantial, of the order of 5-10,000 pages, so that both the commercial attractiveness and potential for abuse are significant.

Insofar as access control is concerned, the two obvious alternatives are either to leave control with the Cable system operator subject to CRTC guidelines or have the CRTC license special Information Providers who in turn would pay the Cable Carrier to broadcast their products. Madden (8) has suggested a third alternative whereby subscribers, via an elected committee or by voting, would make the decisions concerning the Content to be carried.

The first alternative can probably be rejected out of hand since the possibilities for abuse inherent in monopoly control of such a powerful information medium are incompatible with any society that believes in freedom of expression. The second policy is more acceptable since monopoly could be avoided by licensing a number of competing Information Providers in each Cable franchise area in much the same way as broadcasters are licensed today. This would recognize the Cable company as a Carrier. On the other hand, unless multiple channels were utilized, the number of pages available to any one Information Provider could become too small for economic viability. Indeed, ensuring economic viability in any one-way system that incorporates Content/Container separation presents a number of special problems.

For one thing, there is no simple means of implementing a "charge by page" policy since each subscriber automatically has access to all pages on a channel or sub-channel to which he is tuned. Consequently, we are forced to rely on mechanisms whereby the cable operator would charge a subscription fee on a per-channel or possibly sub-channel basis using decoders similar to those used for per-channel pay-TV systems to prevent access by non-subscribers. Alternatively, he could elect not to charge the subscriber at all and depend for his revenues upon the carrying charges imposed upon Information Providers.

The latter, with no possibility of directly charging the subscribers, would obtain their revenues from such classical broadcasting mechanisms as advertising, or, in the case of public service organizations, from charitable donations or government subsidies. In the former case, a real estate company might provide descriptions and prices of property for sale, or a restaurant, sample menus and price lists, either one paying the Information Provider in much the same way as they might pay a newspaper or magazine for ad space. Likewise, a government agency could rent pages for display of informational material, health or welfare services, income tax regulations and so forth.

Greater flexibility would be possible if a number of channels were made available for the teletext service. In this case, each licensed Information Provider could be provided with his own channel so that with suitable channel usage recording equipment on the subscribers' premises he would be able to collect directly from the subscribers as well as from his advertisers. Alternatively, he, rather than the cable operator, could collect subscription fees in the manner of a conventional magazine publisher. Thus, upon payment of the subscription fee, the appropriate channel could be received for the subscription period.

INFORMATION PROCESSING, STORAGE AND RETRIEVAL

Regardless of the communications medium selected for the distribution of information services, one also requires an electronic facility for storing and retrieving information, and, in the case of many interactive systems, for performing a theoretically unlimited number of information processing tasks.

For broadcast systems, this facility is relatively simple, consisting essentially of a small storage system, rudimentary cyclic reading device, coding and modulation equipment. For interactive systems however, the situation is very different. Instead of a cyclic storage system for example, a random-access facility is needed and it may be required to simultaneously satisfy different, independent demands for access from many hundreds or even thousands of customers. The required storage capacity is also very much larger, so that instead of a few hundred pages, or perhaps 10,000 in the case of a full channel broadcast system, space must be provided for an endlessly growing library of hundreds of thousands or conceivably millions of pages. Moreover, in addition to a "read" capability, the system may also incorporate equipment that makes it possible for subscribers to input their own information either into private memory space for their own later use or, in the case of Information Providers, into a public access databank for retrieval by others. Complex information processing services may also be provided as well as person-to-person message services including tele-mail.

Facilities of this size and complexity obviously could involve heavy capital investments and large, skilled, professional, operating staffs. For very large Information Providers (for example, a major newspaper, or a department store) the financial burden may not be excessive and such organizations might elect to provide their own databank and processing facilities. On the other hand, for individual entrepreneurs, smaller companies, and even those large organizations who may not relish the specialized management task of running a computer centre, other approaches are necessary. In the case of the British PRESTEL system, the need is met via public access facilities provided by the BPO as an extension of its normal carriage functions. All Information Providers are permitted to store their data in these facilities for a monthly fee that is proportional to the number of pages stored. The required capital investment for an Information Provider is thus reduced in the limit to the rental cost of a simple Information Provider terminal (currently about £400 per annum) plus the charge for storage space. Of course, the terminal at this price is a pretty rudimentary device permitting only alphanumeric input and primitive character-based graphics. More professional terminals, incorporating local storage, light pens, TV cameras, etc., and designed to exploit the sophisticated graphics and half tone image capabilities of TELIDON, for example, could cost several times as much, but still would represent only a small percentage of the investment involved in a private, remote-access, databank facility.

In the case of Canada, present restrictions on the right of the federally regulated carriers to offer public data processing services could constitute a legal obstacle to the provision of public access databases and processing by these Carriers or by Cable Carriers. However, just as for conventional data processing services, these new services could be provided by arm's length subsidiaries as well as, of course, by any of the myriad remote-access, service bureaux that now cover the country. In this connection, it is likely also that "electronic publishers" will evolve, offering in addition to data storage facilities, a variety of authors' services, including, for example: rental of specialized editing equipment, design of access trees, graphic arts and editorial assistance and marketing services.

DIRECTORY SERVICES

The acceptability and usefulness of any public system such as TELIDON is critically dependent upon the ease with which the desired information or service can be accessed. This in turn is influenced by such factors as: the speed with which connection to the information suppliers or public access databanks is completed, search times in the case of information retrieval services, the design of the access trees, and above all, by the quality of the directory services.

Quality, in this case involves:
1. Comprehensiveness—All services and all service suppliers must be included.
2. Currency—The listings must be up-to-date with each new service listed the instant that it becomes available.
3. Flexibility—The system should be able to handle a variety of different indexing and categorization methods and to provide for natural language (e.g., key word) queries as well as the simple menu selection type.
4. Guidance—Techniques must be incorporated that will automatically steer or guide even the most naive user to the page or service that he wants.
5. Simplicity—The directory must be clear, natural and easy to use.

Incorporating all of these characteristics in any single directory (whose contents are continuously changing and involve potentially millions of entries scattered across the globe) would be almost impossible. Consequently, just as is the case for today's telephone systems, it is likely that there will be many different directories. Master directories, for example, corresponding to the familiar "yellow pages" could be provided on a local basis by the carriers. These will probably include directions for obtaining access to directory services in other locations. Individual directories will be supplied by service providers and electronic publishers. These are also likely to be supplemented by a wide variety of specialized directory services which might for example, cover all listings of a particular category (medical, legal, educational, etc.) independently of geographic location. In fact, in a world where satellites have made communication costs essentially independent of distance, many services are likely to be offered on a national or even world-wide basis. Consequently such "long distance" listings are bound to become increasingly important in the future. Consumer groups, for example, could provide "tested" directories for their own members.

BILL COLLECTION

In an interactive TELIDON system, a customer is likely to be involved with many different services supplied by dozens of different organizations each of which sets its own prices. Pricing structures can also take many different forms, ranging from a simple fixed price per page for information retrieval to complex time, distance, storage and processing charges for services like tele-mail or data-processing. The net result is a costly bill preparation and collection task for service providers and an onerous, time-consuming, payment problem for subscribers.

One obvious solution to the problem involves taking advantage of the fact that all services are delivered via a single organization—the Cable Carrier or Telco—and having it perform the bill collection function on behalf of all service suppliers. Indeed, this is the approach adopted in Britain for the PRESTEL service where the post office simply appends a detailed listing of all charges to the regular monthly telephone bill. Upon receipt of payment, it then deducts its own service charges and sends the remainder to the appropriate service providers.

This approach is attractive to subscribers since they are spared the chore and expense of having to make many separate payments and are presented with a simple, easily understood, but comprehensive statement of all charges. Similar advantages accrue to the information suppliers, while for the carrier it means a source of additional income that can be provided by a complex but natural extension to his existing toll telephone billing equipment.

Unfortunately, however, in the absence of suitable safeguards, having a single organization undertake the billing function could introduce a serious privacy problem. This arises from the fact that the billing process requires a detailed record of every transaction, indeed of every service undertaken via the network. In the case of information retrieval services for example, the records could include the names and page numbers of all material accessed by every subscriber. It requires no surfeit of imagination to see how such information could be misused. The existence of what in time would come to be a complete profile from birth until death of the intellectual affairs of everyone would offer enormous possibilities for blackmail and enforced conformity. Credit organizations, governments, security officials, educators, employers, advertisers, and police—the entire power structure of modern society—all would be natural customers for the sorts of information contained in the computer files, with possibly dangerous consequences for the poor individual whose records might deviate from the norm. In fact, as has been pointed out: "There is an uncomfortable aura of 1984 in all this. Thus it is not difficult to visualize how the computer utility might be perverted until it degenerated into nothing more than an instrument of total political control—the omnipresent eyes and ears of 'big brother' (4).

Given these very real dangers, one is strongly tempted to suggest that we forego the efficiencies of central billing and leave the responsibility with the information suppliers and agents like VISA, Master Charge, etc. Unfortunately however, given the penchant of contemporary commercial organizations and government agencies to share personal information, the way in which computerization facilitates this sharing, and the potentially enormous size of many "electronic publishers", it is doubtful if such an approach by itself would be adequate. Consequently it seems certain that other stringent legal safeguards will be required—safeguards which paradoxically might be most easily implemented in a centralized billing environment. These could include:

1. Creation of a corps of bonded professional computer operators bound by a strict oath of secrecy.

2. A *total ban* on disclosure of personal information from the files except for the individual named.

3. Mandatory security measures, both physical and electronic, for protection of data.

4. Severe criminal penalties, including mandatory jail sentences, for breaches of privacy on the part of the "keepers of the files" and for those, police, government and company officials, etc., who incite, condone or benefit from such breaches.

5. Civil redress for those who may have been damaged by improper disclosure of the contents of their files.

6. Mandatory destruction of certain types of information might also be required, so that certain types of master files cannot be created.

In addition, individuals should have the right to obtain complete access to any files held on them by any organization and to receive amendment, destruction, or abstraction of those records on demand. That is, a phone company may need to know that it received a payment of $10.00 for access to certain information services; it would not need to know from whom the payment was received once its annual audit was completed. Indeed, a system of mandatory, automatic encryption could be imposed on billing service so that operating personnel would not know the names of specific customers involved in individual transactions. The bonded, external auditors would be the only ones allowed to match the coded customer numbers with personal names. Complaints would involve matching the code-number with a real customer, but that would not present a major problem or threat.

Medical records could be held by the individual in the equivalent of an electronic safety-deposit box. These would be in a standard format and a doctor or hospital could request permission each time they needed access to specific portions of those records, but could not store them away in their own master files.

ELECTRONIC MAIL

The use of videotex systems for the provision of electronic message services is a particularly important subject since in time, particularly as auxiliary printers become available, this could make TELIDON a viable substitute for both the normal postal service and Telex/TWX. In its present form, as exemplified for example by the British PRESTEL service, it is a store-and-forward system whereby each customer is assigned an electronic mail box. Messages can then be placed in this box from any videotex terminal for retrieval at the owner's leisure. These may be either pre-formatted, standard messages selected by a minimum-cost, numerical keyboard, or free-form letters if a full alphanumeric keyboard is available.

Services of this type have of course been available in a business environment for some time from many computer service bureaux, albeit not without considerable opposition and harassment from the regular telecommunication Carriers. They are also a natural outgrowth of the development of communicating word-processors. The prospect, however, of having them available to everyone creates an entirely new situation and gives rise to a number of important policy and structural questions. These include:

1. Who should supply the electronic mail boxes: the post office, the telecommunications carriers, the computer service industry or others?

2. If the post office supplies the service should it be as a monopoly or should competition be permitted and if so on what basis: unrestricted, or only from a limited number of regulated organizations?

3. Should the service be universal or optional?

4. What charging mechanisms should be employed?

5. What should be regulated and by whom?

6. What are the obligations of the organization(s) supplying the service?

7. How do we ensure file security, assured delivery and protect privacy?

With respect to the necessary structure, there are two obvious extreme possibilities which might be termed the "telephone based individual responsibility" and "central storage" approaches. The first places the burden of supplying the mail box upon the TELIDON terminal owner where it would take the form of a small and probably very inexpensive memory which could be either incorporated within the normal terminal circuitry or supplied as an optional add-on device. This memory could be accessed for deposit of information via the telephone network in a manner analogous to today's automatic telephone answering devices; the information would be retrieved later via the TV set.

With this approach, one's telephone number becomes one's postal address, no new regulatory or institutional structure is required and the memory capital investment is shared among millions of subscribers as a potentially trivial incremental terminal cost. Insofar as the telephone companies are concerned, the principal investments would involve expanding the current packet switched networks so that they become truly universal, and the provision of equipment at the local exchange for the temporary storage of messages in the event that a subscriber's telephone is busy when a message is received. In addition, of course, if the service is to truly replace the conventional postal service, then the tariffs would have to be made distance independent, at least within the Canadian boundaries.

For those types of mail, advertising for example, where acknowledgement of receipt and privacy is not important, packet radio provides an attractive delivery alternative to the telephone network. Depending upon the volume of information to be transmitted, transmission could take place over either an FM or TV channel and for the latter, either the blanking line or full channel approach could be employed.

Again, the potential volume of information would require new ways of looking at procedures. An individual should have the right to protect his mail-box from the unwanted junk mail (or even from ex-lovers or bill collectors) by putting a lock on messages from specific sources (9). A "box-locked" message could be returned to the sender—but not, of course, when the "broadcast" delivery technique is employed.

The central storage approach has many possible varieties, depending upon who provides the storage. At one extreme this would be the post office operating as a monopoly. At the other, it could be anyone and the environment would be one of unrestricted competition.

It can be argued that having the post office supply the service represents a logical evolution of the delivery function that post offices everywhere have always performed. Over the centuries, a complex international network of local offices has been built up and certain universal principles established that are equally applicable to both physical and electronic mail delivery. These include universality, so that the service is available everywhere, standardized rates; liberty of transit; and cross subsidization, so that profitable services support those which may not be economically viable. Thus, a post office operated electronic mail system should be able to ensure universal access at the lowest possible rates. In addition, it is argued that, by providing new employment opportunities for the tens of thousands of postal workers whose jobs will vanish in an age of electronic mail, this approach could alleviate the individual hardship and general social dislocation that otherwise might occur.

On the negative side however, the capital cost of providing the thousands of complex central facilities that would be required throughout Canada would be enormous, as would be the operating costs. Moreover, the sorts of technical and managerial skills required would be totally unrelated to those currently resident in any postal system with the exception of those where postal and telecommunication services are combined within the same corporation; and unfortunately, the record of the latter with respect to the quality and cost of telecommunications service has in general been far inferior to that of countries like Sweden, Canada and the United States where the services are separated. Likewise, when it comes to universality, access and international standardization, the merits of the postal systems are more than balanced by those of the telecommunications networks. Consequently, if we were to decide upon the centralized approach, it would probably make more sense to grant the monopoly to the telecommunication Carriers rather than to the post office.

The unrestricted competition, centralized-storage approach has even less to recommend it than the monopoly version. Although a few large consumers might benefit slightly from price and quality competition, the chances are that the less profitable areas of the country would not be served at all while in other areas there would be wasteful duplication. Overall, the capital investment required would be just as large and probably larger than for the monopoly case and a wasteful and expensive infrastructure would be required to keep track of who subscribed to which company so that mail could be routed to the proper address.

Obviously a great deal more thought will have to be given to the subject than is possible in this brief essay, but it does seem to me at this time that the "individual responsibility" approach is the correct one. Whether the criteria be technical, economic, regulatory, quality of service to the consumer or ease of implementation, the arguments seem to come down strongly against "centralized storage".

CONCLUSIONS: THE NECESSARY STRUCTURE

It is the writer's hope that out of the discussions in this chapter a clearer picture has emerged of the sorts of policies and institutions that are needed in Canada if we are to grasp the opportunity for human development presented by the "Information Revolution". Basic to this picture is a view of the evolution of computing and communications systems that sees them coming together in the form of a universal, functionally-integrated but institutionally-separated information distribution system metaphorically called an "Electronic Highway Network". Such a network could become the medium for the distribution of a myriad of information services whose number and variety is for all practical purposes unlimited and which would be available to everyone everywhere in Canada.

With a few minor or temporary exceptions, this Electronic Highway Network would be governed by the principle of Content/Container separation in which there is a legal wall of separation between those who distribute the services; i.e., the Electronic Highway operators and those, like pay-TV producers, videotex information providers, etc., who provide them. The former are few in number and function as regulated monopolies, whereas the others are conceptually unlimited in number, competitive and largely unregulated.

As regulated monopolies, the highway operators would be regulated as common carriers and required to fulfill the following obligations:

1. Provide equality of access at tariffed rates to the services distributed by the highways insofar as this is technically and economically feasible.

2. Provide non-discriminatory access to the highways at tariffed rates to *anyone* for the provision and distribution of services.

3. Refrain from participating in or influencing in any way the content of the services carried.

These principles are now generally well established with respect to telephone and normal data services and if in the future picture phone becomes a viable proposition, it is safe to assume that they will also be applied to it. In the case of videotex and pay-TV, they are also fundamental and as we have seen elsewhere in this chapter, their translation into practice leads to the following "necessary structure".

(a) Videotex

1. Information Providers unregulated and with the same freedom to publish and freedom from censorship as for the conventional press.

2. Total Content/Container separation except for over-the-air, vertical blanking interval, broadcast services.

3. Cable systems regulated as common carriers subject to the same rules as telephone companies.

4. All prices set by service providers.

5. Bill collection by either Carrier or service provider at the latter's op-

tion, or by an agency like a bank, credit card company, etc. to which both the subscriber and service provider subscribe.

6. Strict privacy and freedom of access rules with both stringent criminal penalties and civil redress available for enforcement.

7. Directory services provided by Carriers as an obligation and optionally by any one else.

8. Public access databases supplied on a competitive basis by anyone, unregulated except with respect to privacy protection and file security.

9. Electronic mail boxes supplied by consumer as an add-on to the normal videotex terminal with telephone number as mailing address.

10. Electronic mail distribution normally by telephone carriers, with the exception of that material for which an acknowledgement of receipt is not required in which case over the air broadcast or one-way cable distribution can be employed.

11. Individual ability to "lock" the box against unwanted messages.

(b) Pay-TV

The basic structure would be very similar to that proposed for videotex and indeed, in the future, when switched optical fibres put several video channels at everyone's disposal for the price of an audio channel today, the videotex and pay-TV services will probably merge. The structure consequently should embody:

1. Total Content/Container separation as for videotex.

2. Distribution by regulated wide-band Carriers, which could include cable TV companies, telephone carriers, Telesat Canada and conventional TV stations.

3. Same freedom of access rules as for videotex services; i.e., anyone can be a content supplier and suppliers set prices; Carriers must distribute all offerings at tariffed rates without discrimination.

In the short run, limited capacity in the absence of switched optical fibre systems or multiple cables, could lead to peak hour saturation. Consequently, a rationing scheme could be required for some time to come. As an interim measure, for example, some sort of "authorized program packager" scheme might be employed. This could initially allocate a limited number of wide band channels (ten might be a reasonable number to start with) to licensed packagers on a two or three year renewable basis after public hearings, as is done to-day with broadcasting licences. In return for their temporary monopoly, these packagers would be expected to observe certain rules concerning Canadian content, non-discriminatory treatment of producers, fairness, etc. As technology progresses however, and wide band channels cease to be a scarce commodity, the number of packagers or even individual producers could be allowed to grow until eventually any need for government control of access would vanish.

In conclusion, I believe that the future is now inseparably tied to the growth of an *open* Electronic Highway Network that will make the fruits of the Information Revolution available to everyone. As the OECD has noted:

> Out of this widespread availability of information power there will flow social changes and opportunities for human development that promise to make the next few decades among the most critical that mankind has ever faced (10).

During those decades, we in Canada are going to be faced with many critical decisions. Few however, are likely to be of greater long term importance than the policies and structures that we select for fostering and protecting those fundamental rights of free expression and privacy without which a democratic society cannot exist. Hopefully the ideas expressed in this chapter will contribute to the selection process.

REFERENCES TO CHAPTER 3

1. D.F. Parkhill, "Society and Computer Communications Policy", Proceedings of the Third International Conference on Computer Communications, Toronto, 3-6 August 1976.

2. "Computer/Communications Policy—A Position Statement by the Government of Canada" April 1973.

3. The Honourable Jeanne Sauve, Minister of Communications, "New Programs in Communications"—Speech at the Canadian Telecommunications Carriers Association Annual Meeting, Quebec City, June 19, 1978.

4. D.F. Parkhill *The Challenge of the Computer Utility* Addison-Wesley Publishing Company, Reading, Mass. 1966.

5. Edwin B. Parker, "Background Report", Proceedings of the OECD Conference on Computer/Telecommunications Policy, Paris, February 4-6, 1975.

6. Encyclopaedia Britannica, "Public Utilities", Vol. 18, Book 13, pp. 744F-749.

7. "Federally Regulated Carriers and Chartered Banks Paricipation in Commerical Data Processing": Joint Statement of the Ministers of Finance and Communications, 16 January, 1975.

8. John C. Madden, "Videotex in Canada", Discussion Paper, Delta Dialogue Series Seminar #9, Toronto, May 8, 1979.

9. Further information on locked electronic mail-boxes (that is, privately encoded messages) can be found in Martin E. Hellman's "The Mathematics of Public-Key Cryptography", *Scientific American,* Vol. 241, No. 2, August 1979.

10. "Terms of Reference for OECD Panel on Policy Issues of Computer/Telecommunications Interaction: May 1970, in Computers and Telecommunication", Vol. 3, OECD Informatics Studies, Paris, June 1973.

4 SURVIVAL OF THE FASTEST
David Godfrey

Vulnerability Coefficients: The Impact of the New Technologies on Existing Media

"We expected to get quite rich quite quickly." *

The old question. Who will get rich? When?

There are a number of certainties. Information processing and distribution are taking a greater share of the GNP every year. Every advance in information distribution technology has led to rapid wealth for those who were there at the beginning—as long as they managed to stay there. Others have lost their all with equal speed. The other old question. Who will go under? When?

Three stories may be illustrative of the difficulties of predicting the impact of technologies.

Gutenberg devoted his innovations almost entirely to the production of the magnificent Mainz Bible, a task which required 5700 calfskins for vellum, as well as 6 presses and up to 25 workmen operating over a period of at least three years. His venture capitalist friend, Johann Fust,saw other possibilities. At the very moment of triumph, Fust hired Peter Schoeffer, Gutenberg's operations manager, and sued the inventor, probably committing major perjury to convince the good burghers of Mainz to join with him against the patrician Gutenberg. Gutenberg then lost all his rights

From the trial in which the brothers of Andreas Dritzehn (deceased), sought to take his place according to the terms of the contract which Gutenberg had made to initiate Dritzehn, Hans Riffe and Andreas Heilmann into the secrets of the technology in which he was engaged and which did indeed lead to great wealth for many, although certainly not for Gutenberg himself. (1)

to the shop and equipment. (Fust died of the plague while selling books in Paris a few years later.)

The Dominion Telegraph Company, who had helped Alexander Graham Bell set up the first long-distance telephone call (from Paris to Brantford), when offered the Canadian rights to the invention by Alexander's father, felt that $12,000 would be a fair price, being quite content with the profits they were making on the telegraph without risking everything on a consumer item that probably wouldn't sell.

Nor do outside groups necessarily see that manna from heaven has been dropped on them. In 1533, the Sorbonne, confronted with the invention that did more for the status, revenue and influence of the university than all others combined, decided in their collective and objective wisdom that the only satisfactory answer was banning and recommended to Francis I, on July 7, that *"pour sauver la religion... il est indispensable d'abolir pour toujours en France, par un edit severe, l'art de l'imprimerie"*(2).

Patterns clear in retrospect are never so at the moment of innovation. There are two factors in particular, beyond the usual human vagaries, that make it difficult to set the vulnerability coefficients for the various media with the precision that stock analysts might like to see. One of these is government regulation. The second is the changes in definitions and categories that inevitably arrive with each major change in technology. The brothers Dritzehn took Gutenberg to court over an agreement that Gutenberg had created because neither patent law nor copyright existed. With the new Electronic Highways in place, libel, privacy and copyright legislation will have to undergo major revisions. At times, then, regulation and redefinition will go hand in hand, as definitions arise out of new legislation or non-legislative standards (such as ASCII or IBM-format floppy diskettes).

But other definitions and categories will change because of the impact of the new technologies upon market forces and corporational structures. For example, at the moment we all know what Moore Corporation does and where its statistics can be found in an overall view of the economy. It supplies printed forms on which people record information and then distribute according to their own whims and wishes. But now Moore, reading the winds, has made an alliance with Texas Instruments for the production and marketing of a line of minicomputers. In addition, they will supply software according to a strategy enunciated by a Moore spokesman: "The trick is to get volume on a specific application. A lot of little guys wind up customizing their packages until they are too specialized to sell to anyone else"(3). Moore has indentified 150 different industry segments, which could yield an average of 2,600 customers for each package, producing a customer base of 400,000.

In 1990 then, with due respect for what Statistics Canada has accomplished, what will the poor analyst do with the question of categorizing Moore's activities? How much is printing, how much is manufacturing, how much involves communications and services? Given the nature of satellite technology and the desire of Moore/Texas Instruments to provide a full range of services, they might also be engaged directly in communications to offer their clients on-line training, new product information, parts-ordering, or software transfers.

Government regulation will probably be more predictable than such market shifts in categories. Already alliances have been made between groups who previously looked upon themselves only in a client/customer relationship. More will surely follow. Complex though they may be, these alliances will follow the laws of economic advantage. Government regulation, on the other hand, will surely not be as logical and clear-cut as Douglas Parkhill's scheme would indicate (see Chapter 3).

Nonetheless, the Carrier/Content dichotomy which Parkhill outlines is crucial. In order to arrive at the estimates of vulnerability to TELIDON services discussed in this chapter, and to the entire computer/communications revolution, a good deal of statistical background from different media has been compared in new ways. One clear conclusion is that the profits lie in the middle ground of the Carrier/Content polarity, with those who have managed to hang on to rights and power in both areas. Table 4.1 illustrates this point.

CARRIER	CARRIER AND CONTENT	CONTENT
Telephone	Cable Large movie chains Newspapers	Independent film makers Book publishers
Reasonable profits	High and secure profits **Table 4-1**	Occasional block-busters but low returns on average; high risk

Independent producers, at the moment, are like gamblers. When they win, they win big, but the odds are against them. Carriers have the greatest potential for making money, but it is that very potential which raises the spectre of monopoly and leads to their regulation. The surest profits lie with those who are both Carriers and Content producers: newspapers, Cable, large mass-paperback firms.

THE TAMEC REPORT

Before looking at the comparative statistics which underline the estimates of vulnerability coefficients, let us look at the only study so far made public which deals with a specific industry and the impact of TELIDON: the TAMEC Report, *Videotex Services: The Market Potential for Cable* (4). It is not surprising that activity and research into TELIDON services seems most intense with those in the central category, newspapers and Cable, although interest has also been expressed by the Telcos who see both threats and profits in the new structures. Southam, the Toronto Star and the Globe and Mail have formed Infoglobe, which will be preparing material in TELIDON format to be made available for any field trials. A number of such trials are underway or planned. The *Tamec Report* deals with the strategy that should be taken by the Cable industry to recognize, contain, and profit from TELIDON systems.

Although the *Tamec Report* makes a number of assumptions which might be contradicted, it is interesting and the authors are not afraid to go out on a limb and make very specific predictions and recommendations, including:

- projections of a total videotex market by 1990 in Canada of 3 million to 4.3 million units,
- a number of specific vulnerability coefficients for other media,
- a methodology for Cable's containment of the new technology for its own best advantage, and
- a market share for Cable/videotex of 8% to 12% of all advertising revenues: $1 billion to $1.4 billion.

Assuming that home-terminals come down to the price of some of the home-computer units we show in Chapter Seven (which is quite possible even at the moment), and that Cable continues its rapid growth in availability, *Tamec* shows 1,346,900 videotex units in place by 1985 and 4,333,000 by 1990. By 1990, Cable will be available to 8,546,000 of 10,054,000 Canadian households (or 78% versus the current 70%). The pessimistic scenario provides for a cut in the penetration to 30% of all households for videotex/Cable: or approximately 3,000,000 units in place.* Their estimates of Cable/videotex gaining $968,760,700 in advertising revenues by 1990 are based on gains from the other media according to Table 4.2. The $414 million, for example, that will come from classified ads revenue represents the high vulnerability of that particular marketplace. Given 43% penetration of all households and a vulnerability coefficient for the classified advertising in daily newspapers of .80, Cable/videotex's share of the projected market would be (43% x 80%) or 34.4%

4.2 MARKET ESTIMATES OF CABLE VIDEOTEX SYSTEMS $"(OPTIMISTIC SCENARIO)"*

	VULNERA- BILITY COEFFI- CIENT	1980	1985	1990
Cable Videotex overall penetration rate		0.3%	15.4%	43.1%
Dailies—Retail	0.4	657.4	58,744.3	286,165.7
Classified	0.8	769.4	76,875.3	414,940.2
National	0.1	56.1	4,714.0	21,462.4
Sub total		1,483.1	140,333.6	722,568.8
Other newspapers				
Local	0.4	114.1	7,001.8	34,798.2
National	0.1	15.1	823.7	3,611.1
Sub total		129.2	7,825.5	38,409.3
Telephone and city directories	0.8	532.2	50,338.9	259,569.2
General circulation and other magazines	0.1	46.4	3,965.4	18,504.4
Sub total newspapers and periodicals		2,190.9	140,533.3	730,268.5
Direct mail, catalogues and other advertising matters	0.3	502.0	54,462.9	268,625.4
Radio	0.1	114.1	10,326.2	50,931.4
Television (local)	0.1	43.4	4,503.4	25,377.2
TOTAL		2,850.4	187,778.2	968,760.7

*Estimated by TAMEC Inc.

A lot can be said in favour of any report that arrives at such specific forecasts. The *Tamec Report* recommends rigorous action by the industry to ensure that a one-way, full channel system be implemented as quickly as possible.

The first market would be Southern Ontario and the targets would be the directories, large advertisers such as real estate firms, and the classified and retail ads sections of daily newspapers. It recognizes the danger that Cable, once 80-90% penetration is achieved, would be otherwise limited to

Note that they have the titles transposed and accidentally title their optimistic scenerio figures as Pessimistic Scenario on page 118.

growth by rate increases which would not provide it with the profit levels to which it has grown accustomed. It recognizes some of the philosophical implications by pointing out the monopoly position that many newspapers in this region enjoy and suggests that Cable should press its moral advantage as an anti-monopoly force, given that Southam and Thomson have 27 newspapers in "monopoly" positions in Ontario alone. It also recognizes that there will be some costs involved in producing output, but politely ignores Cable's sketchy past record in this area, as demonstrated by table 4.15.

According to the *Tamec Report,* " . . . costs are going to be more closely related to output . . . We cannot very well imagine a Cable operator asking the CRTC for a rate revision because lists of caretakers and dentists have been added to the data bank"(4). The report does not say much about how this programming will come about. It recommends staying away from subscriber-terminal revenues as a base, preferring to rely on advertising revenue and introduces the notion of pay by speed, so that fees would be related to access time. Its position towards regulation then seems to have four major goals:

1) to establish Cable as the Carrier of choice rather than the telephone company,

2) to press for a one-way system (given the "social need" of point-to-mass communications, i.e., advertising) rather than an interactive system,

3) to acknowledge some undefined responsibility to provide information other than ads, but limit this primarily to the transfer of existing databanks (that is, telephone directories, classified ads, professional directories) to the new media and assume that it will have full control of information provided and fees charged, and

4) to ignore the social implications of engaging in this battle, given that its results might well lead to the collapse of a number of newspaper firms.

From the consumer's point of view, there are obvious flaws in this strategy, primarily in that it turns an interactive technology into a one-way delivery system dominated by those who can afford to advertise.

SOME COMPARATIVE STATISTICS

The new technologies force us to look at all the existing media as a group. Unlike previous communications innovations, which tended to be single in their impact and incremental in nature, the Electronic Highway will affect all media and the most general patterns of information collection, storage and distribution. What the following 19 Tables attempt to do, therefore, is sketch in the outline of the existing media. Almost all of the figures come from Statistics Canada; where they come from other sources or where the Stats Can figures have been amended, footnotes are provided. The deductions which I draw from these comparative figures are found in the analysis of individual media which follows these Tables.*

GENERAL NOTES ON THE TABLES

1 . Since Statistics Canada combines Printing and Publishing figures, it is difficult to break some categories out as required by tables such as 4.5, 4.6 4.8 and 4.9; these therefore use aggregate figures or those of specific firms.

2. The Printing and Publishing figures used are from 1976 throughout, while other figures are from 1977. This is spelled out in Table 4.3 and assumed elsewhere.

3. Telcos are usually considered part of the telecommunications carriers sector. We separate them here and in the analysis which follows; Telecommunications is used to refer to the other telecommunications carriers. Stats Can also makes this distinction.

4. Stats Can reports used were 36-203, 56-201, 56-203, 56-204, 56-205, 63-207, 63-256, 87-625.

5. Figures for publishing and film also taken from *The Publishing Industry in Canada* and *The Film Industry in Canada,* reports prepared by the Bureau of Management Consulting for the Arts and Culture Branch, the Department of the Secretary of State of Canada, 1977.

There are a number of other major areas concerned with information distribution which will be equally affected by these changes, including libraries, advertising agencies, education and the post office. Education has a chapter to itself and the Epilogue deals briefly with the impact on advertising agencies; I have ignored the post office. Unless it moves very quickly, the technology will bypass it and the only question will be how strong a rearguard action it will fight. The librarians are adapting very well, judging by their involvement in inter-library computerization of catalogues, and I believe that they will prosper and thrive in the new situation.

4.3 REVENUE—figures to nearest milion

Books 76*	500,000,000
Magazines 76*	500,000,000
Newspapers 76	1,000,000,000
Directories 77	140,000,000
Telephone 77†	3,700,000,000
Telecommunications 77†	120,000,000
Cable 77	235,000,000
TV 77	400,000,000
Radio 77	280,000,000
Film 77 (box office)*	230,000,000
TOTAL TO NEAREST MILLION	7,105,000,000

4.3   *Since it combines printing and publishing, Stats Can does not show retail sales nor take into effect imports. Drawing on figures prepared for the Secretary of State, I have therefore rounded up the figures for books, magazines and film to reflect (conservatively) retail revenues for these media in 4.3, 4.4, 4.10 and 4.11.*
  †Non transmission revenues have been excluded from 4.3, 4.4, 4.10 and 4.11.

4.4 MARKET SHARE—total market—7,105,000,000

Books	.07
Magazines	.07
Newspapers	.14
Directories	.02
Telphone	.52
Telecommunications	.02
Cable	.03
TV	.06
Radio	.04
Film	.03
	1.00

4.5 NUMBER OF EMPLOYEES

	1967	1976/77	% Growth in Period
Printing & Publishing	38,947	43,646	12
Telephone	68,431	95,268	39
Telecommunications	8,961	6,863	− 31
Cable	1,000*	4,946	395
TV	3,913	5,682	45
Radio	5,998	8,286	38
CBC	9,035	11,683	29
Film†	1,205	1,606	33
	137,490	177,980	29.5

4.5 *Stats Can shows a higher figure in 1967 and repeats that figure for 1967 in its 1968 report, but there is either an error in both reports or the industry managed to keep people on staff for $2,000 per annum. The 1,000 employees is an estimate based on salaries paid and Cable's normal growth rate in employment.
†For film, in 4.5 and 4.6, the employees are only those directly involved in production; theatre and distribution staff and performers on fee or contract are not included.*

4.6 NUMBER OF EMPLOYEES AS % OF TOTAL

	1967	1976/77	Change %
Printing and Publishing	28.32	24.52	− 3.8 %
Telephone	49.77	53.58	+ 3.76
Telecommunications	6.52	3.86	− 2.66
Cable	.73	2.78	+ 2.05
TV	2.85	3.19	+ .34
Radio	4.36	4.66	+ .30
CBC	6.57	6.56	− .01
Film	.88	.90	+ .02
TOTAL EMPLOYEES ALL INDUSTRIES	137,490	177,980	

4.7 WAGES, SALARIES (including benefits) PAID OUT ($)

	1967	1976/77
Printing and Publishing	233,923,000	552,847,000
Telephone	408,066,433	1,446,585,036
Telecommunications	55,814,788	115,123,831
Cable	5,637,505	655,392,504
TV	27,144,770	96,774,940
Radio	38,151,676	124,850,038
CBC	80,116,000	259,424,000
Film*	10,205,000	29,362,000

4.8 GROWTH RATES IN WAGES AND SALARIES

	Increase $ 1967–76/77	% Increase in period	Annual % Increase
Publishing and Printing	318,924,000	136.34	15.15
Telephone	1,038,520,000	254.50	25.45
Telecommunications	59,309,043	106.25	10.62
Cable	60,024,999	1118.38	111.84
TV	69,630,170	256.51	25.65
Radio	86,698,362	227.25	22.72
CBC	179,308,000	223.81	22.38
Film	19,157,000	187.72	18.77

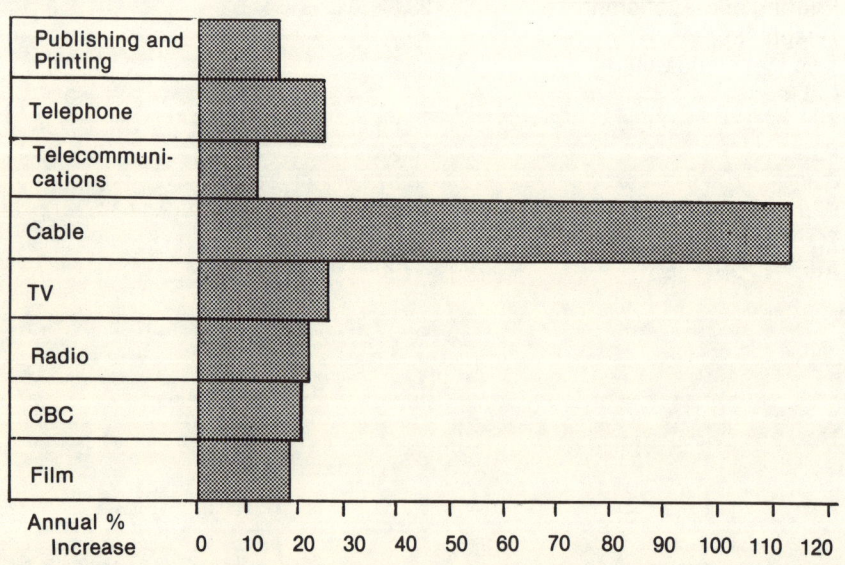

4.9 COMPARATIVE PROFITABILITY (SELECTED) 1977

	Profits after Tax	Profits as % of Revenue
Harlequin (books) 77*	12,514,000	15.39
MacLean Hunter (mags) 77*	9,724,000	4.90
Thomson (newspapers) 77*	47,383,000	18.38
Premier Cablevision*	3,192,000	9.50
Telephones†	384,990,000	9.99
Telecommunications†	47,782,610	15.82
Cablevision	24,425,317	10.47
TV	31,826,660	9.62
Radio	18,940.925	6.97
CBC Net Cost of Operations:	396,770,000	

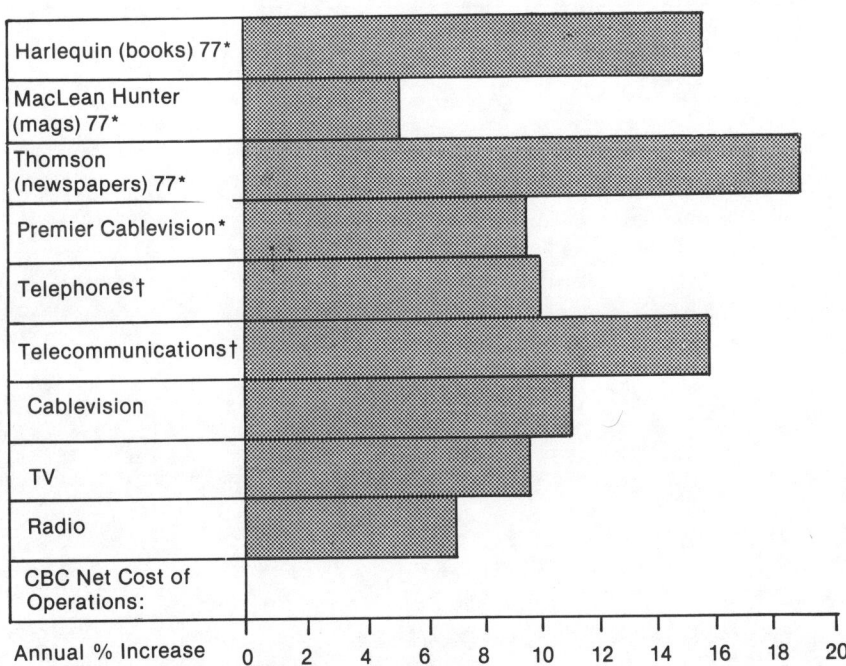

*4.9   *From annual reports, Maclean Hunter is involved in a number of areas of course, in addition to magazines.*
†The revenue figure used here represents all revenues; in 4.3, 4.10 and 4.11, non-transmission revenues were excluded.

4.10 GROWTH IN REVENUE OVER PAST TEN YEARS

	Revenue Increase($) 1967–76/77	% increase over period	Average increase per annum
Books	344,369,000	221	24.6
Magazines	195,817,000	64	7.1
Newspapers	580,249,000	141	15.7
Directories	100,072,000	249	24.9
Telephone	2,632,204,123	231	23.1
Telecommunications	78,478,987	204	20.4
Cable	210,842,869	954	95.4
TV	275,635,953	223	22.3
Radio	181,371,496	200	20.0
Film (box office)	126,129,168	122	12.2

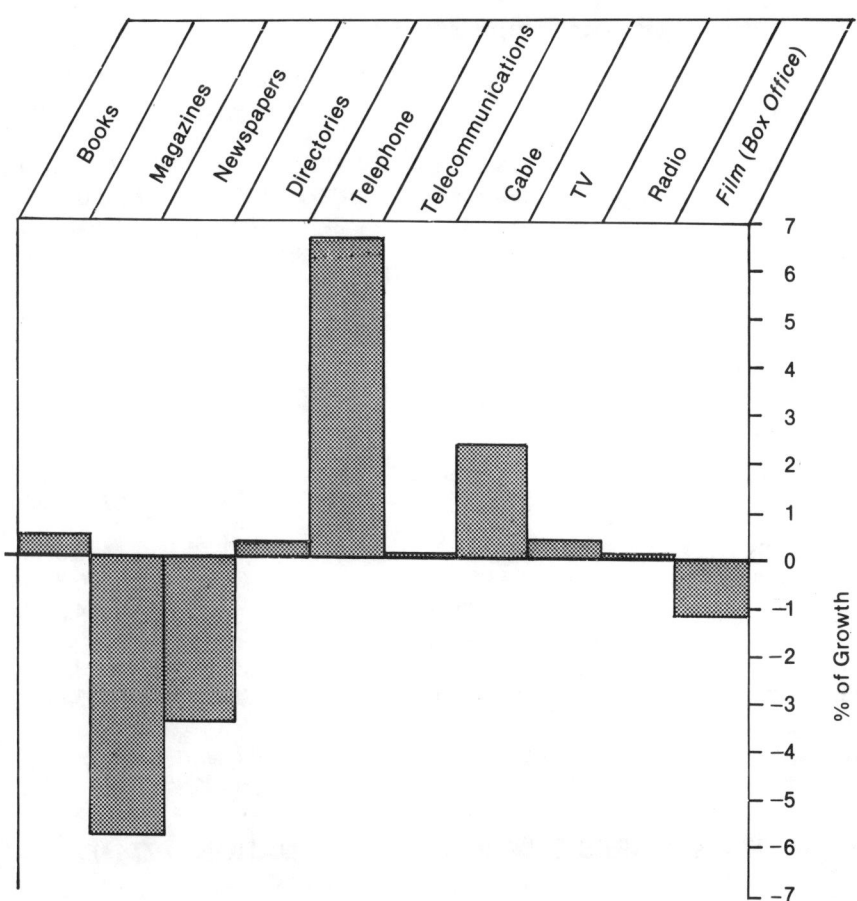

4.11 GROWTH/DECLINE OF REVENUE SHARE OVER PAST TEN YEARS

	1967 % of total	1976/77 % of Total	% of Growth
Books	6.59	7.05	+ .45
Magazines	12.87	7.04	− 5.83
Newspapers	17.42	14.07	− 3.35
Directories	1.70	1.97	+ .27
Telephone	45.40	52.08	+ 6.68
Telecommunications	1.63	1.69	+ .06
Cable	.95	3.30	+ 2.36
TV	5.23	5.63	+ .40
Radio	3.84	3.94	+ .10
Film (box office)	4.38	3.24	− 1.14
TOTAL REVENUES:	$2,363,067,159	$7,105,000.000	

4.12 1977 PLANT AND EQUIPMENT $

	At Cost	Accumulated Depreciation	Net (Book) Value
Telephone	14,531,598,000	3,854,116,000	10,677,482,000
Telecommunications	1,029,688,060	627,783,236	401,904,824
Cable	482,435,462	221,893,353	260,542,109
TV	234,610,256	118,617,452	115,992,804
Radio	136,836,982	68,919,822	67,917,160
CBC	417,014,000	178,483,000	238,531,000

4.13 PLANT AND EQUIPMENT 1967–77 SELECTED (using at-cost figures)

	Increase $ 1967–77	% Increase in Period	% Increase per annum
Telephone	9,520,599,239	189.99	18.99%
Telecommunications	535,201,579	108.23	10.82%
Cable	431,636,643	849.70	84.97%
TV*	134,466,695	134.27	19.18%
Radio*	27,687,322	25.37	3.62%
CBC*	216,577,000	108.05	15.44%

these figures represent the difference between 1970 and 1977 as 1967 figures were not available with CBC as a separate category.

4.14 EXPENDITURES ON PROGRAM ORIGINATION 1977 ($)

Cable	13,539,480
TV	138,047,981
Radio	80,033,147
CBC	262,824,000

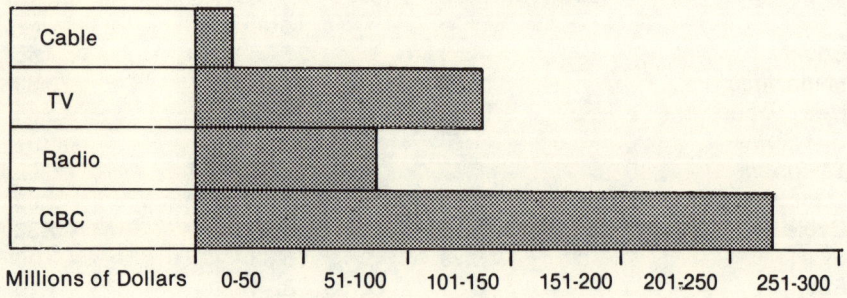

4.15 PROGRAM ORIGINATION AS % of Revenue 1977

Cable	6%
TV	42
Radio	29
CBC*	66

indicates program origination as a % of CBC's net cost of operations

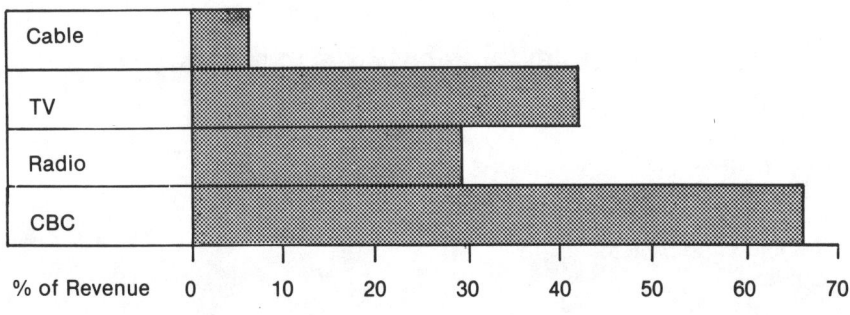

4.16 PROGRAM ORIGINATION AND GENERAL ADMINISTRATION COSTS: CBC AND CABLE INDUSTRY 1977

	Program origination $	General Administration $
Cable	13,539,480	49,841,938
CBC	262,824,000	106,862,000

4.17 1976/77 ADVERTISING REVENUES $

Magazines* 76	193,142,000
Newspapers 76	753,230,000
Directories 76	140,222,000
TV	310,299,943
CBC TV	65,264,000
Radio	268,740,442
CBC Radio	339,000

Canadian Figures only

4.18 ADVERTISING REVENUE BY CATEGORY 1977 $

	Local	Classified	National
Newspapers 76	399,024,000	195,189,000	159,017,000
	Local	National	Network
TV	88,859,260	172,847,643	48,593,040
CBC TV	8,054,000	24,489,000	32,721,000
Radio	195,873,764	72,263,637	630,041
CBC Radio	172,000	68,000	99,000

4.19 ADVERTISING REVENUE AS % OF TOTAL (1976/77)

Books 76	0%
Magazines* 76	76
Newspapers 76	76
Directories 76	100
Telephone	0
Telecommunications	0
Cable	0
TV	94
Radio	99
Film	0

Canadian Magazines only

COMPARATIVE VULNERABILITIES

One could take the vulnerability coefficient I have estimated for any given media and multiply it by the revenue figure in Table 4.3 to come up with a potential loss in revenue under the impact of these new technologies. It must be stressed, however, that the specific firms involved will begin to participate in the new technologies in a variety of ways and at different rates. A book publisher who puts his encyclopedia on a video-disc will remain a book-publisher for quite some time as far as the statisticians are concerned. The degree and rate of involvement will also affect the attitude towards regulation (by which I specifically refer to regulation of Content/Carrier separation in the following summaries) even among firms from the same sector. Nonetheless, there are clear differences of vulnerability among the various media and an attempt at quantification may clarify the nature and extent of the changes due in the next decade.

4.20 COMPARATIVE VULNERABILITY

Books	paperbacks	.15
	hardbacks	.45
Magazines		.40
Newspapers		.60
Directories		.90
Telephone		.05
Cable		.55
TV	Broadcasting	.70
	Production	.00
Radio		.10
Film		.25

Newspapers:

1. Media: Newspapers. Dailies, weeklies, community.
2. Vulnerability coefficient: .60
3. Attitude towards regulation: Supportive. But slowly.
4. Weakest spot: High ratio of advertising revenue to sales revenue. Paper prices.
5. Best move: Become skilled Information Providers as quickly as possible. Stall regulation at first, but press for it in long term.

The vulnerability of newspapers is based on the manner in which they have eroded their role of Content producers in favour of becoming Carriers. The news, as the cynics say, is what fills up the space between the ads. Assume an average $100,000 of revenue. Where does it come from?

Sales: 20,000
Classified advertising: 22,000
Retail: 42,000
National Ads: 16,000

Put another way, the subscription you pay for a newspaper pays for a little more than its delivery costs. A plump Saturday issue could cost up to $4.00 to manufacturer and newsprint is very vulnerable to increased costs of labour and energy. As actual sales revenue only covers 20% of the total revenue a paper needs to survive at a profitable level, a drop of even 25% in an area such as classified advertising could have serious repercussions. Once on a downward spiral, recovery would be difficult.

In any city with at least 30% of the population hooked up to TELIDON, is it unlikely that someone will establish a classified advertising service? For a price of only a few dollars per entry, with billing handled by the Carrier? Assuming that if a customer were looking for a 1927 Maserati, they could inform the Classified Producer service of that fact and be alerted the moment one was listed, thus eliminating the need for a daily search. There would soon be a shift to such a service.

Local retail ads might take a little longer to drift away. TELIDON graphic and production services will have to be provided. But once a restaurant owner can reserve a number of frames, prepared by experts, that show current prices, favourable quotes from reviewers and customers, and the evening's special and many other factors, the limitations of the small ad directed at a mass audience (but missing 80% of them) will become fairly apparent.

As for content, the newspapers will soon find themselves in trouble there also, once a reasonable number of users are hooked-up. The threshold costs of starting a newspaper are now very high. The question is not why so many alternative papers folded in the seventies, but how they managed to get started in the first place and survive even for a few years. A large chain is willing to pay thousands of dollars per subscriber in a well controlled market. Even those owners of small papers who might like to sell to their own young editor, find it difficult to refuse the kind of cash a Thomson or Southam can wave at them.

Imagine that our scenario does begin to come true, and suppose that you are Anne Hardy or Dick Beddoes or any one of a hundred well-known names. Your job function won't change a great deal, but with an initial investment of $10,000 you'll be able to access every TELIDON owner in the country. And, as readers, they won't be limited to your current 1200 words. If they want to see what you said last month about the Deep Cove Chalet, or Guy Lafleur's last game, they'll be able to access that also. At a price of pennies.

You'll have to make sure you remain known to them all, however, so you might join a team, or form a co-operative with your peers, but you won't need the newspapers. Journalists without that kind of a name and established audience will be able to either join a larger team or develop a specialty that isn't overcrowded. And do it on a part-time basis too, perhaps just renting time on an Information Provider Terminal until they can afford their own.

At the international level, the implications are likely to be even more forceful. Given the figures Madden quotes for a long distance call (30 cents per minute for a conversation between Montreal and Cairo), the concept of the foreign correspondent will change greatly. Assuming a civil war in Iran in 1985, one will have a choice of a) your favourite hot-spot traveller if he happens to go there; b) a representative of some foreign service you trust (far right views or far left views as the case may be); or c) Iranian correspondents themselves, who will certainly find translators and get "on the wire" under the circumstances. In addition, the professors will be hard at work updating their background lectures in Iranian religion, sociology and history for those who are really serious.

The high threshold cost of starting a paper also means that large investments in plant and machinery are in place. Once a few of those turn sour, the general environment for newspapers will become much more risky.

On the positive side are some of the side-effects of TELIDON and optical fibre cables. Strangely enough, the British PRESTEL system has turned to print in order to make its services more widely known and accessible. There is now a magazine listing Information Providers, indexing them, showing prices, etc., plus a 160 page handbook for users (5). Given the inevitable explosion of services, the newspaper per se might find its niche as a daily version of the same, essentially making available a printed index to all the services available on the competition. Even now, TV guides are not exactly an unprofitable item for the newspaper.

Another unknown is the reaction of major advertisers, such as grocery chains, department stores and car dealers. How hostile will the new medium be to them? Given almost instant access to information, a well-organized consumer group could provide a service which would let the customer discover the cheapest place to purchase any given item, or group of items, today. Newspapers always could have done something similar, of course, if they had been willing to watch their advertising revenues drop precipitiously. So there may be a certain degree of support for newspapers from major suppliers uneasy with the activities of Information Providers.

At the moment, the newspaper's major psychological advantage is that it is available when you want it. People associate relaxation and choice with their daily read. Television might be far more dramatic, but if you get home at 6:14 instead of 6:00 you've missed the news until 11:00. Your friendly NABU, however, will give you all the news you want, when you want it and the newspaper will lose that advantage also. Those who want to concentrate on sports or the stocks or fashion or new movies, can do so.

PROGNOSIS FOR NEWSPAPERS: At long last, newspapers are about to learn what real hard international competition is all about. They'll lose their traditional position as providers of news and Carriers of advertising in a variety of ways, and will have to undergo major adaptations in order to survive into the 90's.

Magazines

1. Media: Magazines.
2. Vulnerability coefficient: .40
3. Attitude towards regulation: Indifferent.
4. Weakest spot: interest groups tying directly in to advertisers.
5. Best move: Pray that the post office survives.

The visible portion of the magazine world has never been the truly profitable sector, even before the great crunch caused by TV that saw so many of the apparent winners suddenly disappear. *Macleans* survived not because it knew something that *Life* and *Look* didn't, but because that vast array of *Baker, Butcher* and *Officer Supplier* magazines of the Maclean-Hunter empire provided the profits that our national magazine could not.

But the seventies saw even the visible magazines come back into their own, led by very specific targeting learned from the trade sector. Magazines for *Sailors, Spinners,* and *Harrowsmiths* found a ready audience, and any city which didn't receive its own glossy, stapled, ad-fat hymn of praise was really not a city.

So that although much of what has been said about newspapers applies equally to magazines (they are print based and advertising dependent), one is somewhat more sanguine about their prospects; they have already come through the fire and been tested and one suspects that they will be street-wary enough to deal with the NABU in a craftier way than their pulpier cousins. Nor, since few of them promise "hot" news, are they as susceptible to the fast-access of TELIDON systems.

Any magazine that has survived has a much better idea of who its customers are than the average newspaper. Indeed, the magazines like *Quest* and *Homemaker's* which operate under the principal of controlled circulation, have made the fullest acknowledgement of the dominance of the Carrier portion of their activities. What they can do is cut down on waste for the advertiser by denying the pretence that their genuine purpose is information and by admitting that they are a carrier of advertising to the wealthiest consumers.

The one area of regulations that will especially interest these magazines will be the availability of generalized data on NABU owners. Let us suppose that General Foods can discover the electronic mail-box numbers of all house-owners with more than three kids and annual earnings of between twenty-five and thirty-five thousand and offer them, not a coupon for a cake-mix, or whatever, but the actual sample itself. Magazines might well be against the general availability of that degree of precision, even though the concept of target marketing ensured their own success.

Another area of vulnerability for magazines lies in the recognition by non-profit groups of the value of their membership lists. In many cases such lists will already be computerized via the organization's NABU and hooked up to a data-service that will provide software and storage for very low costs. Let us suppose that Seagram's wants to reach dinghy owners with ads for one product and yacht owners with ads for a more expensive product. The economies that *Wind and Sail* might offer Seagram's over a broadcast ad in *Time* are only equal to those that the Dinghy Owners Association themselves can offer them over *Wind and Sail*. So why advertise in *Wind and Sail?* Why not pay for some of the costs of the Dinghy Owners Association databank in exchange for some advertising frames seen by all those who access the databank?

The strength of the magazines will lie in the fact that advertisers will probably respond to the conditions of uncertainty unleashed by these new technologies by increasing their budgets all around, although in cities especially one can expect a great deal of rate-cutting to come from the newspapers as they struggle to survive.

PROGNOSIS FOR MAGAZINES: Continued growth, although at a slower rate than the past decade would indicate. Further specialization and a lot of hand-holding with advertisers. Specialized role as Information Providers. A new awareness of clubs and associations.

Filmakers

1. Media: Film.
2. Vulnerability coefficient: .25
3. Attitude towards regulation: Supportive.
4. Weakest spot: Bootleggers.
5. Best move: Support tough copyright regulations and spectacular films.

Filmakers, too, have been through the fire. In the years after TV was introduced, they saw their growth stopped in its tracks and for a while the charts indicated their inevitable disappearance. The number of paid admissions dropped from 236 million in 1950 to only 100 million in 1964 (6). But we do not seem to have reached the limits of human absorption of media stimulation. With a strong appeal to fantasy, violence, humour, protest and whatever else might possibly sell, the movies have at least held their own. Indeed, their revenues have increased at a reasonable rate as the number of admissions seems to have found a floor at 90 million.

The usefulness of government regulations, in this instance special capital cost allowances, can be seen in the recent high figures for film production in Canada. Depreciation allowances of 100% are likely to be very beneficial to our import/export ratio for films. *Meatballs* may not be much in cultural terms, but as a revenue producer for the economy it sure beats Bricklin hollow. Costing only 1.6 million, it grossed 1.4 million during its first week in New York City after being sold to Paramount for U.S. distribution with an advance of $3.8 million.

As indicated in the Tables, film is directly supported by box-office revenues. On sales to TV, of course, their profit comes indirectly from the prices major advertisers are willing to pay to take advantage of the drawing power of a hit film. But that demand will remain, even though media structures change.

In addition to the protection offered by their non-reliance on advertising revenue, film makers should actually benefit from at least two of the innovations. TELIDON itself will not pose a serious threat, except in terms of alternate activity, because of its current inability to provide film substitute for anything except cartoons. But the multiple channels offered by optical fibre and satellites will create a demand for Content that only film will be able to satisfy in the short term. The life-cycle of a film is quite short, with a re-cycle for most popular films like *The Wizard of Oz* every generation. The new technology will mean that Cable operators will have to use film in far greater quantities, although the average viewer per offering ratio will also decline drastically. The video-disc will also offer the filmmaker a chance to reach the consumer market directly and less expensively than by VTR.

One law of binary activity is that anything which is digitalized can be easily reproduced. At the moment, bootlegging represents a fairly high proportion of the total music market. Video-discs will let filmmakers discover the technical ingenuity of their audience, or at least the part of it that they know about.

PROGNOSIS FOR FILM: Good times ahead. They have learned how to produce spectaculars with a high unit-cost threshold. The new technologies will increase their audience, whoever wins the Carrier battle. Their investment in theatres might suffer as families, clubs and other groups use video-discs and large-size screens to substitute for a night at the Odeon.

Paperbacks

1. Media: Paperbacks.

*For useful comparisons of different models of video-discs and recording costs and methods, see: Heuston, *A Comparison Between the Video tape and Videodisc as Educational Devices.* New York, NY: WICAT. Inc. 1978.

2. Vulnerability coefficient: .15
3. Attitude towards regulation: Indifferent.
4. Weakest spot: How-to-do-it books.
5. Best move: Pray that a lot of newspapers fold and the price of newsprint tumbles.

These figures are somewhat more speculative than the others for a number of reasons. The price at which paperbacks come across the border often bears little resemblance to the real costs of production and almost 95% of our paperbacks do come across that border in one form or another. Again, the definitions of a paperback vary greatly.

We distinguish between mass paperbacks (which sell for under three dollars) and other books, mainly because the distribution chains are so different. The large paperback companies, working with the city wholesalers, represent a distribution chain that is much closer to that of the newspaper world than the hardback book world. There is no choice for the outlet, but there is no fuss and bother either. The space in a rack has a value that can be vended to the highest bidder by the wholesaler. Of course, the purchaser of the space is expert at providing product with fast turn-over, so an uneasy truce is obtained, with market share changing very slowly and each publisher using his best-selling titles to lever space on the racks for those titles that lack the reputation but will sell anyway provided that they have that all-important exposure.

This partial control of the chain of distribution plus non-reliance on advertising contributes to the low vulnerability of the mass paperback, but so does the unit cost. A 300-page book, delivered to the corner newstand for only $2.95, represents a value that the new technologies will find hard to match. With prodution costs on large runs representing less than 10% of that retail price, these traditional Information Providers don't need the economies of the new technology.

Their vulnerability will come from certain segments of their product line, most importantly the how-to-do-it book. Here TELIDON will be far more specific and effective, allowing the consumer to access information about a specific motor or carburetor of a specific year without the cost involved now in finding the right book. Still, even if they lost all of this market, their revenues would decline by only about 10% to 15%.

Two other side effects may affect them more strongly. One will be the high vulnerability of the hardback publishers who, at the moment, provide a fairly large percentage of their content. The other is the larger question of how the new technologies will affect the "mass" nature of our culture. Given access to a wide variety of information sources on a wide variety of subjects, and parallel access to entertainment from different countries and different periods, will there be a gradual weakening of the very notion of best-sellerdom?

PROGNOSIS FOR PAPERBACKS: Continued growth; growing alliances with filmakers and support for their copyright efforts; no loss of adaptability.

Hardback Publishers

1. Media: Hardback book publishers.
2. Vulnerability coefficient: .45
3. Attitude towards regulation: Strong support.
4. Weakest spot: Middle of the line books.
5. Best move: Learn the new technology and sell their printing presses

Book publishers seem most beleaguered by the new technologies, especially by computers. Conservative by nature, many of them still look with regret upon the passing of hot-lead, hand-binding and the intelligent bookstore owner. Now computers seem to be surrounding them. Some of their authors even present manuscripts on floppy diskettes as an inducement to quick publishing. Computers set the books; they handle the accounting (or mis-handle it as the case may be); and now they threaten what remains of the independent bookstore distribution chain by offering the possibility of franchised bookstores, hooked into a wholesaler's warehouse and automatically (by computer) stocking the shelves with best-sellers and only best-sellers.

This sector's vulnerability is almost traditional and is based on their lack of control of distribution and the comparative high ratio of labour per unit produced. Institutions, such as the Alberta Heritage Fund or University Extension Departments, present further competition, without the requirement to turn a profit.

The result is likely to be a further extension of the split between the extremes of the line. Potential best-sellers will earn secondary revenue from mass paperback sales. The really specialized books, such as academic books, make no profit in any case and will disappear from print. Publishers with strong backlists and good contacts will soon adapt to the new technology once they accept the fact that the computer has fully closed the net and they needn't print such books ever again, although they can still make them available to the users by microfiche, diskette, video-disc (for art books) or on-line access (7).

The middle of the line books, titles that now in Canada sell three or four thousand copies, will fall between these two extremes and disappear from the lists and from existence.

The impact upon educational publishers will be softened by transfer of some of their activities to the new field (see Chapter Six). McGraw-Hill Inc., for example, has recently purchased the stock of Data Resources Inc. for $103 million. Data Resources provides more than 600 clients with economic data and forecasts. At the time of the purchase, Harold W. McGraw stated that his firm had "some time ago identified the fields of econometric forecasting and electronic database publishing as particularly appropriate areas to complement our existing publishing activities."

PROGNOSIS FOR HARDBACKS: Major changes, but overall some improvement in prospects for those who adapt quickly. Strong support for Content/Carrier separation based on philosophic grounds and knowing what it's like to be outside the strong distribution chains.

Directories

1. Media: Directories; telephone, city and other.
2. Vulnerability coefficient: .90
3. Attitude towards regulation: Subsumed in larger interests of those involved.
4. Weakest spot: The perfect content for the new technology.
5. Best move: Die a graceful death.

Directories are very profitable. Their rates are much higher than those of newspapers or magazines, but of course they offer to the advertiser a year's currency rather than a few days. Their share of print media advertising revenues has risen to close to 15%. The creation and maintenance of lists, and the cross-indexing thereof, is an ideal task for the computer; indeed many directories are now created in that format and the only change involved will be allowing individuals access to the database rather than sending it all off to the printer once a year. Updates, to telephone books, for example, would take place as soon as the installation was complete. The problems involved in areas of urban sprawl with four or five directories would also disappear as there is no reason why the database should not be at least province-wide with provisions for many search routes.

The practical question is whether the Telcos (and their directories represent about 90% of this market) will rush to implement the technology. In their defense, there is the question of what will happen to the 70% or 40% or even 5% of telephone users who don't own a NABU. The far more difficult question for them is of how to implement and justify an advertising component in this new mode once the Carrier/Content separation battle intensifies.

The new technologies will create at least an interim need for directories of novel content, however, such as the PRESTEL User's Guide and Directory mentioned earlier. As transmission costs shrink, people will begin to utilize information and services from outlets quite beyond their normal range. Before planning a trip to a distant city, for example, one might want to check on what is available there in terms of entertainment, services and culture, and check some background data such as crime rates and food prices. For every specific area, such information searches will increase the utilization of local directories of various kinds. Specific firms may well provide their own new TELIDON directories. Mac's Milk Stores might present a complete list of all their stores with hours of operation; an association of dentists might create a directory of dentists, indicating their location, experience, specialities, etc., together with general information about dental care.

PROGNOSIS FOR DIRECTORIES: A major shift, but no major economic implications since there are few independents involved in this area.

Radio

1. Media: Radio.
2. Vulnerability coefficient: .10
3. Attitude towards regulation: Indifferent.
4. Weakest spot: Digitalization of music recording.
5. Best move: Salt the profits away.

From the point of view of musicians, composers and our balance of trade in records, the CRTC regulations which insist that radio licencees provide certain minimums of Canadian content have been a great success. Those who side with the theoretic vigour of the free market have great difficulty dealing with the contrast in Canadian production before and after these regulations came into force. Although each segment of the broadcast band represents a scarce public resource, and radio stations are therefore licenced, they have managed to establish fairly clearly in the minds of the public their "ownership" of their allocated section of the wave band. With sure and steady profits from mass-oriented programming, they have reacted only under pressure to alternatives suggested by the CRTC and allowed CBC Radio to dominate innovation and variety.

Given CBC Radio's government-dependence for funding and TELIDON'S print and graphics orientation at the moment, radio has little to be concerned about in the short term (8). Their share of revenues has remained fairly constant at 10% and the increasing ratio of local over national advertising lessens their general vulnerability.

The growth in sales of cassette recordings has not affected this, but in the longer term the growth of NABU does present a threat. Assuming that a large number of recordings are stored in digitalized form in databanks and that simple directories are available, an individual could prepare a personal program of music for the afternoon without investing in the records or being distracted by advertising. A single video-disc can now store 400 hours of audio.

PROGNOSIS FOR RADIO: Little to worry about, at least in the 80's.

Other Telecommunications Companies

1. Media: Telecommunications (except Telcos).
2. Vulnerability coefficient: ?
3. Attitude towards regulation: Intense support for regulation of Carriers and presentation of itself as the second-choice option Carrier to ensure competition.
4. Weakest spot: Lack of content and growth.
5. Best move: Ignore the social costs of duplicating all or portions of the Electronic Highway and press the need for competition.

Statistics lovers will note that my figures for revenue in this sector appear low. In fact, of gross revenues of over $300 million in 1977, $71 million came from the telephone service, $72 million from leased circuits, $62 million from other leased plant fees and $50 million from other non-transmission revenues. All these areas show strong growth over the 1967 figures, but the actual transmission area revenues on the whole declined, with any growth coming not from messages but from scheduled transmission services and leased services. The number of telegrams transmitted fell from 10.5 million to 2.5 million in the same period. The value of property and equipment doubled, while miles of wire laid reached 845,000.

My revenue figures do not include the non-transmission revenues, since these are likely to be included in expenses of some of the other media and then passed on to the consumer. Technically, telegraph companies should disappear. CNCP has taken such a strong political stand on the question of connection to the telephone networks primarily because this is an industry seeking new functions for the old shell. It is thus rather difficult to set a vulnerability coefficient. In theory, they are so vulnerable they ought not to be here. The telegram has lost its function because so many large corporations have established nation or continent-wide data networks of their own. Satellites will cause a similar loss of function for ocean cables from continent to continent. Telex is not flourishing.

Nonetheless, by fighting and winning this particular regulatory battle, CNCP has demonstrated its willingness to adapt and its skill at playing on the public's distrust of large monopolies like Bell, however efficient and however closely regulated they may be.

PROGNOSIS FOR TELECOMMUNICATIONS: CNCP is a scrapper, although the odds are against it. The costs of establishing a dual Electronic Highways cannot be justified on economic grounds, but then we do have two major railroads and airlines and we bear those extra costs in the holy name of competition. Access to the telephone network, coupled with a strategy of offering specific services such as word processing in addition to data transmission, might make CNCP the dark horse of the entire race.

Television

1. Media: Television Production.
2. Vulnerability coefficient: .00

1. Media: Television Broadcasting.
2. Vulnerability coefficient: .70

This distinction between Broadcasting and Production must be made, despite the existing structure of the television sector, which is formally subdivided into Broadcasters and Cable with Production as shared ground.

For those involved in production, to the extent that they are involved in production, there is little if any vulnerability. Just as there are few Mainz Bibles left, many early TV productions have disappeared without a trace. Given the nature of the media (mass audiences and limited channels) that was logical. But while cursing that they erased so much material which could now be reshown, television producers will only benefit from new multi-channel and digitalization technologies that provide greater diversity in delivery. Shows that are not now produced will become feasible based on cost-recoveries spread over a larger number of viewings by small but very specific audiences.

Indeed it appears almost inevitable that these factors, plus the greater utilization of display screens in the home, will mean a major increase in TV production of all kinds. Residual sales of popular shows and sports events on video-discs will generate further market revenue and advertisers will need the graphic skills of TV studios for preparation of their digitally-stored messages.

On the other hand, combinations such as Ouimet describes in the next chapter, between satellite and cable technology, would seem to present serious threats to those involved in broadcasting to the extent that their revenue depends on control of delivery through control of the channel allocated to them by the CRTC.

A broadcasting channel will lose its scarcity value in proportion to the availability of other channels. Control of any one channel now obviously still remains, in the famous phrase, a licence to print money. Control of one of thirty-five, or one hundred, or three hundred-odd channels will mean far less.

Broadcasting is an expensive proposition and there are no major cost economies from new technology in sight. Since most of the firms currently involved in production are also involved in broadcasting, but in differing proportions, one can expect a variety of positions to arise in regard to regulation. It would seem to me, however, that the best position for almost all of these firms would be to accept the eventual prominence of non-broadcast methods of transmission and transfer their energies and finances to production and innovation. As Content producers it is true they will have to give up some of their profitable privileges, but short of halting technological advance, such a move is inevitable; in exchange, however, they should be able to quickly occupy a prominent position as Information Providers given that their technical skills and production facilities are more relevant to the new technologies than those of their main competitor, newspaper-based firms.

PROGNOSIS FOR TELEVISION PRODUCTION: Good times ahead.

PROGNOSIS FOR TELEVISION BROADCASTING: In the long term, a traumatic withdrawal from the royal state of Carrier/Content control, but no major economic dislocations since an internal shift can easily be made to television production and information provision.

The Big Battle, Cable versus Telcos

1. Media: Cable TV companies.
2. Vulnerability coefficient: .55
3. Attitude towards regulation: Never will be soon enough.
4. Weakest spot: Public attention on definitions of Carriers.
5. Best move: Make a lot of friends very quickly.

1. Media: Telephone companies (Telcos).
2. Vulnerability coefficient: .05
3. Attitude towards regulation: Always bite the hand that feeds you.
4. Weakest spot: An unholy alliance: optical fibres, Cable companies and satellites.
5. Best move: Accept Parkhill's structure, behind the scenes at least, and make sure that the Cable companies are recognized as Carriers and that a lot of Information Providers get established as quickly as possible. Full speed ahead on optical fibre networks.

Again, one must link two sectors, for what is really involved is Carrier functions. Cable's annual production investment is less than a weekly or monthly production investment of some of the other sectors that we have examined (see Table 4.14).

All that we have said above about television production versus television broadcasting applies to Cable, but Cable's strengths do not lie on the production side of the equation.

In straight economic terms, this is not going to be a battle. The Telcos dominate information distribution in Canada, as the statistics clearly indicate. Their investment in plant and equipment is fourteen or fifteen times that of the telecommunications sector; their revenues account for half of all the revenues of the information media we selected; they are used to dealing with regulation and with the careful implementation of new technologies; they have a clear function and their existing technology is interactive by nature.

Ouimet deals with the red-herring issue of pay-TV and stresses the near absurdity of allowing the structure of television in this country to be determined by the temporary financial clout of the Cable corporations, especially when their quite necessary function of providing some diversity of choice will soon be carried out by a number of newer and more powerful technologies.

The full repatriation of the industry would have to be completed, of course, but except for the pockets of American ownership, the only stumbling block in the way of the Telcos' success is probably the general public's distrust of large corporations in a monopoly position; the Telcos have a good deal to learn about public relations. But the only true alternative would be a second system to match the Telcos' and the costs of that would be very hard to justify. The one simple rule that will help ensure proper economies for the consumer is that all these services should come into the home or business with an absolute minimum of duplication. If one wire (or at least one optical fibre) can do it, than why have three of four or even two?

On the other hand, the Electronic Highway is made up of a number of segments: terminals, local loops, switching centres, databanks, long-distance transmission, etc. Where any of those segments can be duplicated economically, with compatibility and with clear benefit to all consumers, then they should be. Cable's entrepreneurial energies can also be of major benefit to the community, if the industry can maintain them while accepting the responsibilities of a regulated Carrier. There are good economic arguments for Cable establishing a number of two-way channels and certainly their existing investments must be utilized fully wherever possible.

The Telcos reached saturation of their market quite some time ago. It seems fairly apparent that if we are to maintain our lead in this technology and implement a TELIDON system rapidly and with maximum benefit to the consumer, the Telcos must play a major role in development of the network. A serious debate will have to take place concerning the strategies of access that Parkhill has outlined, but the logical losers of this battle are the Cable companies. Despite their recent profits, there is nothing intrinsically valuable in their continued existence and the costs of allowing them to implement the type of strategy outlined in the *Tamec Report* would be enormous. Their profitability is based on regulatory advantages, not on any special complex of skills; their contribution to production is minimal; their technical skills are nothing extraordinary and are not required by the new technologies in any case.

PROGNOSIS FOR CABLE AND TELEPHONE: What is needed is a clear stand by government, with a minimum of delay, federal-provincial wrangling, and submission to vested interests. The questions are too large for any interest but that of the public to dominate. A quickly implemented and clearly defined regulatory structure will minimize vulnerability and encourage creativity. Cable will return to the high-risk days of its conception and may find there a new sense of purpose and a new, improved public image, either as Carrier or perhaps in a few instances as Information Provider. It cannot count on remaining as both. No one likes to give up a licence to have someone else print money for you without cost, but Cable will have to give up some of its privileges sooner or later, despite what will be an impressive, high-cost, professional battle.

In my optimistic scenario, the Telcos will need all the help they can get and will encourage independent Information Providers. Indeed, they will quickly come to recognize that a large portion of their revenues will depend on the availability of a great many Information Providers who will pay them at tariffed rates. Major field tests will demonstrate the superiority of TELIDON over other videotex systems. In my pessimistic scenario, Telcos will forget the historic Carrier/Content separation, decide that here is the route they need to follow to double their capital base more quickly, and attempt to become both Carrier and Information Provider. In the light of Chapter Three, it would then be up to the government to prevent this, fairly but firmly.

Conclusion

One of the worries people have about computers is that they will take over all the jobs. It is true; they have and will continue to take over many jobs. But is there something intrinsically wrong with the twenty hour work week? Have we not seen many instances where new technologies, by expanding the range of human activity, have created new professions and actually increased total employment despite temporary dislocations?

The impact of these new technologies on the general population will be severe, perhaps as severe as Madden suggests in "Julia's Dilemma", but I would be willing to suggest that more jobs will be created than lost by at least a factor of two. As people absorb these skills, there is an incremental effect. Observation of particular solutions leads to ideas for new applications; the attempt to implement the new application requires the absorption of more skills. As more and more of society's mindless and frantic tasks are taken over by the new electronic-level machinery, arts, sports, education, crafts and travel will quickly absorb any excess time and energy.

This chapter has concentrated on the real world implications of these technologies, primarily for major corporations; but the implications for the individual are far more important. As Alphonse Ouimet points out in the following chapter, neither the technology nor the corporate implementation of the technology can be separated from the larger social issues involved. The vulnerability coefficient for the individual ought to be zero. Indeed, the results ought to be very beneficial. If they are not, before we blame the technology, let us at least admit that when we had the choice it would seem we chose the wrong strategy for implementing this revolution.

REFERENCES TO CHAPTER 4

1. Ruppel Aloys *Johannes Gutenberg Sein Leben und Sein Werk,* Nieuw koop: B. De Graaf, 1967, pp. 88-108.

2. Hirsch, Rudolph *Printing, Selling and Reading: 1450-1590*, Wiesbaden: Otto Harrossowitz, 1967, pp. 94-95.

3. *The Globe and Mail,* Monday, June 11, 1979, p. B3, Gillian MacKay.

4. *Videotex Services: The Market Potential for Cable,* January 1979, Tamec Economic Consultants, 2015 Peel, Suite 1116, Montreal, Quebec.

5. *Prestel Handbook.* Compiled by Brian Begg Associates, 6 Hornton Place, London W8 4LZ

The Prestel Users Guide and Directory (with *Teletext Viewdata Magazine*) 2nd ed. Eastern Counties Newspaper Ltd., Prospect House, Rouen, Norwich, England.

6. *Film Industry in Canada,* prepared by The Bureau of Management for the Arts and Culture Branch, Department of the Secretary of State, Ottawa, 1977.

7. There are some basic advantages to computerized storage and transmission of academic books, at least in areas where genuine research is

taking place. From a printed book, one receives the condensed results of the researcher's work completed at least two years in the past. If, instead, the research results are stored and accessed in digital form, then (in theory) there is no time delay whatsoever between accomplishment and dissemination.

8. The radio is another possible medium for the transmission of digitally encoded messages. As community groups of various kinds become used to providing information in these new ways there may well be increasing pressure on governments to allocate radio frequencies to non-commercial interests. Packet or digital use of radio frequencies can be a hundred-fold more economical than use as an analog voice channel.

5 THE COMMUNICATIONS REVOLUTION AND CANADIAN SOVEREIGNTY

Alphonse Ouimet

INTRODUCTION

> With all the force at our command we urge the Government of Canada to take immediate action to alert the people of Canada to the perilous position of their collective sovereignty that has resulted from the new technologies of communications and informatics; and we urge the Government of Canada and of the provinces to take immediate action to establish a rational structure for telecommunications in Canada as a defence against the further loss of sovereignty in all its economic, social, cultural, and political aspects (1).

This concluding paragraph of the Report of the Clyne Committee, together with the fact that most of its recommendations bear on the problems of television, should leave no doubt as to the gravity which the Committee attached to the present television crisis in Canada. The fact that this Committee was composed of Canadians of very diverse backgrounds and origins adds further weight to this pressing exhortation.

Simply stated, this television crisis has three major elements. First, watching American programs has already become by far the most important cultural activity of English Canada. Second, even for equal programming creativity, all the economic and business realities are stacked against reversing that trend. For Cable and the private TV broadcasting industries, the more U.S. programs they carry the more money they make; but the greater the Canadian content the more they lose. Third, with the annihilation of distance by the satellite and the dramatic mulitplication of channels into the home by Cable, all remaining natural obstacles which have remained in the path of the American TV tidal wave have now been removed.

These facts place Canada in a uniquely unenviable situation in the industrial world, as being both a cultural and an economic colony of the most powerful nation on earth. With no historical precedents to reassure us, many of us wonder how much further we can go towards complete cultural and economic assimilation and still claim political sovereignty.

Assuming that we do want to retain political sovereignty, our margin of action is relatively narrow. We can not change the economic reality of the much higher procurement costs of Canadian programming which are inherent in the disproportion between the population and wealth of the United States and Canada. Neither can we deprive Canadians of their acquired right to see those popular U.S. programs which have become their favourites. We can, however, keep a much better check on the business entrepreneurs who exploit this situation to their advantage. We can also try to take advantage of the new developments to organize our efforts and our overall systems in such a way as to remove the natural and artificial handicaps which block the realization of our full Canadian television creative potential.

The solution to the Canadian television crisis will be found in good part in planning, structure, money and enough national will to ensure that the national interest will prevail over private interests, and that Canadian creativity will have a chance to explore new avenues which lie outside the American mould.

Previous chapters have outlined the technologies involved. In the following pages we will discuss how that moment of flux which always accompanies the implementation of new technologies can be seized to support national interests and strengthen our tenuous hold on political sovereignty.

THE COMMUNICATIONS REVOLUTION

Cable is the principal agent of change in television

Television itself was one of the first manifestations of the electronic revolution. Because it is the electronic medium par excellence, the impact of the newer technologies on the hardware of television has already been considerable and positive. The same miniaturized electronic circuits, which have been making the major computers as well as the pocket calculators constantly better and yet smaller and cheaper, have also revolutionized television cameras, amplifiers and recorders. With smaller and more portable equipment, television crews can now move in to cover special events just as fast as their radio and film colleagues have been doing for years.

Still some years away, the almost certain digital transformation of the whole television chain, from the studio camera to the home receiver, will bring major improvements in picture quality and the much-hoped-for development of large TV screens for the home. But actually, the most important contributions of the new electronics to television, have been revolutionary breakthroughs in telecommunications carriage rather than in the technology of television itself.

The communications satellite has in one swoop freed television from all problems of distance. With our own Aniks, CBC can now reach every square inch of our half continent. The satellite does its job so smoothly that no one is even conscious that all the network programs received on CBC channels have already travelled some 75,000 kilometres to and from the equatorial orbit. The world itself has become an electronic village and few viewers are any longer impressed by the instantaneous satellite coverage of world events.

In spite of the satellite's glamour and feats of carriage, it has been the gradual and almost unnoticed development of the venerable coaxial cable as a carrier of television programs to the home that has been the principal agent of change in television. It is revolutionizing not only the means of television delivery, but also our basic concepts of what television should be.

In Canada, which is leading the world of communications in this as in many other respects, more than half of our total population no longer receives television off the air (2). It is Cable which brings television directly to their home. In other words, Cable is rapidly replacing on-air broadcasting in urban and suburban areas and, in so doing, is freeing television from what has been so far its two most important handicaps: the extreme shortage of suitable Hertzian frequencies and the inability to collect directly for its services.

Cable, with its abundance of channels, can become a grave threat to our national survival or can make Canadian television the best in the world. Which it will be depends entirely on the wisdom and political will we can bring to bear on the Cable issues we face today. The basic question is whether Cable will be made to serve our long-term interest, as a nation as well as individuals, or become the prime instrument of our assimilation.

Television in Canada

It would be more accurate to call it "American television in Canada" since already about 75% of our viewing time goes to American programs. People in authority seem to be placing most of the blame for this incongruous situation on the shoulders of CBC rather than recognizing that the marked drop in Canadian viewing in recent years is in good part the result of wrong policies and ad hoc regulatory decision. Little by little, because we do not have any overall long-term plan, we have allowed ourselves to be pushed by the American ethos deeper and deeper into the U.S. broadcasting mould.

Unless we come back to our senses quickly, we are about to give in again to further commercial pressures and clinch our fate forever. I am thinking here about the relentless Cable lobby for per-channel pay-TV (which we all know will end up with at least 90% American content), and also of the pressures to dedicate complete channels on our satellites to feed U.S. networks and superstations to all Cable systems in Canada and, via Cable, to transplant them into every Canadian home.

What worries me so much about all this (judging by their past actions and omissions) is that those with the power to decide seem ready to surrender the most important instrument of communications and cultural survival we have, rather than face and conquer the difficulties of retaining control. Many people whose opinions I respect tell me that it is not politically possible to take away from Cable operators or broadcasters any privilege already granted, whether in the public interest or not. Some even speak of it being too late to "turn the clock back", as if the only way to proceed in this political world of ours were to build as best we can on our past mistakes. I refuse to accept such a proposition. Probably similar arguments were made by those who collected the tolls on the major roads of Canada in the 1800's, and felt the road was their property (3).

The implementation of these new technologies represents a perfect opportunity to reassert political and cultural sovereignty. I think it is a serious mistake to assume that our political leaders do not have the courage to do what is necessary in the best public interest. We have just been through a period of major economic, constitutional and political turmoil which may have left the communications crisis fairly low on the list of Government priorities. Even with just a brief political honeymoon, let us hope that it will now be possible to give the very important communications decisions facing Canada all the attention they deserve.

In particular, it is a long long time since Parliament has refreshed its mind on the fundamental reasons why Canada's broadcasting system is not the same as it is in the U.S. These reasons are even more cogent today than they were fifty years ago, when the Aird Royal Commission recommended that "broadcasting should be placed on the basis of a public service." "From what we have learned in our investigations and studies," the commissioners wrote, "we are impelled to the conclusion that [the] interests [of the listening public and of the nation] can be served only by some form of public ownership and control behind which is the national power and prestige of the whole public of the Dominion of Canada"(4).

It was the recommendations of the Aird Commission which in 1932 led

Parliament to pass, with complete support of all parties and with only one dissenting vote, the Canadian Broadcasting Act, which created Canada's National Broadcasting Service. Here is in part what Prime Minister Bennett said in the House on this this occasion:

> First of all, this country must be assured of complete control of broadcasting from Canadian sources, free from foreign interference or influence. Without such control radio broadcasting can never become a great agency for the communications of matters of national concern and for the diffusion of national thought and ideas, and without such control it can never be the agency by which national consciousness may be fostered and sustained and national unity still further strengthened....
>
> Secondly, no other scheme than that of public ownership can ensure to the public of this country, without regard to class or place, equal enjoyment of the benefits and pleasures of radio broadcasting... (5).

This was of course twenty years before the advent of television, but Canadian radio was then rapidly slipping into much the same position of overdependence on American programming as television has done since the mid sixties.

The second Royal Commission to look into broadcasting was the Massey Commission. Its 1951 report, a year before television, also affirmed in the strongest possible terms the Canadian approach to broadcasting as a public service rather than as a strictly business enterprise, as in the U.S.:

> [It is a] false assumption that broadcasting in Canada is an industry. Broadcasting in Canada, in our view, is a public service directed and controlled in the public interest by a body responsible to Parliament....
>
> We were particularly impressed by the fact that few of the representatives of private stations who appeared before us recognized any public responsibility beyond the provision of acceptable entertainment and community services. The general attitude was that... the private stations must be left free to pursue their business enterprise subject only to the limitations imposed by decency and good taste. We offer no criticism of this frankly commercial attitude; we cite it only as evidence that those who honestly hold these views are not primarily concerned with the national function of radio...(6)

The Fowler Commission was the third and last Royal Enquiry to look into broadcasting in Canada more than twenty years ago, five years after the beginning of television but long before it could anticipate the added perils which Cable and satellites would create for our Canadian sovereignty. Even then, the concern of the Fowler Commission for the survival of Canada is the very foundation of its Report.

> as a nation we cannot accept, in these powerful and persuasive media [radio and television], the natural and complete flow of another nation's

culture without danger to our national identity. Can we resist the tidal wave of American cultural activity? Can we retain a Canadian identity, art and culture—a Canadian nationhood? . . .

Assuming, as we must, that their broadcasting system is satisfactory and suitable for Americans, this is no basis for thinking that it is desirable for Canadians. We may want, and may be better to have, a different system—something distinctively Canadian and not a copy of a system that may be good for Americans but may not be the best for us. . . . This is not a new problem for Canada. . . . There is no doubt that we could have had cheaper railway transportation, cheaper air service and cheaper consumer goods if we had simply tied outselves into the American transportation and economic system. It is equally clear that we could have cheaper radio and television service if Canadian stations became outlets of American networks. However, if the less costly method is always chosen, is it possible to have a Canadian nation at all. The Canadian answer, irrespective of party or race, has been uniformly the same for nearly a century. We are prepared, by measures of assistance, financial aid and a conscious stimulation, to compensate for our disabilities of geography, sparse population and vast distances, and we have accepted this as a legitimate role of government in Canada. . . .

The choice is between a Canadian state-controlled system with some flow of programs east and west across Canada, with some Canadian content and the development of a Canadian sense of identity, at a substantial public cost, and a privately owned system which the forces of economics will necessarily make predominantly dependent on imported American radio and television programmes (7).

It should be pointed out that these conclusions were not those of socialist reformers. The private enterprise convictions of the three great Canadians, Sir John Aird, Vincent Massey and Robert Fowler, who chaired the three Royal Commissions on broadcasting so far, could hardly be questioned.

THE POLICY ISSUES AND THE NEED FOR ACTION*

Given that we are not likely to see a formal policy position as coherent and detailed as that outlined by Parkhill in Chapter Three and that the vested interests as analysed by Godfrey in Chapter Four will be scrambling either for advantage or survival, it is important to look at the policy arguments as they are likely to arise, as arguments that will be made on an ad hoc basis by parties with firm beliefs in their own self-interest. Against these arguments we must set the interests of the consumers and users for, as always, these lack the force and finances of those who stand to profit directly.

*For an earlier version of some of these comments, see my discussion paper for the Delta Dialogue Series Seminars of November and December 1978, entitled "Rationalizing Canadian Communications: A Plan for Action."

So we have a number of tasks. The principle of Content/Carrier separation must be clearly established for TV; the acceptance of the concept of "complementarity" is a prerequisite to our getting the most from the new abundance of Cable channels; and a number of terms which seem to generate fuzzy thinking, including pay-TV, superstations, Satellite-Cable networks, and the freedom to import, must be clearly defined. Unfortunately, the technology will not wait for us to finish these tasks at our own speed. This is why we should tackle them here and now.

Cable is a new kind of carrier

Cable is a new kind of carrier of great potential and versatility. It can already provide 35 interference-free channels, and this is only a beginning. It is no longer the crowding of the spectrum that will determine the number of channels and the kind of television we can have, but economics and our own wisdom.

If Cable is to be the key to future progress in television and informatics, we have to stop thinking of it as an appendix of broadcasting and start getting rid of all its hertzian limitations. Cable will not be television's second chance if it is allowed to perpetuate and exaggerate the very shortcomings of television broadcasting itself.

So, once and for all, let's cut Cable's broadcasting tether. We will not fully realize this potential for public service unless we abandon concepts of the past and recognize Cable, like other carriers, for what it is today: a public utility carriage monopoly, and restructure it accordingly.

The separation of Content and Carriage

To start with, Cable, like other telecommunications carriers, must observe the traditional rules of "Separation of Carriage and Content." According to this rule, a Carrier should not determine what it carries and it should not be in a position to compete with those who have to depend on its carriage.

Naturally, Cable companies are opposed to any of this. They recognize that their primary role is to carry the content of others, but they still want to be free to originate some of their own content for television and for the new services, free to continue the holus bolus transplantation of U. S. border stations into Canada, free to control the content of pay-TV, free to set up multichannel satellite-Cable networks and, obviously, free also from any rate of return regulations.

And why should Cable entrepreneurs feel they ought to have all these privileges, which are denied to other Carriers?

They claim that, while they are Carriers, they do not constitute a monopoly. They make that claim on the grounds that people are free to use antennas and many still do. Surely, this is a specious argument. Even high price antennas cannot compete with Cable for distant signals. Furthermore, many Cable channels will never be available on the air. And, as there are no Hertzian channels left, future TV services will all be on Cable only. Also, what about the likely day when all TV services are available only on Cable?

Furthermore, as Parkhill has made clear, many of the new services will not be receivable on antennas and some may be available by Cable only, even if others are also carried over the telephone.

There is no real doubt that Cable already enjoys in Canada a monopoly position in the carriage of video services to the home, just as the telephone utility does for telephone service.

The Cable corporations use another argument: since they are already involved in production and programming (even if not to a really important extent), it wouldn't be "fair" to take that privilege away from them. It should be stressed here that no one is suggesting that they not be allowed to be involved with Content. There is plenty of room for them in that field, but then they will have to choose between being Carriers or programmers. They cannot be both.

Many who are concerned with this dilemma would like to find some compromise which would both respect the principle of separation and at the same time allow Cable to satisfy their interest in programming. This is how the suggestion came about that Cable should be allowed to engage in program operations through bona fide arm's length subsidiaries. Others see this just as a subterfuge which would eventually destroy the principle. Personally, I think there is a safer arm's length solution.

If it is true, as many Cable people claim, that they have a major contribution to make in the production of high quality Canadian content, why not let them compete, again at arm's length, with other content producers and take their chance with them in finding a "programming undertaking" willing to accept it on its channel or channels.

By "programming undertaking" we mean a group or corporation which is authorized by the regulatory authority to "program" one or more Hertzian or Cable channels. In television terminology, "programming" is the selection or acceptance of individual film, tape or live programs or advertising messages, and their arrangement into daily and weekly program packages or schedules for delivery on a Hertzian or Cable television channel, taking into account the needs and the tastes of the particular audience which the channel is to serve. The "programming undertaking" is also responsible for: the promotion of individual programs and schedules; the sale and acceptance of advertising; the observance of regulations; the negotiation of rights. These activities are common to the programming of both networks and stations. In addition, network programming also involves the procurement of microwave and satellite circuits needed to feed the stations and Cable Carriers on the network.

It is therefore the "programming undertaking" that decides what its channel will carry and where it will carry it. Under my proposal, the conflict would thus be moved from one between carriage and content production to one between carriage and the decision to carry. No Carrier would have the right to decide to carry the content of its own production subsidiary which, like other content producers, would have to seek access through one of the several "programming undertakings" responsible for the programming on the various channels provided by the Cable carrier.

The fact that I have had no takers yet for this proposition should leave no doubt in anyone's mind as to the real reason why Cable people are against separation of Carriage and Content. They want to retain channels for their own use, on which they want to be free to compete with the channels they carry for others. This is the very conflict of interest separation is meant to prevent.

Cable people have another excellent but unspoken reason to oppose the separation principle. As long as they manage to hang on to some Content function, they think they may avoid being treated as a public utility monopoly and regulated on a rate of return basis.

The responsibility for Content

The greater the separation between Carrier and Content, the fewer the problems of responsibility for Content that arise for the Carrier. With the telephone, where separation is complete (as it is the subscriber who generates the content entirely), there are very few problems of responsibility for content: sedition may be plotted, bets laid, robberies planned and sensual messages passed on, but only in the case of pornographic or racist calls to strangers do the problems make the news. On the other hand, as newspapers have become less numerous in cities, problems of responsibilities have increased: to traditional libel and slander responsibilities have been added recent quandries for editors in areas such as cartoons and letters to the editor where the newspaper originally had a pure Carrier role but is now seen as "responsible" for the Content. Radio and television, because of the allocation of channels inherent in their technology, have in a sense demanded their own regulation. One can imagine a case where there was only one owner of a single-channel media of some power and postulate then that problems of responsibility for content would be quite enormous.

Cable, essentially a Carrier, has tried to have the best of both worlds. At the moment, Cable can only be held responsible for the Content of the few channels it programs itself. In fact, the Content of U. S. stations which Cable transplants off the air can only be the responsibility of American originators who are no more concerned with the needs of the Canadian audience than the French or the British could be if we also transplanted their channels into Canada.

We have yet to face the necessity that each television channel on the Cable, as on the air, must be the responsibility of a Canadian Content "programming undertaking" duly authorized for that purpose. A single Content undertaking could be responsible for a number of Cable or Hertzian channels.

Complementary channels: TV's unique content opportunity

The leap from three or four local Hertzian channels to ten times that number on Cable presents us with a fundamental choice. Not very many will be needed for informatics, since many alphanumeric services can be packed in a single wide-band cable channel and other services are better suited for transmission over telephone circuits anyway. This leaves a lot of new channels for television. We could use them, as seems to be the trend already in the U. S., to increase the number of entrepreneurs competing for the same mass audience, all roughly with the same kind of common denominator programming, whether on pay-TV or regular channels.

Or, these new channels could become TV's second chance, giving us at last the ability to serve at the same time all tastes and needs and not just those of some artificial mass. This is what we call "complementary" programming: many channels deliberately specialized so as to appeal to the many different interests in our pluralistic society. While not really competitive amongst themselves, except hopefully for excellence, these complementary channels would compete with the general interest channels which we already have and should retain. It is not a question of taking anything away from anyone, but rather of adding in order to take advantage of the only chance we will ever get to provide complete and mature national television service which, unlike PBS, would serve majority as well as minority preferences.

"Complementarity" requires the non-competitive co-ordination of a number of channels, each dedicated to various segments of the taste spectrum. A fully complementary service could probably be achieved only by a public service programming institution calling heavily on outside sources of content of all kinds. This is possibly why the only opposition I have really heard so far to this principle of complementarity has come from the executives of the private broadcasters association; for to them, the concept of serving all tastes is just the opposite to that of North American commercial philosophy. In any case, they say they are against the opening of additional channels, even just CBC II, which they claim will further fragment their audience and decrease their revenues. This is such an obviously self-serving reaction that it is difficult to attach much importance to it.

For a large number of viewers whose interests are not differentiable, the concept of complementarity as the salvation of Canadian television tends to be rather abstract. Many others, who understand fully its possibilities wonder whether we really can afford it. I wish it were possible to reassure them in this short chapter, with a well documented cost analysis. However, all I can do is state the obvious: one thing we can be sure of is that potential TV channels will not go unused for very long. If they are not used to serve a broader spectrum of tastes and hence more people, through complementary programming, they will be used in a commercially competitive way to replicate the same kind of programming which will only serve the same people with more of the same. And this kind of competitive mass programming is a great deal more costly than the complementary approach. In making this statement, I take it for granted that my readers are sophisticated and no longer believe that commercial TV is free TV. There is another development, which should be kept in mind in the consideration of complementary programming, and that is the probability that, through the development of pay-TV, television is moving towards greater self-financing.

This "complementarity" proposal also envisages a high degree of excellence in the programming of each complementary channel, whatever the level of cultural sophistication of the viewers it may try to serve. To provide the best to all according to their needs and their capacity is a very great challenge. We should tackle it gradually and with a certain humility. We will then soon realize that we cannot do it all ourselves and should not set up targets of Canadian content we cannot possibly meet. Outside the area of news and public affairs, which is well within our resources anyway, I see no shame for a country of modest resources like Canada to rely to a fairly large extent on imports. But these imports should not be made blindly and repetitively as is the case with present Cable transplants. They should also be of a degree of excellence and variety which our best efforts could not hope to attain.

I cannot too strongly stress the vital importance of immediately seizing the opportunity we still have of using the new Cable channels for the development of a complementary Canadian television system. This is the only way we have left of extricating ourselves from the U.S. TV mould, while still enjoying the best and the most popular American (and British and French and Swiss etc.) fare.

Imports: rentals and transplants

Both the development of Cable techniques and satellite technology have introduced important new methods for the importation and distribution of foreign programs. One would think this would be all to the good, and it may still be—in the long run. But for the moment, it is creating a great deal of anxiety among nations with culturally powerful neighbours. International communications specialists all over the world are now talking of the "cultural vulnerability" of some nations and of the "cultural imperialism" of others.

There is probably no other country for which the electronic disappearance of natural borders is of greater national significance than for Canada, but this is obviously not the place for an in-depth examination of our cultural colonialism. It may, however, be useful to remind ourselves that, in terms of television programming self-sufficiency, Canada ranks down with the underdeveloped countries, with only 25% of our TV viewing being of our own programs, as compared to 95% for the U.S. and about 85% in Europe.

Maybe we should consider ourselves lucky to be so culturally similar to the U. S. that we can get what we like best from them, for nothing or at dumping prices. Or is cultural obliteration as dangerous as economic domination?—And what about both? More to the point, do we still care?

"WE'LL WATCH WHAT WE LIKE"

In this brave editorial headline affirming our sovereignty, the *Globe and Mail* has already answered my questions. (One wonders if the *Globe*'s position will remain the same when the new technologies permit the *New York Times* to print a "Toronto" edition and win 30% of the Toronto market.)

I will therefore limit further comments to the mechanics of importation, with one assumption, however. It is that, while we individually continue to watch what we want, spending 75% of our viewing time on foreign programming is not an objective which, as a nation, we collectively would like to exceed.

Only a small percentage of our American viewing is now done directly over the air by people near the border. Most U. S. programs we look at are either "rented" or "transplanted."

Television broadcasters "rent" their foreign content. They select the individual foreign programs they wish to use in Canada, negotiate with their owners for the rights and pay accordingly. This is the way CBC, CTV, Global and other broadcasters proceed, whether the programs come to them on film, tape or live. Broadcasters have never been allowed to appropriate for themselves the programs of others by picking them off the air. Neither have they ever sought to do so.

Cable does not "rent" individual programs in this sense. In effect, Cable "transplants" whole U. S. stations into Canada. In a similar fasion, it also "transplants" Canadian stations into neighbouring Canadian markets. It thus appropriates the total broadcast output of the transplanted station without negotiation or payment. And it does so with full approval of the CRTC.

This "transplanting" of whole stations was the very raison d'etre for the development of Cable in the first place. At that time, Cable's avowed role was simply to complete the natural coverage of a station or to bring some TV reception to areas who did not have any. Now, as we have seen already, time and success have completely transformed the role of Cable and cast serious doubt on the acceptability of transplantation under today's conditions. Here is what is wrong with it:

1. If done without payment and/or consent, it is piracy and, even if declared legal by the court, it is unethical and unfair, specially if the transplants are pruned here and there to satisfy CRTC regulations.

2. Because transplantation blindly appropriates without consideration of rights, it is also unfair to Canadian broadcasters who have already bought these rights.

3. Transplantation becomes a form of "importation overkill." Many of the programs of the transplanted stations are the same as those already legitimately imported by the broadcasting channels also carried by Cable. Second, a large portion of the transplanted programming consists of local border trivia which is of little or no interest to Canadians. Transplantation is therefore a wasteful use of channel space and, through blind repetition and carriage of irrelevant content, it creates an unnecessary overexposure of foreign programs.

4. As opposed to renting which is an act of judgment and so implies accountability, transplantation is blind and irresponsible. Once Cable has dedicated a number of its channels to the transplantation of American border stations, there is no accountability that can be demanded of anyone for the material carried on those channels, surely not of the American stations thus transplanted without their agreement.

The only reason we are still saddled with this brute force approach to importation is that it provides Cable with a lot of content for nothing, content which it carries on its surplus channels at no incremental costs, and then markets to its subscribers as the premium attraction of its service.

If we do not think we should build the future of Canadian television on this kind of questionable practice, it is easy to get rid of it. And not, as has been charged, by depriving Canadians of their favourite American programs. Gradually all the popular U. S. shows Canadian want to see should be imported in a civilized manner and incorporated, as two thirds are already, on regular Canadian network and station channels. As Canadian complementary channels become available, there will be enough room for the other third. This will not increase, but rather decrease, the U.S. content on Cable because importation will eliminate the duplication and chaff we now get with blind transplantation.

There are those who feel that it would be all right to provide all U. S. networks with dedicated cable and satellite channels all over Canada, as long as we place these "showcase" channels on pay-TV. In this way, they argue, we would satisfy public demand and the extra charge would, at the same time, limit their audience and yet produce extra revenues which could be used to encourage Canadian productions. There is more to this suggestion than the usual sophistry of pay-TV advocates who practically suggest that we must watch American pay-TV films to support the Canadian film industry; the logic is: that which is to be avoided, if free, becomes right, once paid for. This somehow reminds me of the oldest profession.

How we can best arrange our Canadian and foreign television content on cable is one of the most important questions of strategy we have to answer in the public interest.

One view is that we should continue to keep the two neatly separated. Thus we would have the foreign package comprising CBS, NBC, ABC, PBS and, once started, I suppose also all U. S. networks and superstations yet to come, as well as HBO 1, 2, etc. And why not BBC 1 & 2, ITV 1 & 2, France's TV 1, 2 & 3, etc.? Each of these networks would be provided with their own Canadian Cable and satellite channels right across the land so that no viewer could possibly feel treated as a second class citizen. Then, there would be the domestic showcase, with only a few channels, but all with 100% Canadian programming, CBC, CTV and Global (if there is a way Canadian commercial networks can survive without a large amount of American content), TVO, ORTQ, and all our own new 100% Canadian superstations.

The second view considers that this first approach will lead to near 100% foreign viewing. It holds that there should eventually be no channel dedicated solely to foreign transplants or even imports. Rather, all channels in Canada, including CBC, should carry a Canadian mixture of the best we can produce ourselves with the best we can get from other countries. It also holds that the ideal percentage of Canadian content would vary between channels and that its average will depend on the money we are willing to spend on it.

Pay-TV

Pay-TV is not a new medium, or even a new type of television as some would like us to believe. It is just a different method of paying for TV and we have had it for a long time. Cable TV is a form of pay-TV which charges a monthly fee for a number of TV channels. The kind of pay-TV which is being pushed at this time is per-channel pay-TV. For an extra payment of $10 a month, Cable would make it possible for subscribers to the pay-TV channel to see films, after their first run in the movie house, but before their availability on the ordinary channels. Pay-TV would also show the odd sporting event and entertainment special. Its content would be over 90% American and necessarily programmed for the greatest possible mass appeal.

At a time when there is already twice as much U. S. content on Cable as Canadian, it would be sheer folly to dedicate, for love or money, even a single additional channel to content which we know beforehand will be almost exclusively American and not necessarily their best.

Why should we further jeopardize our dwindling chances of regaining control of our television channels? There is no demonstrated public demand for pay-TV. The only people who stand to gain anything from its early approval are the Cable operators. They want it for two reasons. First, it could be a highly profitable expansion of their business. Second, and equally important, early control of pay-TV would be another foot in the Content door which they hope could "save" them from becoming straight Carriers, a prospect which, as we have seen from the TAMEC report analysis in Chapter Four, doesn't seem to have much appeal for them.

It is true that some provinces are using pay-TV operations to affirm their jurisdiction over Cable. For Ottawa to respond by a unilateral pay-TV move of its own would just prolong the sterile jurisdictional dispute which has now paralyzed progress in Canadian communications for years.

Before we decide on per-channel pay-TV, we should also have a good look at the per-program type which seems much better suited to our Canadian needs. In any case, the question of pay-TV cannot be dealt with on an ad hoc basis or in isolation. It is only one of the many complex television and Cable issues we have to resolve. It must be studied with all the rest, for it will affect all the rest. In the meantime, there is nothing to lose and everything to gain by delaying a decision until we have decided on the general framework in which these special forms of pay-TV will have to fit.

There is, however, one aspect of pay-TV which can be decided now as a matter of principle. The choice of charging the viewers directly for the programs they look at, rather than indirectly as at present, should be available in principle to *all* purveyors of television content. Pay-TV is just a new method of payment. Who knows that eventually all television services might not be paid for directly by the consumer? How could we then grant a pay-TV monopoly to any one group?

Stations, "Superstations" and "Satellite-Cable Networks"

Life was a little simpler for the regulator before the arrival of Cable and satellites.

In television, there were just local stations and networks. The local station makes local interest programs and the network makes programs for a wide spread audience. Except for a few independents, the local stations are either affiliated to, or owned by, a network. And they broadcast the programs of their network, as well as their own local programs, to the area they are licensed to cover.

Thus, the local stations are licensed for two functions: for local programming and for the local broadcasting of both local and network programs to their franchise area. It is this local broadcasting function which is being rapidly replaced by local, common Cable carriage direct to the home.

Similarly, the network has two functions: network programming and the distribution of those programs for broadcasting by its own or affiliated local stations. The network does not itself physically distribute its programs to its local network outlets. It has it done by regular telecommunication carriers over their general microwave networks. This is still the general television network picture in Canada, except that the satellite has for the most part replaced microwave distribution for the CBC networks.

But this simple picture of local and network television is now becoming more complex. Already, as we have seen, Cable is displacing local broadcasting as the carrier of television into the home. Unfortunately, Cable, which is basically a hardware monopoly, was also encouraged to enter the content production and programming areas. Now, through the satellite, Cable is poised to invade the field of network operation.

The Americans who are really just as far behind as we are in terms of long-term planning and coherent communications policy, seem to have given up any hope of straightening things out. Their most recent strategy seems to be to let the market forces work things out. There is a general move towards de-regulation, the re-definition and repression of monopolies, and the further stimulation of competition. With 15 times our English language population and 20 times our economic base, the three American commercial networks can certainly stand a lot more competition and AT&T may not die if IBM and Xerox cut it down to size. And, as far as the general public interest is concerned, it doesn't really matter much who does what to whom, since large private interest will remain in charge in any case.

In U. S. television, with ratings as the only arbiter, private commercial interest has always been equated with public interest. In any case, how they solve their problems should not be any of our concern, were it not for the fact that, in television at least, we do not seem to realize to what extent the American approach influences our own thinking. And often no less so at the regulatory and policy level than at the private entrepreneurial level.

We seem to have little sense of scale and we constantly mistake ourselves for the United States. What they have we want and it has even become un-Canadian to suggest that some new initiative, which might turn out all right for the most powerful nation in the world, might not be at all suitable for us.

In any case, we are toying with the idea of Canadian superstations because some exist across the border. What happened there is that a few enterprising U. S. local stations, unhappy with the limitations of their local market, rented satellite channels and made the whole U. S. their market by making it attractive for Cable systems to pick up and carry their programs all over the country. Thus was born the "Superstation." It could be more accurately called a "Satellite-Cable Network," that is, a network in which the satellite has replaced microwave carriage and local Cable carriage takes the place of the television broadcasting stations. Whatever it is called, there is nothing wrong with the idea, in itself. Carried to its logical conclusion, however, it may have serious repercussions on the structure and content of the whole American TV system. But this is our neighbour's problem, not ours.

Unless, of course, we jump to the conclusion that we should also have our own Canadian superstations to meet some ad hoc situation, or just to keep up with the Joneses; then it will also become our problem, one which calls for the most careful consideration, not in isolation, but as an integral part of a much broader plan to ensure that all the current and forthcoming technological developments can best serve the long term Canadian public interest.

The "Canadian Satellite-Cable Package"

At present, only CBC networks are using satellite distribution to feed their outlets in all parts of Canada. CTV, Global and TVA, who are not required to cover the whole country, use regular microwave distribution which is cheaper for more limited coverage. So do TVO and Radio-Quebec, which require only regional coverage anyway. It is said that the three private commercial networks are not willing to pay the extra cost of using the satellite to make their programs available to the whole of Canada. The result is that viewers in remote and northern locations cannot see many of the programs, mainly U. S., which are popular in the south but not carried by the CBC national services.

To correct this situation and allegedly also to prevent the further spread of illicit reception of U. S. material, including pay-TV, directly from U.S. satellites (it is reported that the number of TV smugglers is now well over a hundred), the Government would like to provide a broader choice of programming on our own satellites. Hence, this proposal for a "Canadian Satellite-Cable Package," which we call CS-CP for short.

The fact that this seems to be an indigenous proposal should not be allowed to confuse us as to the kind of "deal" this "package" might lead us to. Several questions come to mind. What is Cable doing in a "package" which consists essentially in placing a number of additional networks on Canadian satellites? How will its role differ in the proposed CS-CP from what it is now in relation to the "package" of CBC network channels already on the satellite? In the proposed CS-CP, will Cable do more than provide the local carriage it now provides for all networks?

The danger here again is that the answer to these questions might be based on short-term expediency instead of on basic principles and long-term strategy.

The fundamental responsibilities of providing network television service have not changed because the satellite is in certain cases replacing microwave for network transmission, or because Cable is taking the place of the Hertzian station for local distribution to the home. If they have, will they change again when we get to direct broadcasting satellites and optical fibre transmission?

Whatever the mode of long distance transmission or of local distribution, there must still be a "network operator," as designated in the Broadcasting Act, who can be held responsible for the programming of the network and for the nature and extent of its coverage. These are two inseparable responsibilities, as the choice of programs obviously depends on the audience to whom they are destined. It is the network operator who orders from the Carriers, whether satellite, microwave or Cable, the coverage he requires for his programs. Not vice versa.

In practical terms, however, the Cable industry has great leverage. It has money to invest in the right kind of CS-CP, while private network operators say they haven't, and the CBC's budget has just been cut by 15%. In such circumstances, Cable might just get what it wants: control of pay-TV and some network programming role in return for its banking services.

I hope our decision-makers realize that they are already playing with fire. Surely the status of Cable, as producer, local programmer and carrier, is already sufficiently extensive and confused without making them also programmers or operators of our networks in the hope that they will also become our bankers.

As we begin to look to the Cable industry for money for different television projects, we seem to forget that any funds available from that source come from the comfortable profits of a monopoly not regulated on a rate-of-return basis and utilizing content which is to a large extent "pirated."

The rapid replacement of Hertzian broadcasting by Cable delivery direct to the home will indeed make it possible to collect directly from the consumer for television services. At the same time it will permit a certain equalization of TV costs between more and less profitable areas. But, surely, there are better ways to achieve this than by involving Cable in network programming on top of all the rest. We can also get the Cable industry to become our banker, but the price of its generosity, with our money, will be the control of pay-TV in a form which it chooses on the basis of the highest commercial returns.

It should be self-evident that the Carrier status of Cable has to be settled independently of the short-term financial problems of the particular CS-CP we have been discussing. And there are other CS-CP's, for example CTN, the Cable Television Network, which is also all set to operate television networks, including pay-TV.

CRTC hearings were held in the spring and fall of 1980 and decisions should be forthcoming soon after. We will thus be able to judge whether we are still working on the same *ad hoc* basis as in the past. Or whether, by that time, we will have succeeded in developing the overall national television strategy we so badly need as the basis on which individual regulatory decisions must be founded.

There is no more crucial element in this national plan, than to make it possible for the CBC to continue to play the full role given to it by the Broadcasting Act, as "the provider of the national television service."

The vital role of the CBC

At this time of national soul-searching, it is not surprising to find the CBC at the centre of the great Canadian debate. CBC is Canada's alter ego. Being dissatisfied with ourselves as a nation, or as two, it is perhaps only natural that we should blame our alter ego for our own failures. But this vicarious catharsis has recently become too harsh and unconsidered to be without danger. There is no way I can possibly examine this problem in depth in this paper, for it is the problem of Canada itself. All I can do is to appeal to the many arm-chair CBC Presidents amongst Ottawa's politicians and public servants to jump off their anti-CBC bandwagon before it is too late.

We need the CBC more than ever. Most of the challenges ahead in broadcasting can only be met by an independent public service institution like the CBC—and surely no one would suggest that we should have two.

We cannot seriously look to the private broadcasters or to Cable to develop greater public viewing of Canadian programs. There is two to four times as much viewing of U. S. imports on English language private TV stations as there is on CBC. Cable, with its added U. S. transplants, is an even greater factor of Americanization.

Neither can we ever expect the private sector to develop the kind of complementary programming which Cable now makes possible and which is absolutely necessary for a complete and civilized television service. Generally speaking, it is not possible for private commercial enterprises to abandon common denominator programming no matter how many channels they might be given. Furthermore, they have no mandate to do so. But the CBC has. For the past twenty-five years it has broken its neck trying to serve all tastes and needs on a single channel. An impossible job. We now have the channels, let the CBC show us what it can do when it has the means.

To use Frank Peers' words, we keep "drifting" between "the public and service principle, and the private and commercial;" in the meantime, "the struggle for national broadcasting in Canada" as Austin Weir so perceptively called it 14 years ago, just goes on and on, to our very great collective peril. At the moment, without firm decisions, the new technologies may only intensify the risk.

REFERENCES TO CHAPTER 5

1. *Canada and Telecommunications: The Report of the Consultative Commission on Telecommunications and Canadian Sovereignty,* commissioned by the Department of Communications, Government of Canada, 8 March 1979.

2. In the U. S. A., Cable subscribers represented only about 18% of households in 1977.

3. There were toll roads in Ontario until as late as 1926 according to Edward Guillet, *History of Roads in Canada*, University of Toronto Press, 1966.

4. Aird Royal Commission.

5. Hansard 1932.

6. Massey Commission 1951 Royal Commission report on broadcasting.

7. Fowler Commission (3rd Royal enquiry).

6 NO MORE TEACHER'S DIRTY LOOKS
David Godfrey

> *No more pencils, no more books*
> *No more teacher's dirty looks.*

It is generally agreed that perhaps the most startling of changes envisaged in education over the next 10-15 years will be the extent to which technological systems will be employed. For instance, Information Retrieval Television systems (IRTV) would probably be employed in most schools to provide audio-visual television rather than decentralized type systems. There is also considerable discussion in informed circles of the possible diminution the role of the school itself. Evolving concurrently with the implementation of the technological systems for education, audio-visual communications could transform the home into part-time school. According to a study by Bell Canada, within a decade a significant number of homes could be equipped with home terminals capable of utilizing IRTV and computerized library systems. Consequently, it is quite likely that significant numbers of post secondary students will spend more time working at home or in small groups by 1990. Secondary students could follow by 1993 and primary students by the year 2010 (1).

Before you put too much trust in that prediction you might note that its source was a 1971 document and all that I have done is add ten years to every date mentioned in the original.

Although the media we examined in Chapter Four see growth as well as vulnerability in the new technologies, on the whole the teaching establishment sees, quite rightly, nothing but danger. Why did this revolution predicted by Bell not come about? Partly because of the teaching establishment's relatively firm control of both Content and Carrier aspects of education (can a student bring his own textbook to class?), and partly because those who became involved in the technology early were quickly absorbed by the fascinating techniques available and failed to pose the deeper philosophic questions that will probably have to be answered before the revolution is actually implemented.

Anyone who has taught for a number of years comes to recognize a set of problems which exist beneath the set of problems that occupy one's teaching efforts and hours.

Because these deeper problems seem insoluable, they tend to disappear from view. The evolution of the Electronic Highway and NABU's force one to consider them, however, and once they are considered as solvable, then major structural changes within the educational system become almost inevitable. In many instances, the unhappiness that attends all such structural changes will attach itself to the mechanisms of solution rather than to the deeper set of problems, and it would be unwise to underestimate either the changes or the unhappiness likely to be involved, but in the beginning at least one can concentrate upon the problems themselves.

My personal terms for these problems are a little unusual, but perhaps useful.

LOCKSTEPS	TRANSCRAPS
MR. GRUNDY	BULL CURVES
STUDENT X	PRE-SOLUTIONS

By LOCKSTEPS, I attempt to summarize those problems generated by the requirement to process a large number of students through the same teaching sequence at the same moment. The result, of course, if the teacher is reasonably honest, is that 90% of the students are bored, lost, or out of phase at least 90% of the time and most actual learning takes place outside of the sequence or on its peripheries while the main talents of the teachers are best described in entertainment terms. The result for students is twofold: a general mistrust of education and the development of individual adaptative techniques to bypass the structure they find themselves enmeshed within.

MR GRUNDY refers to those inevitable disasters that occur as LOCKSTEPS ensures that certain teachers will be notched with certain students for fixed periods. All students have had the experience of a year or course of excitement and stimulation followed by one of extreme boredom, non-comprehension, or personality clashes. Teachers sometimes find themselves turned into MR GRUNDY simply by the particular chemistry of a group of students.

The system and the students still make some attempts to grade teachers, but the MR GRUNDY factor makes such comparisons more or less useless. It is possible to grade teachers on their effectiveness within a general population, but their effectiveness range with specific groups of students will likely vary far more than the comparative range of their effectiveness measured against that of other teachers.

The question of defining effectiveness of teaching is thus shuffled to one side and only random attempts can be made to match teachers and students according to such factors as personality type, cultural backgrounds, teaching modes, degree of authoritarianism, libertarianism, intelligence quotients.

STUDENT X represents the other side of the equation. Except at the graduate level, the process of education remains largely exterior to the students. They are processed through a system that must seem almost totally artificial to them and are graded on accomplishment only. Rare indeed are the skylights of a sympathetic and knowledgeable teacher, a well-trained educational counsellor, or a co-op or intern program that demonstrates how the real world goes about its learning.

At the extremes, something is known of STUDENT X as he or she passes through the kinks of the system: honour students and trouble makers impose their presence on the system; but in general, each new teacher takes on STUDENT X as a fully unknown quantity.

After a lecture on *The Heart of Darkness,* I once had a first year student wax enthusiastic over my presentation. I woke up when she said, "That's the first time I ever understood that book." In high school, it turned out, she had studied the text three times. No one had kept track of this fact, nor of her failure to ever understand the book.

The list of factors that can affect learning accomplishment is large: social background, personality factors, motivation, right brain/left brain development, aural/visual/conceptual modes of learning, skill mastery, reading habits, etc., but the system cannot afford to record and report on these factors let alone restructure itself to take account of their impact upon actual learning.

We all know the student who can recite every Vezina Trophy winner from 1904 on, but can't remember the dates of the War of 1812; none of us really have time to understand why that is so.

STUDENT X enters our range of vision, absorbs a vaguely measured quantity of what we push out into his or her domain by methods almost totally unknown to us, and then passes on to the next strange MR GRUNDY with a duly rewarded B- or 63 or Pass or one line comment.

Cumulatively, these strange little marks make up a very formal and imposing document which may allow or prevent STUDENT X from entering Law School or graduating from Veterinarian College. TRANSCRAPS represent just that, scraps of information of very dubious value carried from step to step of the system and acting as cryptic symbols of STUDENT X's contacts with MR GRUNDY. In the aggregate, like tribal scars, they do identify the failures and the superstars.

The fact that TRANSCRAPS can be produced is a major self-ratification of the system, but as anyone knows who has looked at two or three hundred of them, looking for the one best employee or for the thirty most innovative

153

students, the usefulness of the record is not very high; at the best, it records about 10% of what you really want to know.

Looking at the changing ability of certain high schools in Ontario to produce Ontario Scholarship students before and after the elimination of provincial examinations, one can understand the notion of a BULL CURVE as a representation of the system's ability to manipulate its relative grading in order to justify its existence. In B.C., teachers who mark firmly find that their students move to other classes where high grades are easier to obtain and the "offending" teacher discovers that his or her effectiveness is graded downward. In another variation of the BULL CURVE, B.C. secondary schools whose failure rate exceeds a certain percentage may find themselves in trouble with the certification bodies.

The fundamental problem here is that the system finds it difficult to define mastery and degrees of mastery within its disciplines. How much French does STUDENT X know? Not enough. The causes may be diverse, ranging from mere hesitancy, through conflicting approaches and varied environments, to the real problems of advanced disciplines that are in constant flux.

I recently gave some assistance to a student finishing her MA at the Sorbonne on a West Indian writer. There were gaps in her knowledge of literature that absolutely astounded me. She felt, for example, that the writer was racist because many of his characters made racist remarks about Jews in Toronto. Nonetheless, she passed her MA from the Sorbonne. MR GRUNDY'S law of the BULL CURVE might be expressed as follows:

> The knowledge received by any given teacher of any given new student from a TRANSCRAP is always less than 5% of the ideal and the knowledge passed on varies directly with the pecularities of the institution's grading system but is never greater than the original knowledge.

The cumulative result of many of these factors is one I term PRE-SOLUTIONS. A metaphor that seems applicable is that of the meat-grinder; in goes pork, veal, beef and perhaps a little venison, pony and turtle; out comes hamburger. A few students escape almost completely and most learn to learn despite the system, but all are damaged to some extent and the process itself remains unchanged. The amount of adaptation to the variables of time, innovation and personality is miniscule and the awareness of those involved is but a fraction of what it might be.

All the teacher can do is carry into the classroom a set of pre-solutions, ideas, concepts and methods of presentation which have been used in the past, and hope that they will work as well as they did last time; however well that might be. The dedicated teachers manage to change a small percentage of those PRE-SOLUTIONS every year; the less dedicated don't.

The fascination of computers, databanks and cheap long-distance communications for the innovative teacher is obvious and quite enormous. One can now begin to deal with all of these deeper problems. Let me start with a small example. During the seventies, the teaching of English in the secondary schools began at last to stress the creative and personal rather than strict rules of composition. This was quite a break-through, provided that the teachers were excellent and had the necessary time to devote to this quite difficult task. Many teachers were excellent and made the time to encourage students to write out of their own experience and desires.

But the "basics" did suffer, punctuation, grammar, and structure. In fact, of course, these "basics" are much easier to teach than a sense of creativity and provide ideal material for experimental computer-aided courses. I no longer "teach" punctuation in any of my classes. Students who haven't mastered that particular aspect of the discipline receive an 80 page manual covering over 180 rules of punctuation and an introduction to the computer. Then, at their own speed, they master the rules and demonstrate that mastery to the computer/program which is endlessly patient, keeps track of exactly which rules have been mastered and which not, never asks them anything they already know and politely refers them back to the manual if they miss a test question too many times. In addition, it allows the students to decide if they want me to be able to see the computer's evaluation of their current session.

Obviously not all educational material is suitable for this type of CAL (Computed Assisted Learning) presentation, but far more is than is not. There are a number of centres of excellence in the country involved with computer systems and satellites, especially the University of Quebec (2) which has thirteen campuses deliberately linked together by computerized communications to encourage all the segments to function as an Omnibus Network, and the Ontario Institute for Studies in Education (3) which will be one of of the primary foci for experiments involving education.

The National Research Council has sponsored the development of a new language, designed for educational purposes, which makes the writing of courses far easier. Unlike the PLATO and TICCIT systems, NATAL is not restricted to a single terminal type nor to a single manufacturer's equipment with all the limitations and often unnecessary expense implicit in such a restriction. NATAL currently supports a variety of terminals ranging from basic alphanumeric units to graphics units incorporating local processing and is capable of accomodating new hardware developments such as the Telidon terminal.

NATAL now functions on the Digital Equipment Corporation's PDP10 and implementation is underway on other large, general purpose, time-sharing systems and on a dedicated mini-computer. These efforts will result in a standard specification for NATAL, implementations of which are expected to be available from a wide variety of sources.

One of its many features is that it is bilingual. For every command in the language there is a French and English version, so that programmers can work in the language of their own choice with the same system being capable of running both English and French programs (4).

Let us look at my "class" in terms of the six problems:

LOCKSTEPS. Bob does not have to listen as I explain comma splices to Peter for the 27th time. In fact, Bob isn't even present while Peter spends the ten minutes (or fifty minutes) necessary to master this particular unit. If a new student enters the "class" and has problems with only five of the 180 units, then graduation may take place within twenty minutes. All the time-oriented functions of education (periods, days, Grades, Years, Majors and Degrees) are unnecessary for those portions of knowledge available in similar CAL courses. On Monday, the student might improve his mastery of punctuation by three percent, of trigonometry by one percent and of French vocabulary Level Five by six percent. Every student would thus have a completely distinct learning track in all segments of all disciplines.

MR GRUNDY does not completely disappear, but little is left beyond the memory. As students become more aware of the process of learning and more of the routine aspects of teaching are taken over by programs, teachers will be able to be matched with those students with whom they function well rather than those whom the timetable demands. Neither a student nor teacher will have to face a year with a "fink" or a "complete idiot." Most courses will contain a shadow of their originator, of course, but teachers or students will be able to select different courses covering the same material. From the teacher's point of view, dealing with students who have self-selected themselves, with the more theoretical and complex aspects of the subject, all with a minimum of grading, must surely reduce frustration.

The STUDENT X problem will be reduced in a number of ways. Primarily, the student will be able, and ought to be encouraged, to examine the process by which a given body of material is being taught. That is, the program itself will be available to the student and the student's suggestions will be part of the continual amendment of the program. Questions that are ambiguous, elements that are unclear, options that should be added, can all be dealt with in discussions, either group or individual.

Properly constructed programs will also provide a great deal of information to the student about the process of learning so that each student will be able to develop an individual profile of learning skills and difficulties. If some students wish to keep most of this fairly private, they should be allowed to.

In other instances, acceptance into certain learning situations might require some documentation of learning skills rather than merely learning accomplishments, but in these instances the student would at least be able to improve the skills before application.

In the majority of cases, a student moving to a new learning situation would carry with them a great deal of information which would greatly improve their chances of success.

The TRANSCRAP as such would lose most of its functions. Employers would have their own ways of examining in detail for the skills and accomplishments they required and so would graduate schools. Since education would be far less time-bound and place-bound than it is now, one could expect a far greater degree of transfer between the private sector and the formal educational system. The actuality of failure would not disappear, of course, but the recording of it on TRANSCRAPS would. A case can be made that most educational failures represent either inadequate teaching or inadequate self-analysis that draws the student into a particular LOCKSTEPS situation from which the only exit door is marked Failure. Individualized learning should consist of individually established goals as well as individual learning speed, routing and approach.

BULL CURVES are not entirely the educational system's responsibility. The society's general fear of the twenty-hour work week has created a hidden demand on the system, which might be expressed in the vernacular as "teach the buggers anything, movies, bowling, science fiction even sex, but keep them out of the labour market as long as possible."

The universities have listened to this message (suitably translated of course) with more care than most of the community colleges who, out of fear or intelligence, have felt that students might like to be employed once they do graduate. As one result, unlike the universities, many of the community colleges have two applicants for every position.

But much of the responsibility remains within the system. Faced with declining enrolments and uncertain about its functions because of society's own uncertainty about the future, the system becomes terrified at the thought of a fifty percent "failure" rate and the moment of truth is put off, either until university or until the student enters the real work world.

Let us assume, however, that a university develops a computer-based course in Physics with a reasonable effectiveness ratio. What is to prevent secondary schools teachers from taking the course, from letting their best students take the course in their senior year, from revising the course for their other students? Only a few technical considerations which will soon become quite minor.

As such transfers become more common, fraudulent grades will become obviously fraudulent. At the moment, most university departments have learned to recognize the schools which prepare students well and those which don't, but no action can be taken of any real effectiveness. Being able to send back some detailed comparative statistics drawn out automatically by the program and demonstrating that an A in Physics from School Bloat is comparative to a C- from School Honest, will be a start at least.

But it is in the elimination of PRE-SOLUTIONS that the most excitement lies. The creative teacher will be delighted to see 80% of the rote aspects of any discipline adapted for presentation by this methodology for many reasons. First of all, it forces one to examine the content of what is being taught. Since the information presented is public in ways that a lecture or discussion are not, even this initial step can be salutary. Secondly, one must seriously examine one's assumptions about how the material might best be presented. LOCKSTEPS simplifies presentation in many ways. But suppose one needn't worry about holding up the entire class for a half hour while Paul grasps the second law of thermodynamics; suppose it doesn't matter if he needs fifteen examples instead of two. Do you have fifteen? Why didn't the first fourteen work? Perhaps what is needed is more drama, or humour, or a game context?

The program can store data about hundreds of reactions to specific questions and summarize them in patterns that help indicate why some elements didn't work for certain students; the students themselves will discuss their reactions and suggest improvements. Most amendments can be made fairly quickly. In addition, other teachers can utilize the program and report on it to the originator. One thus begins to seriously analyse the educational process itself in additon to participating in it.

Programs should act as a neutral buffer between teacher and student. Both can amend it; both can draw information from it that is not normally available. Rather than guessing as to whether or not a particular segment works, one can compare its effectiveness with other segments of the same course and even with other experiences of that particular class.

The time saved by this method of presentation of rote portions of the material can be spent not only upon specific difficulties and the complexities of a particular discipline, but upon the larger questions of how we acquire and retain knowledge.

This is not to say that adaptation of a large proportion of the curriculum to this teaching method will come about overnight. For every program that is complete and functioning, there seem to be a dozen horror stories of disasters, fantasies, meanderings or brave beginnings best forgotten. There are at least three major categories of error: inadequate equipment, over-ambitious plans, and lack of comprehension of what it is that is to be taught.

Nonetheless, successful programs do exist and if the educational establishment fails to recognize the innovation it will simply have to watch as the new methodology establishes itself outside of the existing institutions.

The establishment of schools as we know them was influenced greatly by Gutenberg's inventions. J. L. Vives was describing a revolution when he wrote in 1531:

> The man desirous of wisdom must make use of books, or of those men who take the place of books . . . Let a school be established in every township, and let there be received into it as teachers men who are of ascertained learning, uprightness and prudence. Let their salary be paid to them from the public treasury . . . Let the teacher know the mother-tongue of the boys exactly, so that by means of their vernacular he may make his instruction easier and more pleasant . . . ; the teacher should keep in his mind the earlier history of his mother-tongue (5).

The innovations we term Gutenberg Two do not have a "schoolroom" as their natural environment: an appendage of a library, a room in which books can be distributed, collected and stored. There is no technical reason why a student in my punctuation "class" couldn't "pass" the course without leaving home. It is inevitable that some of the entrepreneurs we described in Chapter Four will recognize the possibilities of educational content within the new electronic environment and promote the advantages of home learning via the friendly NABU.

Education has existed for a long time without serious competition, partly because of its social function and partly because of its high labour content; competition is about to arrive. As in all instances where a social group faces a threat from mechanical innovation, we can expect a good deal of protest, intensified in this instance by the prior lack of competition and the articulateness of the threatened group. The educational system at the present is a Carrier whose Content is the accepted and valued knowledge of the society. It is place-bound, time-bound and unused to competition or innovation. No other sector of society is more vulnerable to the new technologies. I will predict, however, that within the system (after an initial period of protest), terror will become the mother of adaptation, and although the formal structures will continue to shrink as the work week shortens, creative teachers will have tasks and opportunities that they had previously never even considered possible.

Vulnerability Coefficient: .75
Prognosis: Small craft warnings in the straits at last. High winds. Danger of

capsizing for the ill-prepared. Light in distant harbours for the adventurous.

REFERENCES TO CHAPTER 6

1. *The Film Industry in Canada: Report,* prepared by The Bureau of Management Consulting for the Department of the Secreatary of State, Arts and Culture Branch, Ottawa, 1977, p. 107.

2. The address of the Universite du Quebec is 2875, boulevard Laurier, Sainte-Foy, Quebec, G1V 2M3, Management of Omnibus Network project.

3. The address of the Ontario Institute for Studies in Education is 252 Bloor St. W., Toronto, Ontario, M5S 1V6.

4. For more information on NATAL write J. W. Brahan, Senior Research Officer, Information Science Section, National Research Council, Montreal Road, Ottawa, K1A 0R8.

5. From Hirsch, Rudolf, *Printing, Selling and Reading: 1450-1550*, Otto Harrassowitz, Wiesbaden, 1967, p. 152.

7 APPLES, SORCERERS AND OTHER MONSTERS
David Godfrey Cosmic Upheaval

INTRODUCTION

Except in a few regions selected for experiments, you will not be able to take part directly in the communications revolution for two or three years. You needn't wait, however, simply because the large public networks are only in the planning stage. The data and the intelligence that will eventually flow down the highways can be experimented with already. There once was a clear dividing line between a terminal and a computer. Now the question is, at what point does an intelligent terminal become a microcomputer?

This chapter deals with ways of using small computers to acquaint yourself with terminals, modems, computing languages, data files, operating systems, discs, word-processing, computer games and programming, for a relatively small investment. Prices range from $600 to $3,000.

The key is RS232. This is a standard interface which allows you to connect a computer and a printer, or a computer and a modem. With my own unit working as a small computer, I can load in BASIC (off a cassette) and write simple programs. With the serial port connected to a Modem, however, by simply typing the TERMINAL command, I can turn it into an intelligent terminal and communicate over the NATAL network with the National Research Council's PDP-10 or with a number of other researchers in other universities, some of them using traditional terminals and others using what could be called home computers as intelligent terminals.

The difference is that when the traditional terminal users disconnect from the line they have nothing but a keyboard and screen, whereas the home computer user has a system with some of the attributes of the larger computers.

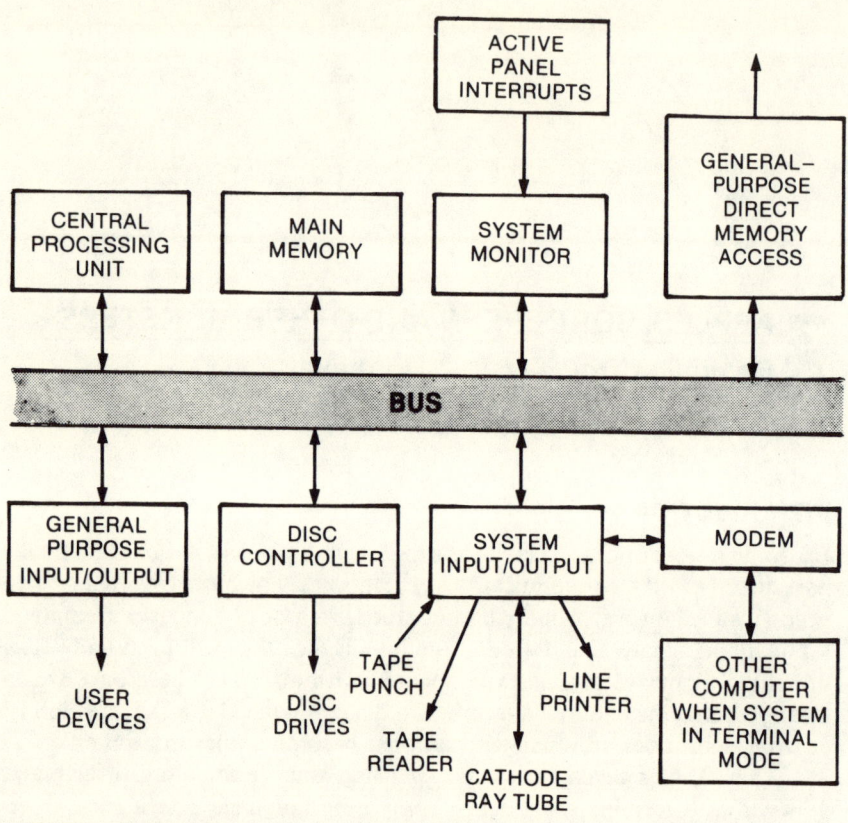

As John Madden has made very clear, the new networks will be interactive. No longer will the world be divided into senders and receivers. Everyone will be both. Now it is true that some people will still chose to remain as receivers only, passively accepting whatever data is stored in the large computers of the new media complexes that arise, but the technology will be working against that and we can hope that the regulatory bodies will follow the natural flow of the technology into diversity and multiplicity rather than opposing it.

The individual will be able to do more than write to the Secretary of State however, or establish a floundering magazine. The individual or collective will be able to produce information for the network with a relatively small investment and to allow access to that information at a price which will be low and should not be subject to monopolistic pricing.

It is true that in five years your existing computer may be available for about the current price of a calculator, but in the meantime you will have learned a great deal about the techniques, languages and equipment necessary to participate in the coming networks as an information producer.

PURCHASE DECISIONS

This chapter is designed for those who might want to make an investment now in order to be better prepared for the future arrival of the networks. What will you be able to do with one of these systems? Certainly not everything that your uncle Fred does with his IBM 370 at Imperial Widgets.

If you have 15 employees and 3000 customers all of whom owe you money and 1900 items in inventory and 40 suppliers clamouring to be paid on time, you'd have to be suicidal to expect that Radio Shack would be your ideal partner, despite the ads. On the other hand, if your uncle Fred laughs at your "toy", you might ask him what the connect and running time cost would be for you to hook up to his IBM 370 long enough to teach yourself how to program in BASIC. Unless you're a genius, those charges could probably pay for your home computer.

Even though you're only starting with a basic system, you might consider pricing the full package: that is, what would it cost to move up to colour graphics, 64K, double density dual-drive floppy discs, with a printer, plus a disc-based operating system, BASIC, FORTRAN, COBOL and PASCAL and enough software to do word-processing and text-editing and run a reasonable accounting system. Not all of that will be required by every user, of course, and not all of it has to be purchased from the original supplier, but some machines are more amenable to expansion than others and an extra three or four hundred dollars spent at the beginning can result in a savings of three or four times that if you ever do expand.

It is very difficult to pick out the best home computer, as most store owners will agree. If they don't, be somewhat suspicious.

There are three major considerations. What do you really want to do with it? Will the company still be around in 12 months? How much do you know about electronics and programming?

The small computer market is right in the middle of a transition from hobby machines to consumer products. There is no ideal unit that is so far ahead of the competition that it ranks as an automatic winner. Nor is it possible really to design such a perfect unit, because if it is to do all that is necessary for all users, it would no longer be priced in the consumer-product range. So the best strategy (we assume you want a computer and have a thousand dollars handy) is to get a working knowledge of the basic components and than to select a machine which *you* can use.

A standard microcomputer in the thousand dollar range is made up of three visible components: the keyboard for input, a TV screen for output, and a cassette recorder for storing data.

We will describe each of these three basic components and the invisible electronics that form the computer system itself.

Current Systems

We will discuss the three most popular computers available in the 1980's: the model I, 16K level 2 TRS–80 from Radio Shack; the basic Apple II Plus from Apple Computer Company; and the 'new' 16K PET (or CBM) with full keyboard. These will be referred to as TRS–80, Apple and PET, respectively. Radio Shack, Commodore and Apple will be producing all-new systems every few years.

New Systems

The newest computers are from Atari, Texas Instruments, APF and Mattel. Details of the Texas Instruments (TI) and Mattel computers are sketchy. By 'Atari' and 'APF' we mean a 16K Atari 800 and the Imagination Machine. TI is the TI 99/4 computer as of 79/80 and 'Intellivision' is the 1980 Intellivision System with keyboard and master units.

Uses

The standard microcomputer system is, in fact, relatively low-powered. The slow speed of the cassette recorder means that you can't store large amounts of data, such as business files or books, for easy availability. You can use a computer for eight digit calculations, games, small-scale teaching programs, etc. One of the best uses of a small computer is to teach its owner about computers. To use this standard computer for anything else, you have to expand it with add-on components. This is the reason many of the professional, large-computer owners feel that most current microcomputers are only toys.

CPU

The Central Processing Unit. A slightly bigger than normal chip. Add logic chips, the memory chips and some input/output control chips, and you have a small computer.

The CPU figures out how to get the input, what to do with it, where to store it and how to output the results. If you want to get a system that is more than just a toy, you will eventually need one of the new 16 bit CPU's. They are faster and can access a lot more memory. However, at the time of this writing, there doesn't seem to be a home system which uses a 16 bit brain and has good software support.

If you want to tell a CPU what to do, you have to tell it in machine language. And the different CPU chips, as 6502, 8080 and Z-80, all speak a different dialect. For this reason, it is much easier to program the CPU in BASIC.

User Programmability

Programming provides the computer with a list of instructions. You may have heard that machines can only understand 1's and 0's. In fact, they accept 'machine language', more complex instructions built from 1's and 0's, usually in 8-bit blocks. Each bit is a 1 or 0. An 8-bit block is called a byte.

The next step to an easier-to-program instruction set is called assembler, but this language still uses obscure mnemonics which makes it difficult. From assembler, high level languages are programmed. These include BASIC and FORTRAN, and use easy to understand words.

There are two types of high level languages: interpreters and compilers. An interpreter executes each command instantly, one at a time. A compiler translates or compiles your whole program (series of commands) into machine language, and then executes them. An interpreter is easier to learn and edit programs in, but a compiler executes commands at a quicker pace.

If you want to write your own software (games, teaching, business programs) or if you want to learn about computers, then you will require some form of computer language. Only Intellivision, at this time, does not have a programming language for the user.

Most computers have the language built in, in ROM memory (see the section on memory for an explanation), since the language itself is a program in machine language.

With a computer language in fixed ROM, however, you can never change to another language. Some systems have removable ROM cartridges so you can change language at will. Atari has BASIC and assembler cartridges available and Pascal and PILOT cartridges are promised. The Sorcerer, from Exidy, also has an assembler cartridge available. TI and APF computers have cartridge capability, but the programming language itself is in normal ROM.

Documentation

If you are a beginner, this is one of the most important areas to consider before buying a computer. There should be several different manuals included and they should clearly explain the capabilities of the computer in non-technical language. If you can, buy the manuals beforehand and read through them. This should also give you an idea of what the system is like. If the computer is new, be careful; the manuals may be full of errors.

Input

In order to 'talk' to a computer, you will need some sort of a device that sends electronic signals into the computer's brain. The usual method is a keyboard that is built into, and comes with, the computer. The keyboard is so named because it is a group of typewriter-like keys. There are some mutant keyboards that respond to heat rather than pressure, or have calculator-like rubber keys. For serious computing, it is best to have a keyboard of typewriter style, one that you will find comfortable over a long period. A keyboard of professional quality doesn't skip, feels good, and will stand up to heavy daily usage.

Options

For gaming and many other applications, some sort of hand held input device(s) will make your computer easier to use. Confusion results if several people are playing a fast-paced computer game and they are all trying to use one keyboard. It is also hard, if not impossible, to program multiple inputs from one device. The commonly used extra inputs are: joysticks, knobs (usually called paddles) and small groups of keys (usually called keypads), such as those found in arcade games. A pair of these devices with long cords and suitable computer attachments may come with your computer. Otherwise, they cost twenty dollars and up.

Another input device that is quite handy for editing computer data and entering pictures is the light pen. It is a pen-like object that can detect the difference between light and dark areas on a computer screen.

These are just a few simple options, but there are more. When you want to start adding complex things, such as vision and speech recognition (also known as cameras and microphones), you will most likely need extra electronics to convert the input signals into a language that the computer can comprehend.

Remember that if you are buying an extra device, regardless of function, you have to make sure the computer knows how to use it. (In other words, a game written for a light pen would not work with joysticks.)

If you want special input devices, you need a computer that can accept them. If you buy from an independent company, make sure that the component you buy is matched to your system, and that it will come with *all* the necessary electronics and connections. Look for detailed documentation and software.

Output

If you are planning to buy a computer system, you'll want it to do something besides make clicking noises while it thinks. The accessory that is taken for granted is the computer display screen. Even if you just want a computer for making synthesized music, you still need a display.

There are two kinds of computer displays. One is a monitor, a television that has been modified or specially built to accept only direct, non-broadcast video. These give a clear display but can be relatively expensive, especially the colour versions. Wherever possible, buy the unit provided or suggested by the manufacturer.

The other option is simply to use a home TV which has been adapted so it can receive the video signals generated by the computer. Such a converter connects into any TV via the antenna connections.

Text

Text consists of letters and numbers. A computer must be able to display small, typewriter quality characters in both upper and lower case. The screen should be large enough to hold at least 24 lines of text.

Some computers cannot have both text and graphics on the same screen at once. Consider whether you need this dual capability before purchase.

Graphics

Most systems provide some method for putting pictures on your display screen. Without such graphics capability a computer presents only typewriter symbols.

The lowest level graphics allow you (the programmer) to select from a predetermined group of shapes (which are the same size as letters) and then to put the shapes on the screen. You have to try and string them together to make a picture. The PET and Sorcerer use this approach, although Sorcerer allows you to create your own small shapes.

Better graphics allow you to turn on (or off) a dot anywhere on the screen and then colour the dot (on a colour TV) and connect it to another dot. The larger the dot, the more 'chunky' a picture will look. Large dots are called lo-res graphics, or just lo-res.

Even better are hi-res graphics, with tiny, tiny dots that allow you to make pictures of almost television quality. Make sure the computer language has easy-to-use graphics commands to draw pictures.

Unfortunately, hi-res graphics also take up a lot of RAM. See the Memory section for more information.

Sound

All of the new computers have either a built-in speaker or can produce sound effects through their TV speakers.

Sound effects can be used in games. Some computers can also play musical notes. Make sure the language chosen has good sound commands, so you can easily make up sound effects and play musical notes.

Speech

There are several ways of making a computer talk. APF, Mattel and Atari computers can control pre-recorded speech on a tape-recorder. This means, however, that to repeat a group of words the cassette recorder must be rewound.

Plug-in components are available for the Apple II and TRS-80 (with expansion box) which allow them to produce speech by selecting phonemes.

The TI computer has a plug-in component which works in the same way as their *Speak and Spell* game. It allows you to select from a group of words stored in ROM.

Printer

Printers are mechanical beasts that print out a variety of data at the computer's will. They are essential to a computerized business or to word-processing. If you are not involved with word-processing, accounting or other long programs, then you can get by without a printer quite well.

There are also printers that can print out some graphic designs as well as letters and numbers, but if you are interested in managing graphical information, a different species of printer called a plotter would be in order.

Some printers are very noisy, very slow, or much too small, so investigate well before purchasing.

In general, printers are expensive tools which are useful because they allow information put into a computer to be sent back in a non-electronic medium: paper.

Active Memory

Active memory uses memory chips inside a computer. All computers have memory. 1K of memory represents storage for about one thousand letters. A screenful of data takes up approximately 1K of memory. There are two kinds of memory chips: RAM and ROM.

RAM, or Random Access Memory, can be written to; that is, you can enter information into the active RAM memory and it will stay there until the machine is turned off. RAM is required if you want to write your own programs, since you need somewhere to store programs while you work on them.

Remember, even if you don't intend to write your own programs, many programs need to be loaded into RAM. Therefore, RAM capacity is an important consideration when purchasing. On systems like Apple and the Atari, RAM is used to store hi-res graphic pictures. So you really need at least

16K of RAM in your computer to store programs, pictures and data. Before you buy a system, find out how much RAM is included, whether or not more is available, and what additional RAM costs. If a manufacturer says that 48 K memory is available, find out how much of that is usable RAM and how much is ROM.

ROM means Read Only Memory. It cannot be used for your programs and data because it has already been pre-programmed, usually with the computer operating system and language. Removable ROM cartridges are also used on some systems. See the sections on User Programming and Expandibility for more information.

Storage Memory

Since RAM memory is lost when the machine is turned off, you need some way to store important programs and data until the computer is turned on again and you can load the information back into the memory. Cassettes and discs are the standard ways.

Cassettes

Tape recorders provide this capability by storing data on standard cassette tapes. Tape is quite inexpensive, but it loads programs and data slowly.

Some systems, such as APF and Intellivision, have their own tape recorders built in. Others, such as Atari, TRS–80 and PET, include a recorder for a standard price. Most other systems require you to provide your own. Hours can be spent adjusting the volume and tone controls on a home tape recorder so that programs can be loaded and saved to and from memory.

Discs

A disc is another means of holding programs and data when the machine is turned off. A disc looks like a flexible 45 record in a square paper envelope. Each disc (also called mini-disc or diskette) can hold about 80K of memory.

To read from and write to a disc, you need a disc drive, a small rectangular box. A few computers, like the Compucolor II, have a disc drive built-in. Disc drives usually cost about $700 and discs cost from $5 to $10 each.

Data is stored on a disc with magnetic pulses and is read off as the drive unit spins the diskette. Data can be read many times faster from a disc than from a cassette unit, allowing you to load large programs into memory in mere seconds.

The major advantage of a disc drive, however, is its ability to store

169

business records, students' progress reports, manuscripts, etc. for easy access and revision.

Discs require Disc Operating System (DOS) software. This can take up a lot of RAM. Adding DOS software to a 16K Atari leaves you with only 4K free memory.

CPM is a standard DOS.

Available Software

If you don't want to write all your own programs, there is a great variety of software available on ROM cartridges, cassette tapes, discs, and paper tapes from your computer maker, independent software vendors or the many computer magazines.

Computer magazines (especially ones for a specific system) will bring you new ideas, news and ads from the software vendors. If you choose a popular system, there should be lots of programs available.

You can get the programs at your computer store or by mail order. Just make sure you have the right system, language, memory size and accessories before ordering.

Magazines also print listings of programs, which you can type in yourself thus saving on the cost of tape or disc.

Software is crucial. Accounting, word-processing, mailing lists and file management all depend on fairly complex programs. So browse through a lot of magazines at a computer store and take a look at what is available before making a final decision on a system.

Expandability

If you ever want to grow or add more components (for example, a disc drive) then this is the most important factor. Right now there are three ways to expand:

1. The Apple Technique

This is the same method used in older systems. Inside Apple there are eight slots. Each slot can hold a small card or board, a collection of electronic components.

Some cards are interface cards. They allow you to hook up to standard printers and modems. There is also a disc controller card, which allows you to hook up two disc drive units.

Advantages: Since this is a standard approach, you are not limited to boards from Apple Company. There are music boards, clock boards, speech boards and even home control boards.

Disadvantages: It is expensive and takes up a lot of space.

2. The Atari Way

The Atari computer has two small slots for ROM programs as well as four larger slots which can hold longer, thinner rectangular boxes, such as the 10K operating system or 8K or 16K memory cartridges.

There is also one peripheral connector. You hook up disc drives and printers in chain. You can hook up a standard interface box to the chain, then hook modems and printers to each other and the interface box.

Advantages: Since you can change both the operating system and the programming language, the machine has great software flexibility. It is somewhat smaller than the Apple.

Disadvantages: There is no replacement operating system available at the time of this writing. There are a number of cords since each peripheral requires its own power supply. It seems likely that there will be a limit to the number of components you can put on the chain.

3. The Radio Shack Idea

This is really just a cheaper version of the Apple method. The standard computer can be connected to an expansion box which is just a number of empty slots, usually with some memory chips thrown in free. In this box, you can put the usual interface cards and disc controllers. This is the most common expansion system, used also by Exidy and APF.

The Exidy Sorcerer expansion box is noteworthy because it uses the standard S-100 bus and larger cards, allowing you an immense range of better peripherals designed for older computers.

Advantages: The actual computer can be inexpensive because no complex connection electronics are required.

Disadvantages: Although the base system is cheap, adding components can be more expensive because you have to buy the expansion box first.

Service

Before you buy, check out the repair shop. How many people are at work there? What's the backlog? How big are the workbenches? What testing equipment is on hand? And once your choice is narrowed down, do all you can to find some people who own the units on your short list. What have their expenses been? What does the owner own himself? What do the technicians own? How long have they been there? And be professional: budget ten percent of your purchase price per year for repairs.

Service varies not only from brand to brand, but from region to region and shop to shop. Repairs are very tricky and service is often the crucial factor in your decision.

Final Words

Chances are that shortly after you finally buy a computer, a newer and better model will appear. So you have to figure out why you need a computer and then select one that can fill your needs. Try to make sure the manufacturer will stay in business to repair your machine and invent new add-on components. If you can't write your own programs, then choose a machine with lots of available software.

And above all, try it. Go to your local computer store and sit down at the keyboard. Type in some programs. Work through the manuals step by step. Browse through the magazines. Make sure that the machine you are looking at is the exact model you will get.

But if you aren't satisfied with the eight bit Apples and Sorcerers, if you want something that is cheaper, easier to use and smarter, then you will have to wait a year or two for machines that can plug into the new TELIDON communications networks.

SHOPPING GUIDE

To aid you in making your decision a Shopping Guide is provided on the following pages. The various components discussed above are broken out so you can evaluate each computer and compare them feature by feature. Then, by comparing how each machine stacks up on the features which are of value to you, you will be able to come to a final decision about the machine you want to purchase.

1. Manuals: _____

_____

_____

2. Languages: _____

_____

_____

_____

3. Operating System: _____

4. Memory: _____

RAM

Max RAM in unit:_____

Max ROM in unit:_____

Cost:_____

Other information:_____

_____

ROM
Is there ROM memory built in? _____
If so, memory size and 'contents': _____
_____
_____

If ROM Pac slots are built in, specify number and memory capacity:
_____
_____
_____

Cassette
Are tape interfaces built in/required? _____
Baud rate: _____
Can a home tape recorder be used? _____
If not, specify price: _____
Other information: _____

Disc
Are disc interfaces built in/available? _____
Disc size (5 inch or 8 inch): _____
Max number of discs: _____
Disc capacity: _____
Price per disc drive (and interface if needed): _____

5. Input/Output
Keyboard
Type of keyboard/number of keys: _____
Other information: _____
Display
RF converters available/built in/required? _____
Monitors available? Price? _____
Extra information: _____
Characters
Rows/columns of alphanumerics: _____
Are lowercase characters built in? _____
Are graphics characters built in? _____
Extra information: _____
_____
_____

Graphics
Individually accessible point resolution is: _____
How many colours are available? _____
Can graphics, text and colour reside simultaneously on the CRT?
_____

Other information: _____

_____

_____

Printers
Are printer interfaces built in/required? _____
Specify type and speed of available printer(s): _____

_____

_____

_____

General
How many serial ports? _____
How many parallel ports? _____

6. Other
Are sound generation capabilities built-in/available? _____
If so, describe capabilities: _____

_____

Are human input devices (i.e. joysticks, keypads) or interfaces built in/available? _____

_____

Other information: _____

_____

_____

7. Available Software
Games: _____
Educational: _____
Text Editor: _____
Accounting: _____

ADDRESSES

Most of the successful models we discussed are available from local dealers. But if you want information only, you may find these addresses convenient.

Apple II
American: Apple Computer
          10260 Bandley Drive
          Cupertino CA 95014

Canadian: Available from Compucentre, Cesco and others.

Atari Models 400 and 800

American: 1265 Borregas Avenue
    Sunnyvale, California. 94086
Canadian: Electrohome of Canada
    809 Wellington Street West
    Kitchener, Ontario
    N2G 4J6

Commodore Pet (Personal Electronic Transactor)

American: Commodore Business Machines
    901 California Avenue
    Palo Alto, CA 94304

Canadian: Commodore Business Machines
    Pharmacy Avenue
    Agincourt, Ontario M1W 2K4
    Telephone: 416 449 4292

Compucolor Corporation Compucolor II

American: Compucolor Corporation
    P O Box 569
    Norcross, GA 30071
Canadian: Dealers in Vancouver, Toronto, Winnipeg.

Exidy Sorcerer

American: Exidy Inc.
    969 W Maude Avenue
    Sunnyvale, CA 94086

Canadian: Toronto, Ottawa, Edmonton, Vancouver, Calgary

Interact Electronics Interact Model I

American: Interact Electronics
    P O Box 8140 Ann Arbor
    MI 48107

    Canadian: Dealers in Toronto and Ottawa

Ohio Scientific Instruments Challengers CIP and C4P

American: Ohio Scientific Instruments
1333 S. Chillicote Road
Aurora OH 44202

Canadian: Available at Becterm Inc., Quebec;
Jackson Electronics, Nova Scotia;
Omega Computing, Ontario.
OJ Microcomputing, British Columbia

Texas Instruments "99/4"

American: Texas Instruments
Dallas, Texas 75265

Canadian: Consumer Product Sales
Richmond Hill, Ontario

SOFTWARE

This list is designed to illustrate just a few of the better software products available.

Digital Research

P O Box 579, Pacific Grove, California 93950.

CP/M (control program for microcomputers) is an operating system for 8080 or Z-80 systems using standard IBM 8-inch discs. It has become the 'de facto' standard for microcomputer disc systems and so there is a great deal of software available for it. The operating system is computer independent and comes with 4 small manuals, an assembler, debugger and editor as well as many built-in and 'transient' commands. CP/M will run with single or double density diskettes.

BASIC-E (also called E-Basic) is a compiler BASIC sometimes associated with CP/M. Avoid it at all costs; it is hard to work with and has many problems.

Contact Digital Research to find out what computers CP/M is operating on. They sell CP/M 2.0 and MP/M 1.0. The latter will let you connect a number of computers together.

Microsoft

10800 NE Eight Street, Suite 819, Bellevue, WA 98004.

Microsoft has written extended BASIC's for many small computers, including the APPLE, PET, TRS-80 Level II, OSI and Interact Level II.

176

Also available is a FORTRAN language for TRS-80 disc systems, a COBOL language for CP/M systems, assemblers and editors. We have found that some of these languages have subtle bugs, but the general workmanship is competent.

Available on disc through Lifeboat, and on ROM or cassette for some common microcomputers.

Lifeboat Associates

164 West 83rd Street, New York, N. Y. 10024.

A good deal of disc software advertised in other places can be purchased from Lifeboat Associates by mail. Microsoft products; XYBASIC; disc sorts; and business systems; for many diskette formats, such as CP/M, North Star, Sol Disc (Helios), and TRS-80.

They have recently announced a C Compiler for $110.00 which is quite satisfactory.

Mark Williams Co

1430 W. Wrightwood Avenue, Chicago, Illinois, 60614

XYBASIC is an excellent BASIC for those buying a language separately from their computer.

XYBASIC has a wide range of bit manipulation and process control functions. XYBASIC is oriented towards the programmer experienced in assembler and machine language, but the BASIC programmer can find normal BASIC commands. It is available on paper tape and disc as well as in ROM.

A good manual can be purchased separately or bought with this professional level basic. The same firm will provide an operating system for 16 bit machines and a number of high-level languages.

Tiny C Associates

P O Box 269, Holmdel, New Jersey. 07733.

Tiny C is a 'structured' language, and a subset of C, which is an advanced version of B (which was developed by Bell Telephone).

Despite the fact that Tiny C has no floating point capability, C itself is well known in academic circles; an excellent manual is included.

Approx. Cost: $100

Available for CP/M discs, TRS-80 Level II, North Star and 'Micropolis' discs, and through Lifeboat.

Books

The following books are divided according to difficulty. While this list does not include all of the good books available on computing, it will give the enthusiastic reader some places to get started.

Beginning Books

My Computer Likes Me When I Speak In Basic
by Robert Albrecht c/o P O Box 310, Menlo Park, CA, 94025

Your Own Computer
by Mitchell Waite and Michael Pardee
Howard Sams

Beginner's Guide to Home Computers
by Marvin Grosswirth
Doubleday Dolphin

A Simple Guide to Home Computers
by Steve Ditlea
A & W Publishers, Inc.

Personal Computing
By the Editors of Electronics Magazine
McGraw-Hill Ryerson

S-100 Bus Handbook
By David Bursky
McGraw-Hill Ryerson — Publishers

Basic For Home Computers
By Bob Albecht, LeRoy Finkel
Jerald R. Brown
John Wiley & Sons. 1978

Advanced Books:

Software Tools
By Brian Kernighan and P. J. Plauger
Addison-Wesley

The Basic Handbook
By Dr. David A Lien
Compusoft Publishing

The C Programming Language
By Brian Kernighan and Dennis Ritchie
Prentice-Hall

Applying Microprocessors
Laurence Altman and Stephen E Scrupski, (Snr. Editors)
Electronics
McGraw-Hill Ryerson

Magazines

Byte, Creative Computing, Interface Age and Kilobaud Microcomputing
are all good, general purpose magazines, (with lots of ads and new products), which attempt to cover all areas of interest. Except for stories on
proven crooks and some letters of complaint, none of them are very good at
tough consumer-oriented evaluation of hardware or software.

Byte (mainly hardware, a good magazine with wide circulation) monthly
  70 Main Street, Peterborough, NH 03458
  Subscriptions: $17.50
  P O Box 590, Martinsville, NJ 08836

Creative Computing (games, some hardware) monthly
  P O Box 789-M Morristown, NJ 07960
  Subscriptions: $23.00
  P O Box 789-M, Morristown, NJ 07960

Interface Age (business and home, software and hardware) monthly
  16704 Marquardt Avenue, Cerritos, CA 90701
  Subscriptions: $17.00
  P O Box 1234, Dept. IA/G, H, I, J, Cerritos, CA 90701

Kilobaud Microcomputing (general, some beginner articles)
  monthly
  Peterborough; N. H. 03458
  Subscriptions: $18.00
  Subscription Department, Box 997, Farmingdale, N.Y.

Other Magazines are more specialized:

Dr Dobbs Journal (Advanced software, reviews) monthly
except for July and December
Box E, 1010 Doyle Street, Menlo Park, CA 94025
Subscriptions: $16.00
Box E, Menlo Park, CA 94025

179

Electronics (Specialized for Engineers, excellent technical articles) monthly
1221 Avenue of the Americas, N. Y. N. Y. 10020
Subscriptions: $19.00
Box 400, Agincourt, Ontario.

On Computing (general and beginner) Quarterly
70 Main Street, Peterborough NH 03458
Subscriptions: $10.00
P O Box 307 Martinsville NJ 08836

Recreational Computing (some beginner articles, educational, games) bimonthly
P O Box 1263 El Camino Real, Box E, Menlo Park CA 94025
Subscriptions: $17.00
P O Box 1263, El Camino Real, Box E, Menlo Park, CA 94025

Computerdata, (for professionals, mainly large systems) monthly.
Suite 2504, 2 Bloor Street W. Toronto, Ontario M4W 3E2.
Subscriptions: $20.00.

Computing Canada (similar to above but some attention to minis and micros) twice monthly
211 Consumers Road, Suite 106, Willowdale, Ontario M2J 4G8
Subscriptions: $15.00
Circulation Department

Cips Review (for large systems, but CIPS will be publishing a magazine for home computers) bimonthly
243 College West, 5th Floor, Toronto, Ontario M5T 2Y1
Subscriptions: $15.00 (CIPS membership necessary)

COMPUTER DEALERS IN CANADA

Note: stores vary greatly in type and quality. There are Byte Shop type stores which are professional and concerned solely with home computers. There are other electronic outlets which carry home computers as one item. And finally there are stores started by people who are hackers themselves. Each type of store has its own advantages and disadvantages, but the ones who specialize in computers and carry products from a wide range of manufacturers can usually give the best advice and service.

British Columbia

Conti Electronics Ltd.
5656 Fraser Street
Vancouver, B.C.
V5W 2Z4
(604) 324-0505

Vulcan Computer System
20571 Fraser Hwy.
Langley, B.C.
(604) 530-8572

Basic Computer Group
1548 West 8th Avenue
Vancouver, B.C.
V6J 4R8
(604) 736-7474

Heathkit Electronic Centre
3058 Kingsway
Vancouver, B.C. V5R 5J7
(604) 437-7626

Kerrisdale Compute Micro
2071 W. 41st Avenue
Vancouver, B.C.
V6M 1Y7
(604) 263-0934

OJ Micro Computer
#1–6340 No. 3 Rd.
Richmond, B.C.
V6Y 2B3
(604) 270–9096

The Byte Shop
2151 Burrard St.
Vancouver, B.C.
V6J 3H7
(604) 738-2181

Victoria Personal Computers Ltd.
780 Fort Street
Victoria, B.C.
V8W 1H2
(604) 388-6212

Alberta

The Computer Shop
3515-18th Street S.W.
Calgary, Alta.
T2T 4T9
(403) 243-0301

TJB Microsystems Ltd.
Box 4844 (10991 124 Street)
Edmonton, Alta
T5M OH9
(403) 455-5298

Orthon Computers
12411 Stony Plain Rd.
Edmonton, Alta.
(403) 488-2921
T5N 3N3

CompuShop
#103-723 14th St. N.W.
Calgary, Alta.
T2N 2A4
(403) 283-0751

Also
#107-4014 Macleod Trail SE
Calgary, Alta.
T2G 2R7
(403) 243-3846

Heathkit Electronic Centre
12863-97th St.
Edmonton, Alta.
T5E 4C2
(403) 475-9331

Spectra Electronic Services Ltd.
329 8th Ave. S.W.
Calgary, Alta.
T2P 1C4
(403) 233-2249

Saskatchewan

Micro Shack Ltd.
Box 3733 (333 Park St.)
Regina, Saskatchewan
S4N 5B2
(306) 543-4079

Digital Service
1310 East Centre
Saskatoon, Sask.
S7J 3A9
(306) 374-8908

Datatec Computer Systems Ltd.
344–2nd Ave. S.
Saskatoon, Sask.
S7M OY6
(306) 653-2641

Custom Computing Systems
#3-204 2nd Ave. North
Saskatoon, Sask.
S7K 2B5
(306) 242-7808

Manitoba

Percomptron Inc.
c/o The Byte Shop
665 Century Street
Winnipeg, Man.
R3H 0L9
(204) 774-1656

Computerland of Winnipeg
715 Portage Ave.
Winnipeg, Man.
R3G OM8
(204) 772-9519

Heathkit Electronic Centre
1315 Portage Ave.
Winnipeg, Man.
R3G 0V3
(204) 783-3334

Advance Industrial Electronics of
Canada Ltd.
576 Wall St.
Winnipeg, Man.
R3G 2T3
(204) 772-0386

Ontario

Toronto

Computer Workshops Ltd.
1240 Bay Street Mall
Toronto, Ont.
M5R 2A7
(416) 923-1917

The Home Computer Centre
6101 Yonge Street
Willowdale, Ont.
M2M 3W2
(416) 222-1165 or 2207

Computer Mart Ltd.
1543 Bayview Avenue
Toronto, Ont.
M4G 3B5
(416) 484-9708

Hamtraders
45 Brisbane Road, Unit 18
Downsview, Ont.
M3J 2K1
(416) 661-8800

Richvale Telecommunications
Unit 18, 10610 Bayview Avenue
Richmond Hill, Ont.
L4C 3N8
(416) 884-4165

T.Eaton Stores

The Bay Stores

The Robert Simpson Co.

The Computer Place
186 Queen St. W.
Toronto, Ont.
M5V 1Z1
(416) 598-0262

Trintronics
186 Queen St. W.
Toronto, Ont.
M5V 1Z1
(416) 598-0260

Compucentre
20 Bloor St. E.
(The Bay Centre)
Toronto, Ont.
M4W 3G7
(416) 961-5978

Hamilton-Avnet
3688 Nashua Drive
Units G&H
Mississauga, Ont.
L4V 1M5
(416) 677-7432

Computer Methods Ltd.
Suite 205, 2249 Yonge Street
Toronto, Ont.
M4S 2B1
(416) 482-5100

Comspec Communications
944 Wilson Avenue
Downsview, Ont.
M3K 1E7
(416) 633-2871

Batteries Included
Village By the Grange
71 McCaul Street
Toronto, Ont.
M5T 2X1
(416) 596-1405

Efstonscience
3500 Bathurst St.
Toronto, Ont.
M6A 2C6
(416) 787-4583

House of Computers Inc.
368 Eglinton Avenue W.
Toronto, Ont.
M5N 1A2
(416) 482-4336

Nakcomm Sales & Service
80 Hale Road, Unit 7
Brampton, Ont.
L6W 3N9
(416) 459-7616

Heathkit Electronic Centre
1478 Dundas St. East
Mississauga, Ont.
L4X 2R7
(416) 277-3191

Datamex
14 Leswyn
Toronto, Ont.
M6A 1K2
(416) 787-1208

Ottawa

Focus Scientific Ltd.
409 Rideau St.
Ottawa, Ont.
K1N 5Y9
(613) 236-7767

Compumart
411 Roosevelt Ave. (show room)
Box 6132, Station J (mailing
    address)
Ottawa, Ont.
K2A 1T2
(613) 725-3192

Computer Innovations
171 Slater St.
Ottawa, Ont.
K1P 5H7
(613) 233-8413

Wackid Radio Television
    Laboratories Ltd.
312 Parkdale Ave.
Ottawa, Ont.
K1Y 1G3
(614) 728-1821

Hamilton Avnet International
    (Canada) Ltd.
1735 Courtwood Crescent
Ottawa, Ont.
K2C 3J2
(613) 226-1700

Heathkit Electronic Centre
866 Merivale Road
Ottawa, Ont.
K1Z 5Z6
(613) 728-3731

Rest of Ontario

BMB Compuscience Canada Ltd.
363 Main St.
Milton, Ont.
L9T 1P7
(416) 878-7890

Custom Electronics
Box 18, R.R. #1
Chalk River, Ontario
K0J 1J0
(619) 589-2083

Colormaster Inc.
3095 Forest Glade Drive
Windsor, Ont.
N8R 1W6
(519) 735-7042

The Computer Circuit Ltd.
737 Richmond,
London, Ont.
N6A 3H2
(519) 672-9370

North Star Computer Ltd.
776 Lasalle Boulevard

Sudbury, Ont.
P3A 4V4
(705) 566-6441

Orion Electronics
40 Lancaster St. W.
Kitchener, Ont.
N2H 4S9
(519) 576-9902

Quebec

Futurbyte
1191 Phillips Square
Montreal, Que.
H3B 3C9
(514) 861-3120

Central Distributors Ltd.
350 Des Erables
Lachine, Que.
H8S 2P9

Hamilton Avnet
2670 Sabourin St.
St. Laurent, Que.
H4S 1G2
(514) 331-6443

Becterm Inc
1277 Cheminx
St. Jean Bernieres
Quebec,
G0S 1C0

Irisco Ordinateurs
537 Boul. Charest Est.
Quebec, Que.
G1K 3J2
(418) 647-4422

T. Eaton Co.
677 Ste. Catherine St. W.
Montreal Que.
H3B 3Y6

Cesco Electronics Ltd.
4050 Jean Talon Street W.
Montreal Que.
H4P 1W1
(514) 735-5511

Heathkit Electronic Centre
795 Legendre St. E.
Montreal, Que.
H2M 1H1
(514) 384-9160

Compucentre Computer Centre
    Ltd./Ltee
9200 Claveau St.
Ville D'Anjou, Que.
H1J 1Z4
Branches in Place Bonaventure,
Montreal, Que. and Toronto
Eaton Centre, Toronto, Ont.

New Brunswick

Interactive Computer Systems,
    Ltd.
105 Fir Court
Fredericton, N.B.
E3A 2E9
(506) 455-8994

Nova Scotia

MiniComp Systems
5666 Stanley St.
Halifax, N.S.
B3K 2G1
(902) 455-5123

Kobetek Systems Ltd.
R.R. #1
Wolfville, N.S.
B0P 1X0
(902) 542–2500

Lantz Electronics Ltd.
15 Clifford St.
North Sydney, N.S.
B2A 1X2
(902) 794-3102

Jackson Electronics
2777 St. Margarets Bay Rd.
Halifax, N.S.

EPILOGUE
David Godfrey

The concepts of time and space reflect the significance of media to civilization. . . . Materials that emphasize time favour decentralization and hierarchical types of institutions, while those that emphasize space favour centralization and systems of government less hierarchical in character. Large-scale political organizations such as empires must be considered from the standpoint of two dimensions, those of space and time, and persist by overcoming the bias of media which over-emphasize either dimension. They have tended to flourish under conditions in which civilization reflects the influence of more than one medium and in which the bias of one medium toward decentralization is offset by the bias of another medium towards centralization. *

Although we may have covered a good deal of ground in these two hundred or so pages, there are still more questions posed than an editor would like to see in a complete and coherent book. Since these range from the philosophical to the mundane, perhaps the best way to proceed is with a sampling: Harold Innis, pornography, the arts, games, advertising, netwirks and netwarks, consumer power and the nature of boundaries.

This book began with two quite diverse questions, whose range Innis would have probably enjoyed. At the practical level, I was led to the work of the TELIDON team by my search for ways to help ensure that the publishing industry in Canada continued its symbolic survival. Over the past few decades, that sector has shown great adaptability in absorbing modern technology quickly in order to stay one step ahead of the American avalanche; as one result, many a small press like Coachhouse is operating with some very sophisticated technology that might not be justified by its size except for the dangers posed to its very survival by the most open border in the world.

* *Harold A. Innis,* Empire and Communications, *University of Toronto Press, 1977, p. 7.*

187

At that practical level, TELIDON represented both a closing of a certain door and a magician's wand. TELIDON was already a book that moved at the speed of light; what chance therefore, did a "real" book have? Time to close down the small presses. But what, in balance, were the possibilities for this new and unreal "book"? Were they as unlimited as they appeared?

At the theoretic level, this quite practical puzzle led me to wonder what that wise old man of communications and power, Harold Innis, would have said if he had managed to stay alive long enough to observe this moment.

A great deal of Innis's theory is rooted in the dichotomy presented above. Innis assumes, with some very thorough historical backup, that media are either hard, permanent and conducive to religious, time-oriented societies, or light, easily transported and conducive to military empires whose goal is the conquering of space.

These modes of communication and thus of society alternate. As one reaches a peak and centralizes power, the other (via some improvement in communication technology such as the invention of papyrus, or the alphabet, or paper, or the printing press) springs up again on the outreaches of the empire and begins its own slow climb towards power and glory and eventual decay.

But what is this new media, computer-communications? Whose "side" is it on in social terms? A case can certainly be made for the conquering of space by militaristic elements; finding someone in this area of research who has not at one time or another worked for "defense" establishments of one kind or another is quite rare. On the other hand, although the permanence may not be apparent and may not be utilized, it is certainly there. What we are dealing with are messages stored in rock and crystal, unnatural though those silicon rocks and bubble-memory crystals might be at their birth. How long could a message last, stored within a silicon chip? The technology is capable at once of both incredible speed and unusual permanence.

Historically, there seems little doubt that we are ready for a hinterland surge of time-oriented, religious forces expressed in a suitable new medium. Innis would find the rise of Ayatollah Khomeini quite significant, representing the resurgence of hierarchical power-centres, with religion playing a prominent role in the conquering of time. The banning of radio in Kohmeini's Iran when that medium was used for banal and secular purposes would cause Innis to nod his head sagely.

But a contemporary application of Innis tends to raise more questions than it answers. Innis himself would say, of course, that like all societies we are doomed not to understand ourselves in any real sense since our mode of understanding is so strongly conditioned by our means of communication. Perhaps all we can say then is that the new medium will create a vantage-point for intellectual thought, from which we may be able to understand how we *were* in the days of print, radio and Hertzian TV, but whose cost will be the inability to perceive how thinking from that very vantage-point affects our ability to see where we *are* and what we are "understanding."

About pornography Innis is more reticent than about empire. And we have imitated him in that respect. But that old art form will obviously not be particularly vulnerable to these new technologies, indeed, quite the opposite. Many channels, private viewing, inexpensive reproduction, sound and colour graphics combined? The best of Yonge Street, we may be sure, will be available, in more than one form, in nearly every home in the country. The only advantage of cheap, instant, eight-colour porn that much of the society may be able to agree on is the pressure it will put on all Carriers to occupy a position as neutral as that of a postman delivering the little package from Loveshops in its brown paper wrapper.

One unexpected aspects, to which we have been able to devote almost no time whatsoever so far, will be the growth of game playing on the media. As befits a Protestant society, there seems little mention of this in the PRESTEL manuals or the early promotion for TELIDON. But if one looks at the current actual utilization of home-computers, or at the common tales from many large systems of how game-playing finally had to be banned since vast amounts of user time were obviously being devoted to such non-productive activities, it is relatively easy to forecast a similar response from larger public participation in these toys; up to 30% of use of the Electronic Highways may be involved with games. Indeed the art/game may become the most natural form of the medium as miniaturization is brought into public acceptance by means of games which utilize the techniques of the new systems in powerful but human ways, allowing artists of a new kind within the society to bring together many diverse elements (myth, simulation, historical databanks, psychology) in order to create new works which will eventually gain a genre/title, just as the novel finally gained a terminology of its own many decades after the printing press made that art form a possibility.

Whether or not advertising follows a path of parallel creativity is an unanswerable question at the moment. The advertising agency will be in some danger unless it adapts quickly. The ad man is a middle-man whose function is to maintain the distance between Carrier and commercial Content. The newspaper or magazine, that is to say, must at least appear to be neutral and avoid the outright blandishments of large advertisers. As the links between advertiser and consumer become more direct, this particular function of the ad man will disappear and agencies will be forced to rely far more on their actual technical skills. Corporations may then find it more economical and reassuring to hire such technical skills directly.

There are two approaches the Electronic Highway might follow in regard to advertising. One would acknowledge the nature of the technology and allow the consumer to recognize messages from corporations as precisely that: information from Ford, Air Canada or Pornography International. The second, and more probable, approach would be to let the form of the prior media influence the content of the new media, just as Gutenberg felt constrained to use vellum and flowered capitals within his Mainz Bibles. Thus, rather than providing information directly, the corporation would attempt to find traditional categories of information, such as news, sports, weather, stock market report, comics, etc., and "sponsor" one or some combination of these. The corporation would pay for the production and updating of these information services; the consumer would receive them "free" but would "pay" the price of watching interspersed frames of traditional advertising adapted to the new media.

Although the first might be considered by the majority to be the ideal, it could not be legislated into being by preventing the second. Given the goal of allowing all citizens and groups the freest possible access to the system, it would be no more possible to censor advertising than any other type of content. The counter-weights, rather than legislation, would be the strength of consumer groups in terms of their own access to the Highways and their provision of hard-nosed evaluations of products and corporations, plus the general cheapness of the information, especially the most popular. Inevitably too, some basement genius will develop a filter tuned to the names of all the major corporations which will easily attach to each NABU and bleep out any frames containing the names of such firms if so requested (1).

One problem which the term Electronic Highway imposes on our understanding of what is likely to happen is that the metaphor counteracts the essential fluidity of the system. We will need some new terms that force us to think of *netwirks* or *floworks* or *netwarks:* specific sub-networks that are designated with some degree of permanence ranging from a few minutes to years. Provided that the overall network was established properly from the beginning, an almost infinite variety of netwirks or netwarks could be available. A given individual might belong to a few or to a great many of these, some of which would be accessed frequently and some only rarely. A farm co-operative might establish a netwark that had its own databank and for which an annual support fee of several hundred dollars might be paid in exchange for a vast array of specific services and information. A smaller netwirk might be nothing more than a group of people who liked to keep in touch in between their annual trip to the Grey Cup.

What this does to the nature of boundaries is not hard to see. The individual group will have a far greater range of choice as to the degree of definition it wishes to impose upon itself. Just as new social groups, some of which are still with us today, formed out of the knowledge they gained from the bibles which Gutenberg and those who followed him provided, so will we have new groups form out of the far larger body of fact, wisdom and revelation they are able to store within their own databanks. In Chapter One, Madden presented one scenario, with a clear split between users and non-users. What seems equally possible is a variety of degrees of firmness attached to any given sub-network. Some might be game clubs of, say, Level III international chess players, others might be based on Greenpeace-type activities, but such examples do not exhaust the possibilities. Just as the earlier electronic systems seemed to have intensified nationalism and regionalism rather than creating a one-world, global village, so may the entirely unexpected happen with this new media. The clanning together of human groups for security, reassurance and expression of the will to state a social and individual presence is one of the forces about which we know the least. It is a force that more than equals the new technologies we have examined as major influences in the coming decades. Any media which we develop seems destined to partially express itself in capturing the mysteries and complexities of human community. But since the media itself, however powerful a force, is ultimately absorbed within the frantic variety of those human communities, it always ends up as part of the mystery and complexity rather than as the means of containment.

This unusual and magical revolution will, perhaps luckily, still not pass beyond that particular historical limit.

Victoria, August, 1980

REFERENCES

1. For further comments on this subject see Godfrey, Dave, "Videotex and the Advertising Media in the 1980's". In *Inside Videotex,* proceedings from the March 13th and 14th 1980 Infomart Seminar in Toronto.

GLOSSARY

absolute address (also known as Direct address): The address or label assigned by the computer manufacturer to an actual memory storage location, as opposed to a relative address, which would not be known until the execution of the program. See also **address.**

absolute assembler: An assembler (or program which translates a symbolic language into the computer's machine language) that produces code in which all references are absolute addresses.

access: The ability to obtain information from, or place information into, storage.

access time: The amount of time required to access the contents of a memory location. This limitation is imposed by the speed of the memory circuitry.

accumulator: A processor register, or electronic counting circuit, to which numbers may be added or subtracted in order to store the accumulated total. A basic part of the Central Processing Unit.

ACIA (Asynchronous Communications Interface Adapter): See **UART.**

acoustic coupler: A form of MODEM that permits attachment of an ordinary telephone handset so that digital information can be transmitted over voice-grade telephone lines.

A/D (Analog-to-Digital) conversion: The conversion of an analog signal into a digital equivalent. An A/D converter measures an input voltage and outputs a digitally encoded number corresponding to that voltage.

address: An identifying number (often hexadecimal or decimal) used to describe a location in computer memory.

ALGOL (ALGOrithmic Language): Used primarily in scientific applications. A mathematical-type compiler or interpreter language. Has gained much wider acceptance in Europe than in North America. Dialects include MAD and JOVIAL.

193

algorithm: An orderly procedure (akin to a recipe) for obtaining a particular result or solving a problem. Algorithms are often expressed in mathematical terms.

Allouette I: The first research satellite sent into orbit by a country (Canada) other than the USA or USSR.

alphanumeric: Alphabetic and numeric characters.

ANSI (American National Standards Institute).

ALU (Arithmetic Logic Unit): The portion of the central processor that executes all mathematical and logical functions.

analog: One of the two main types of computer (the other is the digital). Quantities are represented and processed without the use of a language. The representation and measurement of the performance or behaviour of the system under investigation takes the form of continuously variable physical conditions (analogies) such as voltages, currents, temperatures or pressure.

analog input: A continuously variable quantity which the computer can convert into numbers that can be used by a program. Analog input is used in many game playing programs.

analog output: A voltage or other physical quality which the computer can produce, proportional to a number generated by a program. Controlling a robot with a computer is an example of using analog output. Another example would be a music synthesizer.

Anik I: The first in a series of Canadian domestic satellites. From the Inuit word meaning "brother".

Anik B, Anik C, Anik D: A series of Canadian communications satellites planned to become operational in 1978, 1981 and 1982 respectively.

APL (A Programming Language): Emphasizes operations on groups of data. Most operations are designated by a single symbol rather than a textual verb.

applications program: A program dedicated to a specific purpose or application. Applications programs are considered distinct from systems programs.

architecture: The internal configuration of a processor including its registers and instruction set.

argument: A value (an independent variable) passed to a subroutine or function.

ARPANET (Advanced Research Project Agency NETwork): A communication network developed by the Advanced Research Project Agency in the USA. It was the first large scale *packet switched network.*

array: A list of numbers or strings (or other entities in more sophisticated systems), elements of which can be referred to by their position in the list.

ASCII (American Standard Code for Information Interchange): Computers use a numerical representation for all characters (i.e., the uppercase and lowercase English alphabet, numbers and special symbols). This standard, consisting of all the above characters and 32 control codes, specifies which number will stand for each character. Since each character is represented by a unique 7-bit binary number, one ASCII-encoded character can be stored in one byte of computer memory. All personal computers use this standard.

assembler: A systems program that translates assembly-language programs into executable machine-level code (that is, into the computer's native language).

assembly language: A low-level programming aid that permits the programmer to use mnemonics instead of numerical op codes and alphanumeric labels instead of absolute memory addresses. It is similar in structure to the computer's native language, but is more convenient to use.

asynchronous communication: Data transmission where the time interval between characters is allowed to vary.

asynchronous computer: The performance of each operation starts as a result of a signal either that the previous operation has been completed, or that the parts of the computer required for the next operation are now available.

attenuation: The process of reducing the amplitude of an electrical signal without appreciable distortion. Achieved most successfully using fibre-optics.

automaton: A Machine or control

mechanism that follows automatically a predetermined sequence of operations or responds to encoded instructions. See also **Robot.**

backplane: The circuitry and mechanical elements used to connect the boards of a system. See also **motherboard** and **card frame.**

BASIC **(Beginner's All-purpose Symbolic Instruction Code):** A compiler or interpreter language that is easy to learn. Used with most time-sharing and mini-computer systems. Oriented toward beginners rather than experienced programmers. Numerous incompatible versions exist, often called dialects: CBASIC, MBASIC, XYBASIC.

batch: A group of separate programs loaded together into an intermediate memory of a computer and then later processed as a single unit.

batch processing: The control technique of grouping similar input items (a batch of programs) for handling during the same run. Contrasted with continuous processing.

baud: A measure of the speed with which information can be communicated between two devices. If the information is, for example, in the form of alphabetic characters, then 300 baud usually coresponds to about 30 characters per second. The number of bits transmitted or received per second.

baudot: A 5-bit character code. Since five bits only permit 2^5 or 32 permutations, this character set is limited in comparison to ASCII.

BCD **(Binary-Coded Decimal):** A method of encoding decimal digits in the form of 4-bit binary numbers.

benchmark: A test that compares the performance characteristics of several devices, programs or systems.

binary: The base-two number system. It uses only the digits 0 and 1. The number 10 in the decimal system, which has ten different digits and a base or radix of ten, is represented as 1010 in the binary system.

bipolar: A type of circuit that uses conventional PNP or NPN transistors rather than FET's.

bipolar RAM: The most expensive, ultra-high speed computer memory system; random-access memory with two charges of opposite polarity.

bit: A single binary digit. A unit of information content corresponding to the decision between one of the two possible states. Also, the smallest unit of measurement of capacity in a memory storage device.

board: A card that contains circuitry for one or more specific functions, such as memory or interfacing.

Boolean algebra: A branch of symbolic logic in which logical propositions and operations are indicated by operators such as "and," "or," "not" and "either," analogous to mathematical signs. Used in the design of digital computers. Named after the 19th-century mathematician George Boole.

196

bootstrap: A short loader program that loads a more sophisticated loader into memory. That loader, in turn, loads the desired program. The term bootstrap arises from the idea that the computer is picking itself up by its bootstraps. In other words, it progresses from the bootstrap to the loader to the main program itself.

branch: See **jump.**

breadboard: An electronics design aid that allows a circuit to be constructed, tested and modified more easily than with printed circuit or wire-wrapping techniques.

break: A key which is used to interrupt a computation and return the computer to a user-input mode.

breakpoint: A debugging aid. When a breakpoint is encountered in a program, execution of the program temporarily halts.

broad band: In electronics, a band covering a wide range of frequencies.

bubble memory: See **magnetic-bubble memory.**

buffer: Memory area in a computer or peripheral used for temporary storage of information that has just been received. The information is held in the buffer until the computer or device is ready to process it. Hence, a computer or device with memory designated as a buffer area can process one set of data while more sets are arriving.

buffered computer: A computer which provides for simultaneous input-output and process operations.

bug: A programming error. Also refers to the cause of any hardware or software malfunction.

burning: The process of programming a Read-Only Memory.

bus: The circuitry in a backplane that allows transmission of electrical signals from one board to another.

bus structure: The definition of a bus in terms of its mechanical requirements and the functions of its lines. A memory board designed for the S-100 bus, for example, would not be compatible with a computer using the IEEE-488 bus or the SS-50 bus.

bypass capacitor: A capacitor used to reduce electrical noise from the power supply.

byte: In data processing, a sequence of adjacent binary digits (usually eight) operated on as a word, but usually shorter than a word. The values of the bits can be varied to form as many as 2^8 or 256 permutations. So, one byte of memory can represent an integer from 0 to 255 or from -127 to $+128$.

CAI (Computer-Assisted Instruction).

CAL (Computer-Assisted Learning).

call: An instruction that invokes a subroutine.

capacitance: The property of an electric nonconductor that permits the storage of energy as a result of electric displacement when opposite surfaces of the non-conductor are maintained at a difference of potential.

capacitor: An assembly on one or more pairs of conductors separated by insulators, used to obtain an appreciable capacitance, sometimes of a specified value. The two conductors are called electrodes or plates, and the insulator, which may be solid, liquid, or gaseous, is called the dielectric.

card frame: An enclosure that holds a system's boards in place.

Cathode Ray Tube: See CRT.

CCD's (Charged-Coupled Devices): A medium speed, volatile memory system, less expensive than magnetic-bubble memory. A CCD stores packets of electrical charge in movable chains, and as the charges pass by a station, they can be "read".

CEEFAX: The largest fully operational teletext service. It's run by the BBC in the UK.

Central Processing Unit: See **CPU**

chaining: The process of having one program transfer control to another program.

chalcogen: Any of the elements oxygen, sulfur, selenium and tellurium.

chalcogenide: A binary compound of a chalcogen with a more electropositive element or radical.

character set: The repertoire of characters that an output device can display or print. Two common character sets are 96-character ACSCII, which includes all ASCII

197

characters except the 32 control codes, and 64-character ASCII, which includes all ASCII characters except the control codes, the lowercase alphabet and several other symbols.

Charged-Couple Devices: See CCD's.

checksum: A method of detecting errors when information is being loaded into a computer from magnetic tape or paper tape. The checksum is the sum of the numerical values of the bytes on the tape. As the tape is loaded, the checksum is computed. After the loading is complete, this value is compared with the checksum value that was placed on the tape when it was generated. If the two are equal, the information is assumed to have been loaded without error. Of course, two or more errors may have balanced out.

chip: An integrated circuit.

clock: A device that generates electronic timing signals. Clock signals are often used to synchronize certain system operations.

CMOS (Complementary Metal-Oxide Semiconductor): A type of integrated circuit whose output structure consists of an N-type MOSFET and a P-type MOSFET in series.

coaxial cable: A transmission line that consists of a tube of electrically conducting material surrounding a central conductor held in place by insulators. Used to transmit telegraph, telephone and television signals of high frequency. Also called coaxial line.

COBOL(COmmon Business Oriented Language): A compiler or interpreter language developed in the USA as a possible international common language program for commercial applications of computers.

code: To write instructions for a computer system; to classify data according to arbitrary tables; to use a machine language; to program; to convert analog signals to digital.

CODEC (COder-DECoder): an electrical circuit which converts (or codes) an analog waveform into a digital code (i.e. a series of pulses) which, conversely, decodes a digital signal back into an analog waveform. These devices are much used in the telephone industry since a telephone headset receives and transmits an analog waveform of the appropriate speech (or other). signals whereas for a variety of reasons having to do with economy and the ability to transmit digital signals over long distances without degradation, much of the telephone network now works with digital signals.

coded program: Instructions, usually in the form of a list coded in the computer's native or machine language, for solving a problem. Often shortened to code.

coder: A person who prepares instructions sequences from detailed flowcharts and other algorithmic procedures prepared by others, as contrasted with a programmer, who prepares the procedures and flow charts. Also, a device that is capable of translating one type of data representation into another type.

coding: The design and application of a coded program. The process of writing the detailed step-by-step instructions for the computer to follow. This is done by a coder.

command: A request to the computer that is executed as soon as it has been received. Sometimes this word is used interchangeably with the terms "instruction" and "statement". Those terms properly refer to portions of programs and not to commands, which are carried out immediately.

compiler: A systems program that translates high-level language programs into binary machine-level code.

computer: A device which can accept and supply information and in which the information supplied is derived from information accepted by logical processes. The two main types are digital computers and analog computers, and they make extensive use of electronic devices and circuits.

concatenation: The process of joining two strings to make a longer string.

concentrator: A device used in data communications to multiplex numerous low-speed communications lines onto a single high-speed communications line.

conditional jump: An instruction that executes a jump only if a certain condition is true.

continuous processing: The constant handling of disparate input items without grouping them.

CONTRAN (CONtrol TRANslator): A high level programming language combining many features of FORTRAN IV and ALGOL 60

control character: A character or command obtained by holding down the key marked "CTRL" while pressing another key on a keyboard. Any of the 32 ASCII control codes. Their functions range from generating a carriage return to controlling remote devices.

core memory: A type of memory that stores information on magnetically charged, doughnut-shaped cores made of ferrite and lithium. Core memories have largely been superseded by semi-conductor memories.

counter: A register or memory location used to count the number of times a certain event occurs.

CPS (Characters Per Second).

CPS (Conversation Programming System): Generally refers to a computer system in which input and output are handled by a remote terminal and employing time sharing so that the user obtains what appears to be an immediate response.

CPU (Central Processing Unit): The primary component of all computer systems. It is responsible for controlling system operation as directed by the program it is executing.

crash: A system shutdown caused by a hardware or software malfunction.

CRC (Cyclic Redundancy Check): An error-detection scheme (usually hardware implemented) that is often employed in disc devices. Although the mechanics are different, it is similar in principle to the checksum method. When information is stored, a CRC value is computed and stored. Whenever it is reread, the CRC value is computed once again. If the two values are equal, the information is assumed to be error-free.

cross-assembler: An assembler that runs on a machine other than the one for which it is designed to assemble code.

cross-compiler: A compiler that runs on a machine other than the one for which it is designed to compile code.

crowbar: A circuit that protects a system from dangerously high voltage surges.

CRT (Cathode Ray Tube) terminal: A type of communications terminal that displays its output on a television-like screen. Synonym of video terminal.

CS-CP (Canadian Satellite-Cable Package).

current loop: A type of serial communication where the presence or absence of an electrical signal (usually 60 mA) indicates the state of the bit being transmitted.

cursor: A symbol on the display of a video terminal that indicates where the next character is to be located.

cycle stealing: A technique that allows an external device to temporarily disable processor control of the bus. This, in turn, allows the device to access main memory.

Cyclic Redundancy Check: See CRC.

DAC (Data Acquisition and Control system): A system designed to handle a wide variety of real-time applications, process control and high-speed data acquisition. Each system is individually tailored with modular building blocks which are easily integrated to meet specific system requirements. A large family of real-time process input/output (I/0) devices is included, as well as data processing I/0 units. Data are received and transmitted on either a high-speed cycle-steal basis or under program control, depending on the intrinsic data rate of the I/0 device.

databank: A collection of data organized for rapid search and retrieval. This collection of data, stored in the form of a complex set of tables, describes some aspect of the world outside of the computer (i.e., a library catalogue, a student record file or a budget).

database: A collection of information in a form that can be manipulated by a computer.

data vs. information: Data are the basic elements of information which can be processed or produced by a computer. Sometimes data are considered to be expressible only in numerical form, but information is not so limited.

db (decibels).

debugging: The process of searching for and removing errors from a computer program.

decibel: A unit (= one-tenth of a bel) used in comparison of power levels in electrical communications or intensities of sound, one of the compared values often being an understood standard.

decode: To apply a code so as to reverse some previous encoding; to determine the meaning of individual characters or groups of characters in a message; to determine the meaning of an instruction from the set of pulses describing the instruction to be performed; to translate coded characters to a more understandable form.

decoder: A circuitry that receives pulses in one pattern and emits pulses in another pattern; a circuitry that produces a single output from a combination of inputs; a converter of digital data into analog form; a circuit that accepts only one signal; a matrix.

decoding: The process whereby an operation is performed as a result of the equipment translating the operation code; the act of translating a code into readily understood language.

dedicated device: A device that is used exclusively for one function.

device: A computer peripheral or an electronic component.

diagnostic: A systems program used as a hardware troubleshooting aid.

digitcasting: Use of radio broadcasting for the transmission of digital information.

digital: information that can be represented by a collection of bits. Most modern computers store information in digital form. The digital (as opposed to analog) computer can represent information only as separate, discontinuous numbers and works on data mathematically (that is, it does calculations by adding binary numbers), rather than physically.

DIP (Dual In-line Package): The most common type of integrated circuit packaging. It is characterized by a rectangular shape and by pins that point downward. The pins are arranged on two sides of the rectangle. See **integrated circuit.**

direct address: See **absolute address.**

direct memory access: See **DMA.**

disassembler: A systems program that converts machine-language code back into assembly language.

discrete component: An electronic component that contains only one function, as opposed to an integrated circuit.

disc: A circular piece of material which has a magnetic coating similar to that found on ordinary recording tape. Digital information can be stored magnetically on a disc much as musical information is stored on a magnetic tape. This term is often (and confusingly) used also to refer to a disc drive.

disc drive: A peripheral which can store information on and retrieve information from a disc. A floppy disc drive can store information from a floppy disc and can retrieve that information.

diskette: A small floppy disc in a square plastic envelope commonly either about 13 or 20 cm on a side. See **Floppy disc.**

disc storage: A type of mass memory in which information is stored on a magnetically sensitive rotating disc. Disc drives are generally both faster and more expensive than paper tape or magnetic tape devices

dispersion (pulse): The spreading out of an electrical pulse waveform due to a difference in transmission velocity of its high and low frequency components. (Note that any waveform can be broken down into a number of sine waves of different frequency and phase.)

DMA (Direct Memory Access): An arrangement where blocks of data can be transferred between main memory and a peripheral device (such as a disc drive) without processor intervention. It is a fast and convenient method of data transfer, enabling a peripheral device to transfer data directly from the memory circuits, without requiring action from the main processor (except to start the transfer, if needed). It is used frequently in video display systems and in disc systems. See also **programmed data transfer.**

Dopants: Impurities (commonly of boron and phosphorus) needed in the composition of transistors to make the silicon wafers electrically conducting or non-conducting.

Doping: The process of adding impurities to specific areas of the silicon wafers used in transistors, thus creating a *P* (electrically positive) zone or an *N* (electrically negative) zone.

DOS (Disc Operating System): A systems program that controls a disc system.

Driver: A program that controls (or drives) a device.

Dual In-line Package: See **DIP**.

dump: To transfer the contents of one section of storage into another section of storage; to inadvertently cause stored data to be lost. Also, a display or printout of part or all of the contents of a storage device.

dyadic: An operation that uses two operands.

dynamic memory: A type of programmable semiconductor memory. Data is held in the form of electrical charges on tiny capacitors inside integrated circuits. Dynamic memory, unlike static memory, must be refreshed or recharged periodically to prevent loss of data. It is usually cheaper and often faster than static memory, but less reliable.

EAROM (Electrically Alterable Read-Only Memory): A type of memory that combines the characteristics of RAM and ROM. It is non-volatile (like ROM), but can be written into by the processor (like RAM). The EAROM, however, has a substantially longer writing time (currently about 2 microseconds vs. 400 nanoseconds) as well as a limited number of writes (about 1,000,000) before the chip can no longer be reprogrammed.

EBCDIC (Extended Binary Coded Decimal Interchange Code): An 8-bit character code used primarily in IBM equipment.

editor: A program that facilitates the editing of textual material or computer software.

Electronic mail: The transmission of messages normally transmitted via the postal system, using electronic communications systems in lieu of the physical transportation and delivery of paper messages.

Elie project: A rural area in Manitoba to be wired-up with an optical fibre network in 1980. One of the first tests of the practicality of a unified telephone and cable TV delivery system. Jointly sponsored by the Canadian Telecommunications Carriers Association and the federal Department of Communications.

eliza program: A computer program (developed by Joseph Weizenbaum at MIT in 1966) that imitated the conversation technique of Rogerian psychologists. The computer printed out questions based on the previous statement typed in by the human "patient."

emulator: A program that allows one processor to simulate the instruction set of another processor.

encrypt: To encipher or encode, that is, to convert information from one system of communication to another.

ENIAC (Electronic Numeral Integrator and Calculator): The first fully electronic computer: a giant calculator made up of 18,000 vacuum tubes which filled a large room. Completed in 1946. Consumed 130,000 watts of power, but had only one-fifth the computation power of a 1979 microprocessor, which takes about 50 watts of power.

EPROM (Erasable and reProgrammable Read-Only Memory): See EROM.

EROM (Erasable Read-Only Memory): A read-only memory that can be erased and reprogrammed. Most EROMs are erased through exposure to ultraviolet light. Also spelled EPROM.

execute: To perform a computer instruction or run a program.

executive: See **monitor.**

extender board: A trouble-shooting aid. It physically raises another board above the other boards in a system, where it can be monitored more conveniently.

FET (Field-Effect Transistor): A unipolar transistor. That is, it contains only P-type or N-type doping (but not both).

fibre-optics: The study of the physics involved in communications that involve the transmission of information by pulses of light down hair-thin tunnels made of glass, that is, down optical fibres.

FIFO (First-In, First-Out): A stack arrangement.

file: A group of related information records that are treated as a unit. The records may consist of data or program instructions.

firmware: Software stored in read-only memory. Also a synonym for microcode.

fixed-point arithmetic: Arithmetic where the decimal point always remains at a predetermined position. Integer arithmetic is a type of fixed-point arithmetic, because the decimal point is always to the right of the mantissa.

flag: A bit whose state signifies whether a certain condition has occurred.

flat pack: A type of integrated-circuit packaging in which the pins extend outward, rather than pointing down as on a DIP.

flip-flop: A circuit that changes its logical state when signaled to do so by another device.

floating-point arithmetic: Arithmetic where the decimal point may occupy any position.

floating-point BASIC: A type of BASIC language that allows the use of decimal numbers. The name comes from the fact that the decimal point "floats" to a new position in a number, as required, following a calculation.

floppy disc: A slow-speed, inexpensive type of memory storage that uses flexible, or "floppy," discs (or diskettes), made of a material similar to magnetic tape, as opposed to "hard" discs made from rigid materials. It is a convenient method for the "bulk storage" of data, but slower than main computer memory (by 10,000 times) since data is stored in serial form.

flowchart: A diagram representing the logic of a computer program.

FORTRAN (FORmula TRANslator): The first high-level (compiler or interpreter) language. Emphasizes algebraic operations. Used primarily in scientific applications. RATFOR and WATFOR are dialects.

Frequency Shift Keying: See FSK.

FSK (Frequency Shift Keying): A method of data transmission in which the state of the bit being transmitted is indicated by an audible tone. Three common types of FSK are those used by acoustic couplers (2225 Hz for logic 1, 2025 Hz for 0), radio teletypewriters (2125 Hz/2975 Hz) and the Kansas City cassette format (2400Hz/1200 Hz).

full duplex: Communication where data may be simultaneously transmitted and received by both ends of the circuit.

gate: A basic building block in computers. A circuit that performs a Boolean logic operation; that is, the circuit can handle more than one input (symbolized by the logical functions AND, OR and NOT), but only one output.

gating: The process of selecting those portions of a wave which occur during one or more time intervals, or which have magnitudes between selected limits. Also, electronic switching using a square wave of desired time and duration.

geostationary satellite: An artificial satellite that travels above the equator at the same speed as the earth rotates, so that the satellite seems to remain in the same place.

germanium: A relatively rare element once used as a semiconductor in the manufacture of transistors. Now replaced in transistor manufacture by the far more abundant element, silicon.

ghz (gigahertz): A unit of frequency equal to one billion hertz.

graphics terminal: A video terminal capable of displaying user-programmed graphics.

hacker: A computer enthusiast, prone to sleeping near the computer.

half duplex: Communications where only one end may transmit at a time.

handshaking: The exchange of a sequence of signals required to complete an I/0 operation.

hard copy: Information printed on paper or other durable surface. This term is used to distinguish printed information from the temporary image presented on the computer's CRT screen.

hard disc: Disc storage that uses rigid discs rather than flexible discs as the storage medium. Hard-disc devices can generally store more information and access it faster. Cost considerations, however, currently restrict their usage to medium and large-scale applications. Smaller, cheaper units are now coming to market.

hard sectoring: Defining the sectors on a disc through hardware.

hardware: A popular expression used to distinguish the physical parts making up any electronic equipment from the software.

hardware multiply/divide: A feature that allows a processor to perform multiplication and division entirely within hardware. Processors without multiply and divide instructions require special software routines for these operations.

Hermes satellite: A joint Canada-USA project using a high frequency radio band, launched January, 1976.

hertz (hz): A unit of frequency equal to one cycle per second.

hexadecimal: The base-16 number system.

high-level language: Computer language that allows the programmer to write programs using verbs, symbols and commands rather than machine code. Some common high-level languages are: ALGOL, APL, BASIC, COBOL, FORTRAN, NATAL, PL/1, PL/M and SNOBOL.

Hi-Ovis experiment: An experiment in Japan using optical fibre and TV broadcasting channels to provide on-demand, pay-per-program video communications. Hi Res. See **resolution.**

Hz (hertz).

IAS (Immediate Access Storage): The form of storage that has the shortest access time and where no delay occurs before or during the execution of instructions.

IC's (Integrated Circuits): A development of micro-electronics in which a whole circuit is constructed by micro-manipulation and processing of a single block or chip of semiconductor, usually crystalline silicon. Separate con-

205

tainers and wire connections between circuit elements are completely eliminated, so extremely compact structures can be achieved.

IEEE (Institute of Electrical & Electronic Engineers).

Impact printer: A printer that prints characters by mechanical means, such as a type ball (as opposed to thermal or ink jet methods).

informatics: Information science; that is, the collection, classification, storage, retrieval & dissemination of recorded knowledge treated both as a pure & as an applied science.

initialize: To set up the starting conditions necessary for the execution of the remainder of a program. For example, in a program that draws a circle, the initialization might include specifying the radius of the circle. To prepare a diskette so that the computer can later store data on it.

input: Information arriving at a device. The very same data moving around in a computer system will be output one instant (from one part of the computer) and input the next instant (to some other part of the computer). You must be careful when using the terms input and output to specify what they are input to or output from. The word "input" is sometimes used as a verb, even though it feels a bit strange to do so. For example: You must input the data before doing the calculations.

instruction: The smallest portion of a program that a computer can execute. The term is used with a number of other less clearly

defined meanings. Its meaning in such cases parallels its usual meaning in English: a statement directing something to perform an action. See **Program.**

integer BASIC: A type of BASIC that can process whole numbers only; no decimal numbers are allowed. See BASIC and floating-point BASIC.

integrated circuits: See IC's.

interactive: Said of a computer system which responds to the user quickly—usually less than a second for a typical action. All personal computer systems are interactive.

intelligent device: A device that contains its own processor.

INTELSAT: A geostationary communications satellite.

interface: An electronic device that allows two other devices to communicate with one another by converting signals from one into a format that can be processed by the other.

interpreter: A systems program that executes high-level language programs instruction by instruction. Interpretive language processors are considered distinct from compilers, which convert the entire program directly into machine-level code.

interrupt: Temporary suspension of normal system operations while the processor responds to a request from another device.

invisible refresh: A scheme that refreshes dynamic memories without disturbing the rest of the system. The refresh requirements of the memories might otherwise reduce system performance and interfere with DMA operations.

I/0 (input and/or output): A keyboard, a floppy disc and a printer are all I/0 devices.

ionosphere: The region of the earth's atmosphere extending from about 90 to 450 kilometres above the surface of the earth. This region contains several layers of ionized gas.

Josephson junction: Superconducting switching devices based on Brian Josephson's theory that an electrical current, or flow of electrons, can tunnel through barriers that would ordinarily restrain them (called electron tunneling). Depending on the presence or absence of a small magnetic field, electrons cross from one side of the barrier to the other, as in a transistor, but with a significant difference: the amount of current in a Josephson junction is infinitesimally small.

joystick: A type of input device. It has a stick that is manipulated by the user to produce different inputs. Joysticks are often used in conjunction with graphics terminals.

jump: An instruction that causes the processor to transfer control to another instruction. Normally, a computer executes the statements of a program in the order of appearance. Statements that tell the computer to break out of this normal mode are said to cause a branch, or jump. In BASIC, one such statement is GOTO.

K (kilo): A unit of one thousand, but when measuring bytes of memory in a computer, it usually means 1024. (64 × 16).

KANSAS CITY STANDARD: A low-speed cassette storage format.

keyword or key word: A word that has meaning in a computer language. See **Reserved word**.

kilobaud: A unit of measure of data transmission speed consisting of 1,000 bits per second.

kludge: Makeshift, as in this program is a real kludge.

label: A name comprised of letters, numbers or symbols used to identify a statement or instruction or segment in a program.

language: A set of conventions specifying how to tell a computer what to do.

language processor: A systems program, typically either a compiler or an interpreter, that permits a computer to execute code written in a high-level language.

LED (Light-Emitting Diode): A type of digital output display that is frequently used in calculators.

LIFO (Last-In, First-Out): A stack arrangement.

light pen: An input device used in conjunction with a video display. When the user touches the display screen with the light pen, the electronics associated with the pen will determine the coordinates of the point that the user touched. These coordinates will then be transmitted to the computer.

linear IC: An analog integrated circuit, as opposed to a digital integrated circuit.

line printer: An output device that prints an entire line of information at a time.

loader: A program that loads information into main memory.

loop: A program segment that is executed several times in a row.

lpm (lines per minute): Usually used to describe the speed of a line printer.

LSI (Large-Scale Integration): The class of integrated circuits that contain the largest number of functions per chip except for **VLSI**. Microprocessors are LSI devices.

M (mega): A unit of one million (10^6). 1024^2 (1,048,576).

machine code: Programming in **machine language.**

machine language: Binary code that can be directly executed by the processor, as opposed to assembly or high-level language.

macro: See **Pseudo-op.**

macro assembler: An assembler that allows the programmer to define his own macros, that is, his own methods of assigning a name to a block of coding. After every appearance of that name as an operator, the assembler inserts a copy of that coding into the object program.

macro instruction: An instruction that combines several operations as an overall instruction. The extent to which a number of operations can be performed for each macro instruction indicates the power of the computer. Compare with micro instruction.

magnetic-bubble memory: A medium-speed, non-volatile memory system that is more expensive than charged-coupled devices. These microscopic pockets of magnetism (or "bubbles") move along orderly pathways through electric or magnetic fields. As they pass fixed stations, the presence or absence of bubble is read as coded information.

mag tape: Magnetic tape, similar to that used by audio tape recorders, on which information can be stored in a computer-readable format.

mainframe: The computer itself, including the processor, main memory, 1/0 interfaces and backplane.

main memory: The memory that the processor accesses directly, as opposed to peripherals such as disc and tape devices.

mark sense: A data-input method where the user designates information by placing pencil marks on cards. The cards are then fed into a special reader that translates the marks into a format that can be understood by the computer.

mask ROM: A read-only memory that is permanently programmed by the chip manufacturer.

mass storage: Auxiliary or bulk memory as opposed to main memory. Disc drives and tape drives are common mass-storage devices.

matrix: A group of numbers organized on a rectangular grid and treated as a unit. The numbers can be referenced by their position on the grid.

memory: The portion of a computer which stores information. See **ROM** and **RAM.**

menu: A list of options from which to choose.

microcode: Software that defines the instruction set of a microprogrammable processor.

microcomputer: A computer based on a microprocessor.

micro instruction: An instruction that performs only one machine operation. Compare with macro instruction.

microprocessor: A one-chip Central Processing Unit developed in 1971. An integrated circuit that performs the task of executing instructions.

milli-: One thousandth (10^{-3}).

microprogrammable processor: A processor whose actual instruction set is not accessed by the programmer. Instead, another, more versatile, instruction set is simulated by microcode.

mnemonic: An abbreviation for a computer instruction. For example, jump to subroutine might be represented by the mnemonic JSR.

mode: One of several states of electro-magnetic wave oscillation

which may be sustained in a given resonant system; or, one of several methods of exciting a resonant system.

MODEM (MODulator-DEModulator): A device that allows a computer to communicate over the telephone lines (and other communications media). It does this by changing the digital information into musical tones (modulating) and from musical tones to digital information (demodulating). It is used with frequency-shift-keying (FSK) data transmission.

modulator: A device that lets a computer use any ordinary television set for output. This term is understood in this sense mainly with respect to personal computers as such modulators are not generally used with larger machines. It is sometimes referred to as an RF modulator. RF stands for "Radio Frequency," meaning Television Broadcasting Frequency.

modulo: A mathematical operator that yields the remainder function of division. For example, 100 modulo 97 equals the remainder of 100/97, or 3.

monadic: An operation that uses only one operand.

monitor: A television set. Often one that is specially manufactured to be connected to a computer. Also a program supplied by the manufacturer that allows the user to control the operation of a computer. With computers that operate directly in a higher level language, such as BASIC, the monitor may often be built into the language.

MOS (Metal-Oxide Semiconductor): A semiconductor structure that is used in many FETs and integrated circuits, which are then referred to as MOSFETs and MOS ICs.

MOS RAM (Metal Oxide Semiconductor Random-Access Memory): An expensive random-access memory system which is faster than CCD's and magnetic-bubble systems, but which is slower and cheaper than RAM systems using bipolar technology.

motherboard: Synonym for backplane.

MPU (Microprocessor Unit).

MSI (Medium-Scale Integration): The class of integrated circuits having a density between those of LSI and SSI devices.

MTBF (Mean Time Between Failures): The length of time for which a device can reasonably be expected to operate without malfunction.

MTTR (Mean Time to Repair): The length of time typically required to service a device following a breakdown.

multilayer: A type of printed circuit board that has several circuit layers connected by electroplated holes.

multiprocessing system: A system that includes more than one processor, each of which works concurrently on separate tasks.

multiprogramming system: A system that can execute more than one program at a time.

multitasking system: See **Multiprogramming system.**

NABU (Natural Access to Bi-directional Utilities): An electronic communication computer system for the home.

Nanoseconds: A billionth (10^{-9}) of a second. The fraction of time it takes for light to travel almost one foot.

NATAL: A high level, structured language for CAI.

native language: The language that a computer was built to understand. It is different for each brand of computer. Synonymous with machine language.

nesting: The practice of placing one loop inside of another or having one subroutine reference another.

niladic: An operation for which no operands are specified.

nim: A junction point that receives synchronous or asynchronous circuits in a packet switched network.

NMOS (N-type Metal Oxide Semiconductor).

node: In electronics, a point of zero current or zero voltage on a conductor. A point in a radio wave where the amplitude is zero. A junction point in a network. In computer programming, the dots used in decision trees to represent the situations that can occur in the course of solving a problem.

noise: An unwanted signal.

noise immunity: A device's ability

to accept valid signals while rejecting unwanted signals.

non-volatile memory: Memory storage that retains data when operating power is removed, as opposed to volatile memory, where information is lost when the power is removed. Core, disc, magnetic drum and magnetic-bubble memory are all forms of non-volatile storage.

ns (nanosecond): A billionth (10^{-9}) of a second.

N-type: The condition of semi-conductor (silicon) crystals doped to provide a surplus of electrons, thus creating a negative zone.

nybble: A group of four bits, or one-half of a byte.

null string: A string consisting of no characters whatever. If it doesn't seem like a useful idea, think about how useful the number zero is.

object code: Machine-language code.

OCR (Optical Character Recognition): Computer recognition of printed characters.

octal: The base-8 number system.

OEM (Original Equipment Manufacturer): A manufacturer who buys equipment from other suppliers and integrates it into a single system for resale.

off-line: A process or device not under control of the CPU. A key-punch is an example of an off-line device. Printing output recorded on tape, done some time after the output has been generated by the computer, is an example of an off-line process.

on-board regulation: An arrangement where each board in a system contains its own voltage regulator.

on-line: A device that is connected directly to the CPU.

op code (operation code): A binary number or mnemonic that specifies the instruction to be executed by the computer. Also called machine code.

operand: A number which is operated on in a computer program. The value being processed by the operator. For example, in the expression $2 + 3$ the operands are two and three.

operator: A symbol or command that specifies the operation to be performed.

optical couplers: Devices for connecting optical fibres.

optical fibres: The actual fibres of glass (used in fibre-optic networks) which are specially manufactured so that light can be transmitted for a long distance and still be detected at the far end.

ORACLE: A teletext service in the UK.

OS (Operating System): A collection of programs to aid a person in controlling a computer. This term is usually used in reference to large computers. A small computer operating system is often called a monitor. See **monitor**.

output: Information leaving a

211

device or process. For example, the output from a computer can be displayed by a printer or CRT. This term can also be used as a verb, even if it does sound a bit awkward, as in: Watch the computer output a graph. See **input**.

overlaying: A technique used to increase the apparent size of main memory. This is accomplished by keeping only the code or data that is currently being accessed in main memory. The rest is kept on a mass-storage device until needed.

packet switching: A data transmission process that transmits addressed packets so that a channel is occupied only for the duration of transmission of a packet.

page: A segment of memory that is treated as a unit. For example, 65,536 bytes of memory (64K) might be divided into 16 pages of 4096 bytes.

paper tape: A length of narrow paper punched in a pattern decodable by a paper-tape reader. Paper tape is bulkier than magnetic forms of data storage. On the other hand, paper tape cannot be erased accidentally and is easier to edit by splicing.

parallel I/O: Data transmission where each bit has its own wire. All of the bits are transmitted simultaneously, as opposed to being sent one at a time (serially).

parity check: An error-detection scheme in which an additional bit, the parity bit, is appended to each word or byte. Under even parity, the parity bit is 1 if there is an

even number of 1s in the rest of the word. Under odd parity, the parity bit is 1 if there is an odd number of 1s in the rest of the word.

parsing: Analyzing a character string and breaking it down into a group of more easily processed components.

pass: A scanning of source code by an assembler or a compiler. For example, a two-pass assembler is one that processes the source code in two separate steps.

pay TV: A scheme whereby the TV viewer pays directly for the TV programs he watches either by "renting" access to a pay TV channel (per channel pay TV) or by paying a specific charge for each program watched (per program pay TV). Pay TV can be contrasted with the more usual modes of TV where the viewer pays only indirectly for the programs either through taxes or through purchase of advertised products.

PC (Printed Circuit) board: A circuit board whose electrical connections are made through conductive material that is contained on the board itself, rather than with individual wires.

PCM (Pulse Code Modulation): A form of pulse modulation in which a code is used; usually the code represents the quantized values of instantaneous samples of the signal wave.

PEEK: A BASIC instruction that allows the programmer to look at (peek at) any location in programmable memory. This instruction is often used to scan the memory locations which hold the information displayed on the video monitor in order to determine what is being displayed.

peripheral: A unit, such as a communications terminal, that is external to the system processor. Some typical peripherals are floppy disc drives, printers, MODEM's and television sets.

Photodetector: A device for converting incoming light into electricity.

Photolithography: The process of printing from photographically pre-pared plates on which the image to be printed is ink-receptive and the blank area ink-repellant. The process used in transistor manufacturing, especially to produce miniaturized integrated circuits on silicon chips.

PLA (Programmable Logic Array): A device (usually an integrated cir-cuit) containing a set of logic gates whose interconnections may be programmed.

PL/1 (Programming Language/One): Possesses qualities of many languages, especially ALGOL.

PL/M (Programming Language/Meta): A subset of PL/1. Usually implemented as a cross-compiler.

plotter: A hard-copy device that produces line drawings such as X/Y graphs. The coordinates of the points or lines to be plotted are normally supplied by the computer.

PMOS (P-type MOS).

POKE: A BASIC instruction used to place a value (poke) into any lo-cation in programmable memory. This instruction is often used in conjunction with the PEEK instruction to display graphics on a video screen.

Polling: The interrogation of the devices in a system by the processor to determine if and where any I/O operations are pending.

Populated board: A circuit board that contains all of its electronic components. The components for an unpopulated board, conversely, must be supplied by the purchaser.

Port: That portion of a computer through which a peripheral may communicate. Sometimes confused with **Interface** since almost all ports are associated with interfaces.

POTS (plain old telephone service).

Power fail/restart: A facility that enables a computer to return to normal operation after a power failure.

PRESTEL: A British electronic mail box system, using videotex. Operated by the Post Office.

processor: Synonym for CPU.

program: A sequence of instructions that permit a computer to perform a task. A pro-gram must be in a language that the computer can understand.

programmable logic array: See PLA.

programmable memory: Content changeable memory, as opposed

213

to read-only memory (the contents of which are fixed during manufacture). Programmable memory can be both read from and written into by the processor, and is where most programs and data are stored. Sometimes called RAM, but this is a slight misnomer.

programmable read-only memory: See **PROM**.

Programming Language /One: See **PL/1**.

programmed data transfer: The most common method of data transfer in microcomputers. Each byte of data passes from the memory circuits, through the main processor, and out to the peripheral device in the case of output; and in the opposite direction in the case of input. Programmed data transfer requires the constant attention of the computer program for the transfer to continue, hence its name. See also **direct memory access**.

prom (programmable read-only memory): A type of read-only memory that can be programmed by the user. This programming usually requires special equipment. See **burning**.

prompt: A symbol that appears on your computer's display to let you know that it is ready to pay attention to your commands.

protected memory: Programmable memory that cannot be written into, usually on a temporary basis.

pseudo-op (pseudo-operation): An instruction that is implemented by an assembler but is not in the processor's instruction set. It is often used to give information to the

assembler. Or, if the pseudo-op is part of the program itself, the assembler will assemble in its place a sequence of instructions that simulates the pseudo-op.

p-type: The condition of semiconductor (silicon) crystals doped to give the semiconductor a deficiency of electrons, thus creating a positive zone.

pulse code: The patterns of electrical pulses which represent characters; the binary bit representations of characters.

quantizer: A device used to convert an analog measurement into digital form.

quantization: In communications, a process by which the range of values of a wave is divided into a finite number of smaller subranges, each of which is represented by an assigned or "quantized" value within the subrange.

queue: A waiting line of tasks or data.

RAM (Random-Access Memory): The main memory of any computer. Information and programs are stored in RAM, and they may be retrieved or changed by a program. For some computers, the information in RAM is lost whenever the power is turned off.

Random-Access Memory: See **RAM**.

Random Number Generator: A program that, when executed, provides a number whose value is difficult to predict. In many computer systems a random number generator is built into the language rather than appearing as a subroutine.

Read-Only Memory: See **ROM.**

real time: A system function that is controlled by external events. For example, a system that reacts to inputs from a temperature sensor would be considered a real-time system.

real-time clock: An electronic timekeeping device within the computer.

recursive subroutine: A subroutine that invokes itself. Or, a subroutine that invokes another subroutine, which, in turn, invokes the original subroutine again.

reentrant subroutine: In a multiprogramming system, a sub-routine of which only one copy resides in main memory. This copy is shared by several programs.

register: A place in a computer where numbers can be temporarily stored and operated on. A unit of memory that is contained within the processor circuitry itself, as opposed to main memory or mass storage.

relative addressing: An addressing mode in which the target memory location is specified as the sum of a variable and a constant. The variable is referred to as the origin and is usually the address of the instruction currently being executed. The constant is specified within the instruction. For example, the relative address + 10 is the same as the absolute address × + 10, where × is the origin.

relocatable code: Code that can occupy any position in main memory.

reserved word: A word that you cannot use as a variable name, since it has been pre-empted for use in the computer's language You also may be restricted from using reserved words in other ways as well. Key words are often reserved words. See **key word.**

resolution: The density and overall quality of a video display. Also refers to the number of distinct points that can be plotted by a graphics terminal. Hi Res. A comparative term.

response time: The amount of time required for a computer to respond to an input from one of its terminals.

robot: An automatic machine capable of sensing conditions, evaluating the conditions and causing a reaction to such evaluations without any operator guidance.

robotics: A field of interest concerned with the construction, maintenance and behaviour of robots.

roll-over: A property of some keyboards. Keys may be depressed in more rapid succession on a keyboard with roll-over.

ROM (Read-Only Memory): Memory in which the information is stored once, usually by the manufacturer, and cannot be changed. Programs such as BASIC interpreter (used by most owners of personal computers) are often stored in ROM.

RPN (Reverse Polish Notation): A mathematical notation in which the operator is placed after its operands, rather than between them. For example, the expression 2 + 3 would be written 2, 3 + in RPN.

RS-232: A data communications industry standard for the serial transmission of data to a peripheral device, such as a printer, a video monitor, a plotter, etc. Most personal computers have an RS-232 interface port.

RTTY (radio teletypewriter): Radio communication between teletypewriters.

run time: The time at which the program is executed. Also, the amount of time required to execute the program.

Saint Hubert experiment: A Pay TV experiment operated by Telecable-Videotron in Quebec.

satellite: A man-made object or vehicle intended to orbit the earth, the moon, or another celestial body.

Satellite Business Systems: See **SBS**.

save: To store a program anywhere other than in the computer's memory, for example on a diskette or cassette tape.

SBS (Satellite Business Systems): A joint venture of IBM, Comsat and Aetna Casualty and Surety to launch a high-frequency satellite in 1980 that will be able to communicate directly with customer-owned roof top antennae.

scratchpad memory: Programmable memory that is being used for storage of "housekeeping" value, or information that is internal to the program.

scrolling: A property of some video terminals. If the screen of such a video terminal is filled, it will move the entire display image upwards; the top line of text will be lost; and a blank line will appear at the bottom.

second source: A manufacturer who produces a product that is interchangeable with the product of another manufacturer.

seed: An argument that is used as the initial value for a pseudo-random number generator.

semiconductor memory: Memory consisting of integrated circuits rather than magnetic cores.

serial I/O: Data transmission in which the bits are sent one by one over a single wire.

silicon: An element used in the manufacturing of transistors and optical fibres. It is used as a semiconductor because it can be either electrically conducting or non-conducting, depending on the impurities added to it. See doping.

simulation: A computer program that mathematically models a process.

single stepping: Having the computer execute a program slowly so that the user can watch each step and its effects.

slot: A single-board position in a backplane.

216

SNOBOL (String Oriented Business Language): A computer programming language for manipulating strings of symbols.

sociobiology: The systematic study of the biological basis of all social behaviour.

soft copy: Output printed on a video display.

soft sectoring: Defining the sector format of a disk through software.

software: A general term for all programs and routines used to implement and extend the capabilities of the computer: e.g., assemblers, compilers and subroutines. "Software" sometimes means data as well as programs.

software license: A contract signed by the purchaser of a software product in which he is usually made to agree not to make copies of the software for resale.

source code: Code that is to be processed by a systems program such as a compiler or an assembler.

speech synthesization: The generation of human speech by electronic means. This is done by "synthesizing" or combining the appropriate electrical waveforms to reproduce the phonemes, which are the basic sounds of which all words can be composed.

square wave: The rectangular wave form of a quantity that varies periodically and abruptly from one to the other of two uniform values.

SSI (Small-Scale Integration): The class of integrated circuits that have the fewest number of functions per chip.

stack: A sequential data list stored in main memory. Rather than addressing the stack elements by their memory location, the processor retrieves information from the stack by popping elements from the top (LIFO) or from the bottom (FIFO).

statement: A single computer instruction within a computer program.

static memory: A type of programmable memory. Data is held by changing the position of an electronic "switch", a transistor flip-flop, contained in integrated circuits. It does not require refresh operations, as does dynamic memory.

string: A sequence of alphanumeric text, or letters, numerals and other characters. See **null string.**

structured programming: An attempt has been made to formalize the elements of good programming. These practices have influenced the development of structured languages like Pascal which stress modularity, clear pathways and simplicity.

subroutine: A portion of a program that can be executed by a special statement. In BASIC, that statement is "GO-SUB". This effectively gives a single statement the strength of a whole program. A subroutine call differs from a simple jump instruction in that after completion of the subroutine, execution of the program will return to the program section that invoked it.

switching: The relaying of electrical impulses.

switching power supply: An efficient type of power supply that produces power in a compact package.

synchronizing signal: An electrical signal used to provide timing information. For example, the horizontal synchronizing signal in a TV set is used to time the start of each horizontal sweep of the electron beam in the TV tube.

synchronous communications: Data transmission where the bits are transmitted at a fixed rate. The transmitter and receiver both use the same clock signals for synchronization.

syntax: The rules that specify exactly how an instruction can be written.

systems program: A program that does not perform actual problem solving but rather is used to control system operations or act as a programming aid.

Telcos (telephone companies).

TELESAT CANADA: The world's first domestic geostationary communications satellite system; incorporated by statute in 1969.

teletext: An inexpensive, one-way information delivery system designed for mass market home and business use. It makes use of the spare signal carrying capacity in existing television broadcasting channels. It can present from 100 to 300 "pages" or "TV screens of information." See also **videotex** and **vertical blanking interval.**

TELIDON: The specific name given to an information system developed in Canada. It's capable of operating in either a one-way teletext or a two-way videotex mode and has superior graphic capabilities.

terminal: A device for communication with a computer. A typical terminal consists of a keyboard and a printer or video display.

text: Data other than numbers.

thermal printer: A hard-copy device that produces output on heat-sensitive paper.

throughput: A loosely defined term that refers to the speed of a processor.

time-sharing: See multiprogramming.

trace command: A command in some high level languages (such as some BASIC's) which causes the computer to list the exact order of program steps executed while running a program. The trace command is useful for debugging programs.

transistor: An active semiconductor device with three or more electrodes.

transparent: A process that is not visible to the user or to other devices. Transparent memory refresh is an example.

transponder: A radio or radar set that emits a radio signal of its own upon receiving a designated signal. (From transmitter + responder.)

trap: A hardware- or software-implemented function that signals the processor whenever a specified condition occurs.

TTL (transistor-transistor logic): A family of integrated circuits characterized by relatively high speed and low power consumption. These are usually SSI devices, so named because of the dual-transistor arrangement used by the output stage.

TTY (teletypewriter): A hard-copy terminal.

turnkey: A computer whose format panel is blank or contains few controls. Also refers to a product delivered ready to run.

TVT (television typewriter): A basic or low-end video terminal.

UART (Universal Asynchronous Receiver-Transmitter): An integrated circuit that converts parallel input into serial form, or vice-versa.

unary: See monadic.

universal asynchronous receiver-transmitter: See **UART.**

users' group: An association of people who all have an interest in a particular computer or group of computers. They usually meet to exchange information, share programs, trade equipment and show off their accomplishments.

User Service Routine: See USR.

USR (User Service Routine): A machine-language subroutine that may be invoked by a high-level language program.

utility: A frequently used program or subroutine. Utility routines are most often associated with systems programs rather than applications programs.

vacuum tube: the dominant electronic element found in computers prior to the advent of the transistor. It acts as a two-state device and can be made to turn off or on by changing the characteristics of the electrical conditions of the tube. Computers using vacuum tubes are referred to as first generation computers.

VBI: See **Vertical Blanking Interval.**

vendor: Supplier.

Vertical Blanking Interval: Spare signal-carrying capacity is found in what is called the 'vertical blanking interval' or VBI. This is a pause in the TV signal transmission between the completion of one TV frame and the start of the next. In order to allow the electron beam of the TV tube to move from the bottom left hand corner of the screen back to the top right hand corner ready for the new frame to begin. Approximately 22 lines out of the 525 horizontal sweeps made by the electron beam occur during the vertical blanking interval. Several of these lines are, or could be made, available for teletext signal transmission.

219

video-disc: a method for storing large quantities of information in tracks, each of which has an address; the information is read by a laser or other light source. The technology is still in flux and few standards have been established. Quantity of storage is the key factor. There are now 54,000 tracks per disc; each track can store a still photograph or a video frame. A single disc could store 400 hours of digitalized audio. In addition, this material can be individually accessed (2 to 3 seconds) and intermingled. Video-disc should come to dominate the delivery of audio-visual materials in the coming decade. At the moment, preparation is expensive, although replication averages $1.00. Unlike other storage methods used with computers, video-disc requires preparation of a master, from which duplicates are pressed. A duplicate even of the Encyclopedia Britannica would cost at most $4.00 to manufacture, but the master would cost $1,500 plus preparation costs of the 2-inch master video tape. Full production facilities for preparing masters could cost up to $2,000,000. Second generation equipment, with DRAW and answer processing capabilities, will be slower but far more flexible. Major differences exist between consumer (Magnavox) and industrial/educational (Thompson-CSF) type players and these will remain, especially in terms of editing the stored content and programmed access.

video monitor: A device that is functionally identical to a television set, except that it has no channel selector. It receives its picture signal from an external source such as a video terminal board.

video phone: A communications system which transmits both speech and pictorial information between two communicating entities. The best known is *picturephone,* an A T & T product. Thus far videophones have not been a commercial success, largely because they require much greater communications capacity than voice-only transmission, and hence are more expensive to use.

video teleconference: A teleconference which communicates both visual and audio information. Such systems are considerably more expensive than audio only teleconference systems and tend to be used only in special cases.

video terminal: Synonymous with CRT terminal.

videotex: An information delivery system that makes use of the telephone for two-way communications. It may also be linked into two-way cable TV or hybrid cable TV/telephone systems. Electronic mail is made possible by this system.

viewdata: an early name for videotex, and still used as the generic name for the British Prestel system.

virtual device: An imaginary device that the processor assumes to be present. Automatic memory overlaying, or virtual memory, is an example.

VLSI: Very Large Scale Integrated Circuits. Electronic components containing over one hundred thousand gates on a single substrate or chip. VLSI's are larger than LSI's. The crucial factor is getting line widths below 2 micrometers.

voder: A speech synthesizer.

volatile memory: Memory that loses its contents when operating power is removed.

VTR's (videotape recorders): A product that permits both the recording and the playback of TV pictures. Available to consumers in the late 1970's.

window: A portion of the computer's display that is dedicated to some special purpose.

wire-wrap: A type of circuit board construction. Electrical connections are made through wires connected to the posts that correspond to the proper component lead.

word: A basic unit of computer memory (synonomous with cell or register). The length of the word may vary from processor to processor. The most common microcomputer word length is 8 bits, or one byte.

workspace: A loosely defined term that usually refers to the amount of main memory available for programs and data. Also, the APL name for all of the memory-resident functions and variables that the programmer has defined.

xerography: A copy process of fixing magnetized particles on a surface as an image of a master.

zero-address instruction: A particular instruction which does not refer to any memory location; that is, a shifting instruction.

zeroise: To replace the contents of a storage area by pulses representing zero. To reset a mechanical register to its zero position.

zone bits: In computers, the various bits other than the four used to represent the digits in a dense binary code.

About the Authors

DAVID GODFREY

David Godfrey is currently Associate Professor and Chairman of the Department of Creative Writing at the University of Victoria. He holds a B.A., M.A., Ph.D in English Literature. Author of the Governor-General's Award winning novel *The New Ancestors* as well as *Death Goes Better with Coca-Cola, I Ching Kanada,* and *Dark Must Yield,* he is also co-editor of *Man Deserves Man* and *Gordon to Watkins to You: The Battle for Control of our Economy.*

Co-founder of three publishing companies: House of Anansi, New Press and Press Porcepic, he has served as President of the Association of Canadian Publishers and is a Director of the Association for the Export of Canadian Books.

Dr. Godfrey has written widely on the issue of cultural nationalism and his articles and stories have been frequently anthologized. He is a member of the Canadian Information Processing Society and has been appointed first editor of the National Research Council's newsletter for NATAL users. He is currently involved in CAI research.

JOHN MADDEN

John Madden received a B.A., and an M.Sc., from U.B.C., and obtained a D.Phil. in experimental nuclear physics in 1964 from Oxford University.

On his return to Canada in 1965, Dr. Madden joined Computing Devices of Canada in the Research and Development side where he was involved in problems related to signal processing and pattern recognition using specialized computer systems.

Beginning in 1970, Dr. Madden consulted with the Department of Communications as a member of the Canadian Computer/Communications Task Force and as a member of the Computers and Privacy Task Force.

Since that time he has served in the Research Sector of the Department of Communications as Director-General, Technology and Systems Research and Development and as Director-General, Special Research Programs. He is presently President, Pacific Microtel Research Ltd.

The two chapters which he wrote for this book were written while he was on leave of absence from the government and was a Visiting Professor at the Department of Communications Studies at Simon Fraser University in Burnaby, B.C.

DOUGLAS F PARKHILL

Douglas F Parkhill is currently Assistant Deputy Minister (Research) for the Canadian Department of Communications. Earlier he held the position of Assistant Deputy Minister (Planning) and was appointed to his current position in December 1974. He came to the Department in October 1969 from the MITRE Corporation of Bedford, Massachusetts, where he was Head of the Satellite Communications Systems Department. He has also worked for the General Dynamics Corporation, Information Technology Division, as Chief Engineer of the Advanced Development Department, AVCO Corporation as Deputy Manager of the Computer and Electronic Systems Department and Computing Devices of Canada.

Mr Parkhill has led a number of major policy and technical activities concerned with communications satellites, computer/communications systems, command and control systems and telecommunications, and has published widely in these fields. He is the author of *The Challenge of the Computer Utility,* published by Addison-Wesley in 1966, and a winner of the McKinsey Award for an outstanding contribution to management literature. He received his B.Sc. in Electrical Engineering from the University of Toronto in 1949, and an Honorary Doctorate in Engineering from the University of Ottawa in 1971.

ALPHONSE OUIMET

Alphonse Ouimet, C.C., is a member of the International Broadcast Institute and the International Editorial Board of *Telecommunications Policy.* He is chairman of the Communications Research Advisory Board and Chairman of the Board of Telesat Canada.

M. Ouimet is a graduate in Engineering from McGill University and holds many honorary degrees. After serving as a Research Engineer in Television and the Electronics industry he went to the CBC where he served successively as Operations Engineer, Co-ordinator of TV, Chief Engineer, General Manager then as President (1958-1967).

M. Ouimet has received many decorations and awards including Companion of the Order of Canada, the Gold Medal of the Canadian Council of Professional Engineers, International EMMY Directorate Award, International Communications Society Public Service Award and the Greater Montrealer Award.

COSMIC UPHEAVAL

Is living proof that those under fifteen absorb complexity much more rapidly than those under thirty. The members are heavily involved in micro computer use and the development of software for them.

Acknowledgements

Dave Godfrey would like to express his appreciation to Sharon Sterling, Charlane Etherington, Theresa Robertson and Murray Robertson for research, typing and invaluable discussion (about points both fine and philosophical). John Madden provided an editorial touch for these sections, much of it by long distance, that was firm and insightful.

John Madden wishes to acknowledge the assistance of the two co-editors, Dave Godfrey and Douglas Parkhill, most particularly the latter whose friendship and assistance over many years is much valued. He would also like to express his appreciation to the faculty and staff of the Department of Communications Studies, Simon Fraser University, whose hospitality and help during a year's visit made the writing possible; and to Ms. Sherry Toye at the Department of Communications in Ottawa whose efficient and friendly assistance in completing the final draft was essential to meeting publication deadlines.